Many of us think somehow that we have to live dramatic, highly visible lives of success to be used by God. But the Lord most often works to touch others through our quiet obedience in the everyday matters of life. Bert and Colleen Elliot exemplified that truth through more than six decades of faithful service in Peru. This account will inspire you, encourage you, and challenge you.

Jim Daly, president, Focus on the Family

The love of Bert and Colleen Elliot for Jesus is a shining example of dedication and obedience. They lived out the example of Christ as leaders who serve. Where we might see self-sacrifice, they saw His kingdom—kingdom first. They responded to the tasks Christ set before them. Their remarkable, inspiring story is now carefully and eloquently pieced together by Gilbert Gleason in *Love So Amazing*.

Marshall Christensen, PhD, cofounder, Co-Serve International

I often spoke of Bert and Colleen from the platform as examples of stick-to-it-tive-ness, godly self-sacrifice, and simple perseverance in jungle heat, mildew, mud, and rain in the high Andes, humbly ministering to lonely people. Amy Carmichael wrote, "Can he have followed far / Who hath no wound nor scar?" Jim often quoted those lines. Bert and Colleen lived them.

Elisabeth Elliot, sister-in-law, author of *Shadow of the Almighty: The Life and Testament of Jim Elliot*

For sixty-five years the world has been enriched and challenged by the story of Jim Elliot told by his wife, Elisabeth. Now Gilbert Gleason brings us the equally fascinating account of another brother in that family. Bert's quest was to discover "what God made me for." He found it as he loved on, listened to, prayed with, healed, and taught people throughout the jungles, mountains, and coasts of Peru. Colleen and Bert were models and mentors for my work in Bolivia. It's a treat to know their full story.

Dr. Steve Hawthorne, nephew, SIM medical missionary

Bert and Colleen Elliot invested their lives into developing strong church leaders. Peruvian men and women accompanied them on their river voyages and mountain trips, watching firsthand their commitment to obeying God and loving people. Principles of godly living and church leadership are often better caught than taught. Bert and Colleen modeled that. As a result, an indigenous church planting movement continues to thrive in Peru. This is true apostolic Christianity in action—the Great Commission on display. *Love So Amazing* tells their captivating story.

Alexander Strauch, author of *Biblical Eldership* and *Paul's Vision for the Deacons*

As a seminary student I was privileged to know Bert and Colleen Elliot as friends. In *Love So Amazing* his nephew, Gilbert Gleason uses Bert and Colleen's own words to portray their lives through every season and illumine their personalities, grace, perseverance, and love for the Lord, which informed all they did. Here is a guide for living the Christ-centered, obedient life, from one who had sought to know "what I was created for" in the shadow of his younger brother's mighty, yet martyred life. These two together cultivated faithfulness with love so amazing that over sixty years . . . a whole nation was transformed!

Bill MacLeod, founder and director, Mission ConneXion

This story of the lives of Bert and Colleen Elliot is a treasure trove of amazing quotes that will bring tears to your eyes, a smile to your face, and a challenge to your heart. Christian Missions in Many Lands had the privilege of serving both Jim and Elisabeth and Bert and Colleen. Our prayer is that the Lord of the Harvest will send out more men and women like them, willing to pour out their lives for the Lord on the mission field.

John Peasland, executive director, Christian Missions in Many Lands

Love So Amazing

The Missionary Biography of Bert and Colleen Elliot

GILBERT A. GLEASON

Dedicated to

Susan Colleen Gleason
My wife
My love
My best friend

Who loved her Uncle Bert and Aunt Colleen,
is honored to be Colleen's namesake,
and cherishes the memory of listening
to her grandmother Clara Elliot read their letters.

Love so amazing, so divine,
demands my soul, my life, my all.

—Isaac Watts

Contents

Northwest Peru

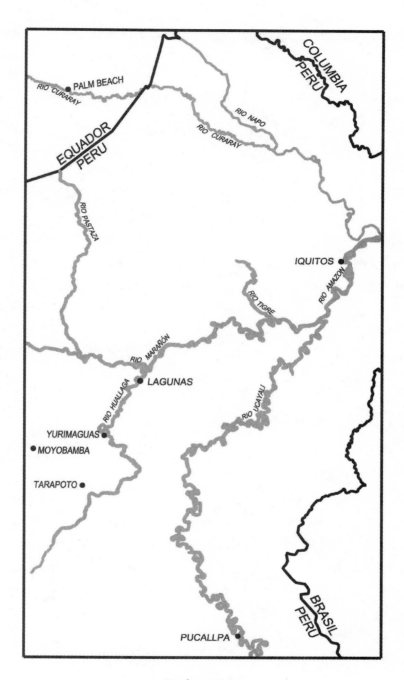

Northeast Peru

Foreword

At my home church in January 2006—the fiftieth anniversary of the death of five missionaries in Ecuador—I interviewed Steve Saint, son of martyr Nate Saint; Steve McCully, son of martyr Ed McCully; and Mincaye, one of the tribal warriors who killed the missionaries and later came to faith in Christ.

Afterward, my wife, Nanci, and I, along with our friends Stu and Linda Weber, joined Bert and Colleen and other Elliot family members, including Gilbert and Susan Gleason, for dinner at Jim and Bert's childhood home in Portland, Oregon. We spent an unforgettable afternoon with members of three of the five martyred missionaries' families.

What I most enjoyed that day was time spent talking alone with Bert Elliot. When I asked him about their ministry in Peru, Bert's eyes lit up as he said, "I can't wait to get back from furlough!" At that time, he and Colleen were in their eighties and nearing their sixtieth year as missionaries, with no intention of retiring. They were vibrant—still joyfully excited about reaching people for Christ.

Prior to that Sunday I knew a great deal about Jim Elliot and Nate Saint, and a little about the three other missionary martyrs. I knew absolutely nothing about Bert and Colleen. Though aware their home was less than two miles from where my wife grew up in Portland, we didn't even realize that Jim had a brother. We had no clue that in the 1940s Bert and Colleen attended the same college that Nanci and I had attended in the seventies, then known as Multnomah School of the Bible.

After returning home that night, I searched online and found only one article with much information about Bert and Colleen. It said they'd planted over 158 churches in Peru. (Of course, Bert didn't tell me that.) They served Christ faithfully, almost completely under the radar of the church at large.

I will never forget what Bert said about Jim that day in his childhood home. Tears formed in his eyes as he spoke. "Jim and I both served Christ, but differently." He paused and cleared his throat. "Jim was a great meteor, streaking through the sky."

Bert stopped there. He didn't go on to describe himself, but here is what came to my mind: Unlike his brother Jim—the shooting star everyone learned about in *LIFE* magazine and numerous books—Bert was a fifth-magnitude star, a mere pinpoint of light, rising night after night, faithfully crossing the same path in the sky, to God's glory. A star so faint that no one knew its name or pointed it out. Millions have quoted his younger brother, Jim, who went to Ecuador three years after Bert went to Peru. But I've never heard a sermon or read a book quoting from Bert Elliot. Not until this one.

Gilbert Gleason writes in this book, "Bert and Colleen serve as the right kind of examples for 'average' followers of Jesus, proving that, for most of us, substantial, supernatural impact is achieved through simple daily faithfulness, listening to Jesus and loving people in His name." I'm struck by Gilbert's description of Bert and Colleen being "average." Of the well-known modern martyrs, Jim Elliot has become—and in some ways, in real life truly was—an almost mythical character. I've read what he said and did, and, while

14

he's had great impact on my life, at times he seems far beyond me and other mortals. I'm tempted to think of Jim as a superhero to admire, rather than an example to follow.

Bert was different. He wasn't like the sprinter who wins the Olympic gold medal. He was like the clerk or custodian who jogs a nine-minute mile three miles a day and, over his lifetime, runs much farther than the pro who retires at thirty. Bert and Colleen just kept serving, faithfully and joyfully, for sixty-two years. They modeled true humility and sacrificial love for God and others.

Missionary work sometimes culminates in unforgettable martyrdom. More often it involves what Eugene Peterson called "a long obedience in the same direction"—years spent dying daily to self and living moment-after-moment for Jesus. Certainly I believe Jim Elliot's reward is considerable, but it wouldn't surprise me to discover that Bert and Colleen's is greater still.

After visiting Bert and Colleen in Peru, Lars Gren, Elisabeth Elliot's husband, wrote, "They are available for any who call or ring the doorbell, whether expected or unexpected. Along with open doors, there are the Bible studies, their involvement in the Christian School . . . Plus an exceptional drug program leading addicts into a new life based on Scripture . . . All this after fifty-six years on the field with no thought of the rocking chair or hanging out a shingle saying, 'Busy. Please call again.' What a life of service."

Bert and Colleen may not have made much difference on Google and Twitter, but God was their Audience of One. He says a book of remembrance is written for his faithful servants (see Malachi 3:16), and Jesus promised, "If anyone gives even a cup of cold water to one of these little ones who is my disciple, truly I tell you, that person will certainly not lose their reward" (Matthew 10:42, NIV).

Bert and Colleen's life reminds me of the man Jesus described in a parable: "The Kingdom of Heaven is like a treasure that a man discovered hidden in a field. In his excitement, he hid it again and sold everything he owned to get enough money to buy the field" (Matthew 13:44, NLT).

When we read he "sold everything he owned" to obtain the treasure, we might feel sorry for him, because his sacrifice was great. But he didn't feel sorry for himself; on the contrary, he couldn't believe how fortunate he was! (The point, of course, is not the value of temporary treasure, but the eternal treasure it represents.)

Though Bert and Colleen served in Peru over 75 percent of their lives, they would say the sacrifice was nothing compared to what they gained, *even in this life!* And gauged by their forever lives, the payoff will be unimaginable and eternal! Because their sacrifices were eclipsed by joy, to them they seemed small.

In 2012, a few days after Bert died, I wrote an article about him that, in God's providence, was reprinted by many, including Focus on the Family. I'm delighted to say you can now find far more about Bert and Colleen than I was able to when I first tried. Certainly *Love So Amazing* provides a great wealth of information unavailable until now.

It was a great honor to be asked to speak at Bert's memorial service, but I had to decline because of a prior commitment I couldn't cancel. I was amazed to learn that Colleen died the day before Bert's service! It became a memorial for both of them. I wished I could have been there. But there's something far better than a wish, and that's the promise of Jesus: I will see Bert and Colleen again—and will partake in a joyful reunion with countless Christ followers I've known and far more I haven't met but will. It is not wishful thinking that one day all of us who know Jesus will walk the New Earth together. It is a certainty bought, paid for, and written in Jesus' blood.

So as you read this book, if you love and follow Jesus as the Elliots did, you won't have to regret that you didn't know Bert and Colleen. Because one day you will. In countless magnificent dinners and other celebrations, full of laughter and delight, we will meet and hear the stories of thousands of people from those 150-plus churches God raised up through his faithful, humble, and happy servants, Bert and Colleen Elliot. And that will be a tiny sampling of the adventures that await us, by the grace of our Lord Jesus Christ.

As you read *Love So Amazing,* may you better grasp the meaning of Christ's words: "Give, and it will be given to you. A good measure, pressed down, shaken together and running over, will be poured into your lap. For with the measure you use, it will be measured to you" (Luke 6:38, ESV).

Randy Alcorn
Eternal Perspective Ministries

Introduction

The septuagenarians strode onto the platform holding hands like teenagers in the bloom of first love. Bert and Colleen Elliot turned to face the crowd of 300,000 gathered for the Luis Palau Festival in Lima, Peru. It was October 2004.

International evangelist Palau had invited Bert and Colleen to attend the festival as his special guests, to publicly honor them for their lifelong ministry in Peru. Before this audience Palau drew attention to the hardships the Elliots had endured, the challenges they'd faced, the opposition they'd withstood, and the commitment they had needed to finish well. For fifty-five years they had served in relative obscurity in remote villages in the jungle, mountains, and coastal regions of northern Peru, routinely traveling hundreds of miles between their local churches to sustain the physical and spiritual health of real people like us—people the rest of the world knew nothing about. Every bend in the river, fork in the road, lonely mountain trail, and isolated village presented a fresh opportunity to share the love of God. While they knew the geography like the features of each other's faces, it was the people—precious, eternal souls—who were embedded in their hearts. As they celebrated with

Palau in Lima, they could not know they still had seven more fruitful years ahead of them.

Colleen wrote of the Palau festival,

> That evening we looked out over the largest group of people we had ever seen together in one place and listened to a clear and simple message with an invitation. Palau's team had prepared thirty-seven thousand counselors. In those two nights about forty thousand people made professions of faith and received his little book *Say Yes to Life*. We couldn't help think of the tremendous contrast to the Peru fifty years earlier when it was against the law to preach in the open air. None of what we saw [in 2004] would have been remotely possible [in the 1950s]. Praise the Lord for all He has done and is doing in this beautiful country.

As they sat on the speaker's platform, tears flowed. Bert said to Colleen, "What we are seeing is nothing less than a miracle. Remember when there were only fourteen local churches in Lima?" Lima was a city of eight million. "And to think God allowed us to be a part of it."

Palau had been watching the couple and said to Bert, "Man, you really love that woman!"

Bert beamed. "Have you seen how pretty she is? You know, when you don't have children, you can spend all your love on just her!"

This couple deserved the accolades, but they never sought them. Bert and Colleen Elliot didn't begin their missionary journey with the intention of living a noteworthy life. They simply made themselves available for God to use wherever and however He wanted. They didn't craft a master plan or write a life purpose statement. They didn't establish a set of lofty goals. The question they asked each step of the way was simply, "What would God have us do next?"

The jungles of Peru in the late forties and into the fifties and sixties were still very much a pioneer setting that required great sacrifice.

Besides forgoing life's modern conveniences in the States, Bert and Colleen faced tropical diseases, poisonous creatures, hazardous travel conditions, and at times life-threatening opposition to their ministry. They chose to walk, not the easy road, but the obedient one.

One of my life's privileges was that my road intersected that of Bert and Colleen. I also count it a privilege to tell their story. When Elisabeth Elliot—bestselling author and wife of Bert's martyred brother, Jim—first encouraged me to write Bert and Colleen's biography, I recoiled at the thought. What words could I put on a piece of paper that would effectively communicate their heart's passion, their infectious personalities, and their commitment to be a "living and holy sacrifice, acceptable to God"?[1] How do I adequately describe Uncle Bert's warm bear hug, dynamic preaching and scriptural observations, love of nature, robust sense of humor, delight in telling a good story, and appreciation for Colleen? And then there's Aunt Colleen—her perceptive insights, her anticipation for each day, her genuine interest in each person, and her admiration for Bert.

But I found myself in an unusual position to follow through with the task. I first met Bert and Colleen when I was "evicted" from the downstairs apartment at "7272"[2] so they could live there during their furlough in 1976. I fell in love with their niece and married into the family in 1979 and then became their pastor in 1981. I found in Uncle Bert an impactful mentor for my life and ministry. With Aunt Colleen I shared a kindred spirit and could always count on her being in my corner. The Elliots were a treasured aunt and uncle, dear friends, and incredible role models.

In writing this book, I have relied greatly on Bert and Colleen's personal correspondence. Colleen especially was a voluminous letter writer. She saw her letters as a lifeline to those who loved and prayed

1   Romans 12:1.
2   The family nickname for the Elliot home where Bert grew up in Portland, Oregon, on the east slope of Mt. Tabor. Six generations of the Luginbuhl/Elliot/Gleason family have lived in it.

for them. Most of her letters were two to three pages of single-spaced typewritten news with virtually no margins. She didn't like to waste the paper! Living before the advent of copiers or email, Colleen would type six or seven letters at one time using carbon paper. She sent these to family members, encouraging them to share the letters with friends, family, and church. She usually included a handwritten note on each individual letter, filling whatever margin remained. She realized how important communication was to the effectiveness of their ministry, so keeping up with correspondence was a constant pressure. She would sometimes add a note that she had as many as forty or more letters on her desk to answer. Bert frequently wrote letters or added notes to the bottom of Colleen's letters, but the bulk of the correspondence was hers.

Bert and Colleen gave me permission to write their biography, but they voiced their skepticism: "Gilbert, who would want to read about our simple life?" In my initial efforts I read their letters and then attempted to retell their story in my own words as eruditely as I could. Two factors changed my approach. First, I found that I was wearing out my thesaurus trying to find words that told the couple's story with more color and authenticity than their own writings, while at the same time avoiding plagiarism. Second, after reading these first attempts, my wife, Sue, said, "It would be better if you let Uncle Bert and Aunt Colleen tell their own story." One of Sue's fondest childhood memories was sitting in the kitchen nook at 7272 listening to her Grandmother Clara read the real-life adventures that Colleen described so vividly. Yes, they do tell their story better.

So I have attempted to let Bert and Colleen communicate their own story as much as possible by quoting extensively from their correspondence. They wrote their letters as personal correspondence, not for publication. I have limited my editing and quoted much of the material verbatim. At times I have taken the liberty to shorten sentences, change some words for clarification, correct spelling (Bert was a notoriously poor speller!), or leave out unrelated details, while maintaining the integrity of the quoted content.

This book is my humble attempt to introduce to you this couple with all their strengths, weaknesses, challenges, and accomplishments, who epitomized what it means "to give what [you] cannot keep to gain what [you] cannot lose."[3]

In their later years, on numerous occasions Bert and Colleen said, "If we had sat down at the beginning of our marriage and tried to write out what we would have liked our life to look like, in our wildest dreams we could not have imagined anything as joyful and fulfilling as the life that God has given us."

To love and obey God and to love and serve His people . . . as the Elliots would say, "What a privilege!" Theirs is indeed a love story.

---

3   This widely quoted statement comes from Bert's brother Jim, published in Elisabeth Elliot, ed., *The Journals of Jim Elliot* (Old Tappan, New Jersey: Revell, 1978), 174. The original reads, "He is no fool who gives what he cannot keep to gain what he cannot lose."

1

A Twig Consumed

"I remember spending some time blessing God for such a spiritual heritage," wrote Bert, "for a father who towers in spirituality head and shoulders above other men, and for a mother the size of whose heart can never be measured, but is hinted at in all she has suffered to bring us all up and then give us back to God."

His father, Fred, was a traveling evangelist who believed Bible teaching needed to begin at home. Bert recalled, "For breakfast we had oatmeal and the Bible." No matter what demands the day held, it started with an in-depth Bible lesson in the kitchen nook.

Fred was the oldest of eight children born to John and Margaret Elliot in the hardwood bush country of Ontario, Canada. They were one couple from among the marriages of four Elliot siblings to four McAllister siblings, producing thirty-six double cousins. John was a livestock trader who maintained a farm and believed in hard work. Margaret suffered from frequent violent asthma attacks. Consequently Fred had to quit school to help out at home. He never finished his formal education but compensated by becoming an avid reader. He decided to follow Christ at age thirteen after hearing of His imminent return.

Immediately following the dawning of the twentieth century, while still in his late teens, Fred traveled with his younger brother Will to work in the wheat fields of Saskatchewan and then on to British Columbia. It was there he sat under the teaching of Harry Ironside and learned that it was only by living a life totally committed to God that one could find fulfillment. He married at twenty-seven but lost his wife and child in childbirth on their first anniversary. He began traveling with Mr. Ironside, who at that time was preaching in rural communities across the Pacific Northwest. One of his regular stops was to a pair of neighboring sheep ranches near Roosevelt, Washington, one owned by Emil and Emma (Maurer) Luginbuhl, the other by the family of Emma's sister Clara (Maurer) Berney. Fred first met Clara Luginbuhl, named after her aunt, at the Berney ranch. She was eighteen and unavailable, as she was very much in love with her uncle's foreman.

Clara's parents, Emil and Emma, had sung together in a choir in Switzerland. When Emil, after settling in Eastern Washington, learned this ribbon maker's daughter had arrived in America, he wrote immediately and persuaded her to join him on his homestead. They were married by the local Methodist preacher. Clara was their second child, born in 1895. Along with sheep, her family raised apples, pears, plums, cherries, apricots, grapes, strawberries, and an assortment of vegetables and flowers. Except for an hour reserved for playtime, the children's day was filled with chores; Clara's were housekeeping, bread baking, and caring for the orphan lambs. In 1907 the Luginbuhls purchased "7272," a simple four-room farmhouse on the east slope of Mount Tabor in Portland, Oregon, for reprieves from the isolation of the Washington farm and so the children could continue their education. It quickly became the hub of family activity. In fact, Clara's cousin Ted Berney was born in the house in 1908. On a personal note, I had the privilege of being at his bedside when he passed away ninety-six years later.

Three years after their initial meeting Fred spotted Clara in the audience at the little Baptist church in Portland where he was preaching. He assumed her escort that Monday night was her intended. But on Tuesday night she showed up with a different fellow. When he saw her with a third one on Wednesday night, he began to think there might be hope for him and asked if he could escort her home on Thursday night. That began daily visits, leading up to the lily he sent her for Easter. Fred and Clara corresponded for two years and married after Clara graduated from Pacific Chiropractic College in 1918.

They lived in Seattle for the first four years of their marriage. Fred did evangelistic work in the Puget Sound area while Clara began her chiropractic practice. Their son Bob was born in 1921. They returned to Portland a year later, purchased 7272 from her parents, and lived there for the remainder of their lives. Bert was born in 1924, Jim in 1927, and Jane in 1932.

Although Clara conducted an active chiropractic practice in her home, she saw the children's care as her primary responsibility. She was the heart of the home. Affection and discipline were equal expressions of her love. A lifelong bond of love was nurtured between those six. Their letters to each other, even through their adult years, reflected that bond, and it grew stronger with each crisis and tragedy they faced together.

Chores were part of their routine. The children fed the chickens, rabbits, and goats, did the yard work, stoked the furnace, maintained the house, cooked the meals, and cleaned up. Everyone pitched in. Fred did not hesitate to administer punishment when needed, but spankings were usually delayed until they could be dispensed in private. The parents tried to follow through consistently, because they thought idle threats were dishonest and damaging to the child. When each child turned fourteen, Fred and Clara told that child that the primary responsibility for his or her attitudes and behavior was now to the Lord. They were His children, and He would watch over them and discipline them.

Sunday was reserved for church—Grace and Truth Gospel Hall (now Grace Bible Fellowship), which was part of an international association of churches or "assemblies" called Plymouth Brethren. The children attended from the age of six weeks. "I don't think it hurts any child to sit quietly through an adult meeting," said Clara. "It's good for his nerves." Family, friends, and church relationships were closely intertwined. Fred was a key leader and preacher in the church.

The gift of hospitality was on full display in the Elliot home. The children loved this, even though it meant extra work and inconvenience for them—like giving up one's bed for a night. They met missionaries from around the world, broadening their perspective on the needs and opportunities for overseas ministry. Other guests came because they needed a place to stay while in transition or recovering from an illness.

One guest stayed permanently. "Auntie Frostie" was an ailing English lady whom Clara nursed back to health. She stayed twenty years and literally died in the home. She helped keep the household functioning while Clara maintained her chiropractic practice and Fred traveled on his itinerant preaching trips. As Bert put it, "She was trying her hardest to bring a little of her British good manners into our very laidback American family." But sometimes she could get on the nerves of various family members. One time Bert and his dad were working on the roof when Auntie Frostie came out and announced, "Fred, you'd better come down now. The guests are coming in five minutes."

Under his breath Fred muttered, "Ah, go mind your own business, you old battle-ax!"

Bert then helpfully shouted down, "He said, 'Mind your own business, you old battle-ax!'"

Fred laughed so hard he fell over and would have fallen off the roof except for a valley between two peaks!

Fred's impact on his children was immeasurable. In a letter to his future wife, Elisabeth, Bert's brother, Jim, wrote, "My father's

Bob, Jim, Clara, Bert, Fred holding Jane

religion is of a sort which I have seen nowhere else. His theology is wholly undeveloped, but so real and practical a thing that it shatters every 'system' of doctrine I have seen. He cannot define theism, but he knows God."[1] He loved his children and poured his life into them.

---

1   Elisabeth Elliot, *Shadow of the Almighty* (Grand Rapids: Zondervan, 1958), 90.

Much of the credit for raising the children goes to Clara. She was a remarkable woman. As a teenager on the sheep ranch, she fell off a horse and sustained a leg injury that never completely healed. She probably had chronic osteomyelitis, which somewhat crippled her the rest of her life. In her later years, when I first met her, she was confined to a wheelchair.

For a young woman to become a chiropractor in that day was unusual. This medical discipline was still in its infancy. She was the family's primary financial provider; she kept her business in the home, her office a room off the living room, so she could stay home with the family. Fred didn't bring in much income as an itinerant preacher and was often away from home for months at a time on his circuit. Clara fully supported his ministry and appreciated that she was able to play a role in it.

"Bert" Ironside Elliot was born November 3, 1924, in Portland. I have discovered that a person's middle name is often a window into what or whom the parents deem significant—even more than the first name. Bert's middle name was a tribute to Harry Ironside, who introduced Fred and Clara and made a profound impact on Fred's life and ministry. Bert came to value that significance.

The family spent many happy summers on the Luginbuhl ranch in Roosevelt, Washington, where they learned about sheep, cows, and coyotes. Bert said of his older brother, "Bob was great at getting me into trouble. I had a Benjamin pump pellet gun. He said he was sure I couldn't hit the license that hung in the middle of the radiator on the old '29 Chev. He was right—I hit the radiator instead and put a hole in it, draining out all the water."

When Bert was twelve, his family visited the Charles Berney farm in Corbett, Oregon. While playing by himself in the barn, Bert slid between two haystacks, became trapped, and thought he was going to die. He was rescued, but that night he couldn't sleep. He wasn't prepared to die. His father asked him what was wrong. Together they wrestled through John 5:24 (KJV): "Verily, verily, I say unto you, he that heareth My word, and believeth on Him that sent Me, hath everlasting life, and shall not come into condemnation; but is passed from death unto life." He put his faith in Christ and found peace with God.

But he did not experience the full impact of that decision until his midteen years. Bert reflected, "In my first years of high school I was just a wretch. My dad said one day, 'Bert, what can we do with you? Your mother and I have tried everything. We've tried kindness and goodness. We've tried the switch. We've tried everything. What can we do with you?' I didn't even know I had a problem!" First Bert confirmed his salvation.

> When I was sure my sins were forgiven, I began to read in Romans. I found I had an obligation—He who gave His life for me demanded my life for Him. I offered my life and began to renew that commitment daily. *Lord, what would You have me do today? What would You have me say today?* It is the daily consecration. He purchased me with His own blood on the cross. He forgave all my sins. He made me a new creature. He has given me His Holy Spirit. I am now under a new authority.

Bert followed in the steps of his older brother, Bob, and attended Benson Polytechnic High School. With an all-male student body of 2,800, it was Portland's largest school, a trade school focusing on the industrial arts. As a technical mechanical major, Bert took classes in subjects like electrical systems, gas engines, machine shop, woodworking, printing, sheet metal, plumbing, foundry, blacksmithing, and drawing, in addition to the usual academic studies. This was a perfect combination for a student like Bert, who struggled with academics but excelled in the hands-on mechanical skills. It was also great training for his role as a missionary who would often have to be the jack of all trades in remote settings. Through the years Bert relied heavily on his Benson education.

To round out his high school career, Bert was also involved in public speaking and football and was elected senior class president.

Jim, Jane, Bob, Bert

Looking back after his many years navigating the tributaries of the Amazon River, it is fitting to read Bert's entry under "class will" in his year book: "Bert 'Ironsides' Elliot leaves his boating ability to someone who can't paddle straight." He graduated in June 1943.

At a youth meeting around a bonfire, Bert put a twig in the fire and said, "Lord, I want my life to be consumed, giving light and heat in a world full of darkness and cold." That became the passion of his life. Later in life he commented, "I did not realize this is an attitude for all of life, for every day, to put my life on the altar."

A couple months before graduation, Bert purchased a garbage collecting business for three thousand dollars with the financial help of Ray Berney, his mother's cousin. The purchase included a 1939 GMC truck retrofitted with a steel garbage-carrying body and hydraulic hoist. He excelled in operating the business. As a side benefit, out of the garbage he was able to reclaim some useful items— several stoves, a bed, chairs, and a bear rug complete with head. His brother Jim helped him on Saturday mornings and picked up a set of autopsy tools, which inspired Jim to take taxidermy lessons. They accumulated enough bricks over time to build a fireplace on the patio at 7272.

This was a successful enterprise, but by the end of the year Bert was questioning its place in his long-range plans. His three options were to grow the business, in which case he would "clean up materially but, as I see it, lose out spiritually"; to cut back on the business and balance work and ministry; or to sell the business and "trust the Lord for guidance."

He clarified the impetus for this evaluation of his life's direction in a letter to his father dated December 20, 1943:

> My heart has been stirred through the ministry of Mr. Bernam [a traveling preacher] during the past two weeks. First, the Lord has placed in my heart the one desire, that from this day forward my life might be spent for His glory. Second, at the present time my life is falling far short of that desire—the reason being that I don't spend enough time in the Word. Third, if the desires of my heart are to be fulfilled, more time must be spent in the Word. If more time is spent in the Word, less time must be spent in business. If less time is spent in business, income is less. If income is less, hard feelings are caused [with his investor].

For the time being he decided to maintain the status quo and try to balance business and spiritual interests. However, his heart was drawn to overseas missions, a growing burden for the entire family, as evidenced in this undated letter to his father from this period:

> As I think of the different trails but the common call of yourself, Bob, Jim, Dick [Fisher, a family friend], and myself, my heart has been devising certain things, but we are trusting Him to direct our path. Proverbs 16:9.
>
> One cannot help but ponder the outcome of these five men, and such women as the Lord directs, as their lives converge to carry out a common purpose—to spread by lip and by life the glad tidings of our Lord Jesus Christ, perhaps in some uncharted field in South America. The potentiality is beyond our very conception. Yet just below the surface of the sea as we sail are jagged rocks placed strategically by our arch enemy, Satan, so as to spell shipwreck for the most courageous men guided by the most skillful pilots. Consequently, at the helm of our frail bark[2] is none other than the master of every tempest, even the Lord Christ.
>
> The days before sailing must be spent in rigid preparation. But at each bend in the road we travel lurks an enemy to our cause, seeking at all cost to lure us out of the hearing of our Helmsman for a short season, and to escort us to the wharf. But then we would find the Lord's bark far out to sea without us and experience the heartbreak of a shipwrecked life.
>
> Therefore, realizing more fully the hazards along our path, let us spend much time daily in the presence of our compassionate Shepherd, becoming more fully acquainted with His voice *so that* we might *come* when He speaks our name, *go* when He puts us forth, and *follow* wherever He leads, anticipating the day when we experience the joy of hearing from His lips, "Well done, thou good and faithful servant."

---

2   A small sailing ship, also spelled *barque*.

But those plans were interrupted by the United States' involvement in World War II. By this time Bob was married to Ruby and had a temporary deferral from the draft, because he was training in the medical field. When the deferral expired upon his graduation from chiropractic college, he and Bert became eligible for the draft at the same time. Many of their closest Christian friends joined the military and served with distinction. But Bob and Bert were convinced that military service was incompatible with the teaching of Scripture. Elisabeth's explanation of Jim's view on military service reflected that of his brothers:

> He believed the church of Christ, in contrast to the community of Israel in Old Testament times, has abandoned national and political ties. In the words of [the apostle Paul]: "But we are citizens of heaven. Our outlook goes beyond this world to the hopeful expectation of the Savior who will come from heaven, the Lord Jesus Christ." The principle of nonresistance which Jesus demonstrated once and for all on the Cross was one which Jim felt must be obeyed, in public life as well as in personal.[3]

Consequently they registered as conscientious objectors.

The government established the Civilian Public Service (CPS) in 1941 to give conscientious objectors the opportunity to perform "work of national importance" without joining the war effort, as an alternative to military induction. The government provided camp housing, transportation, and $2.50 a month. The churches and families of the men often provided funds for maintaining the CPS camps and to meet their needs. In total about twelve thousand men served in 152 locations across the US. At the outset government agencies were skeptical of the CPS, but then came to appreciate their contribution and often requested these workers for their programs.

---

3   Elliot, *Shadow of the Almighty*, 33. Scripture quotation paraphrased from Philippians 3:20.

Bob and Bert joined the CPS in September 1944 and were assigned to a forestry camp two and a half miles outside Belden, California, along the Feather River. Like many of the CPS camps, this was originally built for the Civilian Conservation Corps. Their main responsibility was to fight forest fires. When not occupied with that, they did timber cruising, evaluating the grassland for grazing and the forest for Christmas trees and timber harvest. They typically worked nine hours a day, six days a week.

Bert's graduation from Benson

There were 153 men assigned to the main camp at Belden, some of whom were distributed among six to eight satellite sites. The camp supervisor was a minister from Colorado. One of the CPS camps' distinct features was the demographics of the fellows. By definition, CPS camps employed only conscientious objectors. Most had come to their conviction based on deeply held religious beliefs. The majority were from the peace churches—Church of the Brethren (different from Plymouth Brethren), Religious Society of Friends (Quakers), and Mennonites. But many like Bob and Bert came from smaller denominations and church associations.

Consequently Sunday services were regular occurrences, as were discussions over various interpretations of Scripture. On at least one occasion Fred preached in the camp service while visiting his sons. This setting was free from many distractions, so the brothers found themselves spending much time in the Word.

The camp provided regular training classes on various skills. Bert reported, "These last two days we have been studying the standard first aid course. It's kind of fun but certainly gets monotonous four hours in a row. We both have taken it before, so that makes us the brains, quite a change for me."

Bert found he was not out of the reach of his mother's heart, to whom he wrote,

I see you are still worried about my love affairs, Mom. I appreciate your observations. I always told you Margie had something. She is a sweet gal. So is Marylou, but I'm sorry to hear she thinks she is first on my list. This would be a bit difficult as I have no list. There are times, when a fellow is alone watching a sunset or a full moon shining through the sugar pines, that his heart and affections go out to someone. But lately mine have been embracing the Person who created that lovely sunset and who by the word of His power made and holds that moon in its course, these being only the work of His fingers. When I stop and consider His love for me, it nearly overwhelms me. Think of it. This very same *almighty* one spent Himself at Calvary to redeem us from sin; such was His love for us. Can it be that we go from day to day, week to week without just *telling* Him we love Him? May it not be so with us. But as time goes, may it be more and more and *more* of Christ (Philippians 2:9–11).

Partway through their seven-month assignment in California, Bob and Bert were transferred to the satellite camp at Brush Creek. They found a great improvement in both the cooking and the morale—a predictable correlation! The Christian fellowship was also much more to their liking. Bert wrote,

> Most of the fellows in this camp are German Baptist (G. B.) or Old Order Brethren, which on the whole are much sounder than the Church of the Brethren. Occasionally the fellows have their relatives come from the Modesto area [about a three-hour drive]. One of them is usually a minister. Today there were about four carloads of folks up, all with their quaint dress—black suits with no collar, a broad-brim black hat, and lots of whiskers for the men and little white hats and plain clothes for the women.
>
> This has been the best Lord's Day since we left home. The G. B.s are plain but godly folks. They really love our Lord. The service started by singing from a hymnbook very much like the *Believers Hymn Book* with many of the same hymns. When they pray, everyone goes down on their knees. The preaching is without eloquence but Christ exalting. After meeting we had a real old-time sing. They can really do it. Bob and I sang in a quartet, which seemed to sound pretty good. Anyway, we had a grand time, almost like home.

He added a postscript stating they tossed several packages of tobacco and cigarettes in the stove as several of the men made a commitment to quit smoking.

In spring 1945 Bob and Bert were transferred to the Springfield State Hospital in Sykesville, Maryland. This was a mental hospital, and the living conditions were a vast improvement over the forest camps. A major benefit for Bob was that, due to the living arrangements, Ruby was able to join him. Bert's primary responsibility was giving shaves and haircuts to the men. Ruby was an aide on the ward, and Bob was the staff director.

The Elliots' hearts for ministry were again evident. They started a Bible study in the hospital. Several times they were able to get away on Sundays to fellowship with DC-area believers who were Elliot family friends. On one of those visits Bert met for the first time Joe Hocking of Pucallpa, Peru, and learned about opportunities for ministry there.

At one point Bert applied for a transfer to a building project in Puerto Rico, because he reasoned the experience would be more valuable than a year of college, providing carpentry skills useful in missions. Alas, the transfer never materialized.

After reading a missions magazine describing a particular financial need, Bert committed to pray and give. He wrote his brother Jim, "Large corporations are successful because they can supply *sufficient capital quickly* where it can be most wisely invested. The greater shortage in God's supply house is not for capital but for *yielded young lives.* May He not find His warehouse at Sixth and Prescott [Grace and Truth] with a depleted stock."

Bob and Bert were discharged from the CPS in fall 1946 after serving two full years.

2

Old "Percy"

When preparing for her older sister's wedding, Colleen Collison wrote, "Anyway, I've been doing exercises for two whole nights now. For about fifteen minutes Ann and I get out in the hall and do back bends, flip flops, and I don't know what all—until I'm so stiff today I can hardly walk. But you know me, old 'Percy' (short for perseverance). I can't let a little thing like stiffness keep me from getting *slim* and *trim*—especially for such an important event."

The apostle James wrote, "Perseverance must finish its work so that you may be mature and complete, not lacking anything" (1:4, NIV). Old "Percy" learned that steady persistence in spite of difficulties, obstacles, and discouragement reaped lasting rewards. Perseverance was in the Collison family DNA.

Colleen's father, George Collison, was born in 1899 and attended the High School of Commerce, which focused on business education and eventually became Cleveland High School. This prepared him to become a bookkeeper/accountant for Pacific Power and Light for forty-five years. He briefly attended the Oregon State College

ROTC program, but this military training was cut short when World War I ended. He was a tall lanky man who never drove a car or rode in an airplane. He enjoyed walking and used public transportation to get around. Although he did not become a Christian until the end of his life, he was very supportive of his family's involvement in church and Colleen's decision to become a missionary.

Colleen's mother, Catherine "Kate" Olga Muschalik, was born in 1901, the sixth of ten children. Although she only completed the eighth grade, she picked up skills in typing and shorthand. She initially worked for the Union Pacific Railroad. During World War II the War Production Training Company hired her to edit and print training manuals for building ships. She worked the swing shift and learned to run the mimeograph machine, which launched her into a career in printing. Following the war she worked for the Pacific Pumping Company and then US National Bank, from which she retired. She was a noted proofreader, and many of her coworkers brought their forms, letters, and reports for her to edit. Having read more than a thousand of Colleen's letters, I can attest that she inherited her mother's verbal skills and spelling acuity.

George and Kate's 1925 wedding was not photographed, but Colleen's sister Joan remembers playing dress-up as girls with some of their mom's dresses, including one fancy brown satin dress that her mom called her wedding dress. Patricia was born in 1926, followed by Colleen in 1928 and Joan in 1931.

Colleen was born on July 5, 1928, with blond hair and blue eyes. Her birth weight of twelve pounds portended her large adult frame, which stood out among the much smaller Peruvians.

The early years of their family life were marked by the Great Depression. George was blessed to remain employed during those years, although at a lower salary.

For several years during the Depression Kate and the girls, along with some extended family members, spent about eight weeks each summer picking berries—strawberries, raspberries, blackcaps (black raspberries), boysenberries, youngberries, and loganberries—in

Pat, Colleen, Kate, George, Joan

the fields east of Portland. They all camped out near the fields in a chicken coop equipped with a wood stove and some beds. George and his brother-in-law would come out to help on the weekends. Everyone pitched in to make ends meet, instilling a tremendous work ethic in Colleen.

The family grew up spending many summers in Ocean Park, Washington, at a small cabin owned by Grandma Collison. It was located on the Long Beach Peninsula with the Willapa Bay on one side and the Pacific Ocean on the other. The family didn't own a car, so getting to the cabin was a challenge. They traveled from Portland to Astoria by train, then crossed the Columbia River by ferry to Megler, Washington, then bused to Long Beach. There they used their persuasive powers to get the driver to take them the extra seven miles to Ocean Park. Since they were packed for the summer, they usually had a number of trunks and duffel bags. Upon their arrival the water pump had to be primed and a path cleared to the outhouse on the property's backside.

Colleen's graduation from Jefferson

George would leave the family and return to Portland to work for the summer. Kate was responsible for the girls, along with gathering wood, cooking, washing clothes, and otherwise keeping house in rustic conditions. Near the end of August George would make the return trek for his two-week vacation. The family made many happy memories playing on the beach in the icy water, searching for driftwood for the woodstove, crabbing, and clamming. It was an inexpensive vacation that paid great dividends in family time.

Much of family life for Kate and the girls centered around their involvement at Grace and Truth Gospel Hall. They had been attending another church when Edwin Gill (a lay leader who was an accountant) visited their home and invited them to Grace and Truth, located twelve blocks from their home.

Fellowshipping in the same church led to a strong bond between the Elliot and Collison families. They were often in each other's homes for meals, and the children enjoyed the friendships. When they first met, Bert was a gangly fourteen-year-old trying to adjust to the challenges of high school while Colleen was an inquisitive ten-year-old on the verge of blossoming into a young lady. The Elliots frequently gave the Collisons rides home from church and family activities.

Although George didn't attend church, he often walked the girls home when Kate stayed for an additional meeting. Kate taught Sunday School, cooked for church gatherings, and helped around the church in other ways. Between meetings, potlucks, and time with friends, the entire Sunday was often spent at church or church-related activities. On Sunday afternoon the youth usually visited the elderly at the Patten Home, went downtown to do open-air preaching, or ministered in the local jail. They often organized "sings" with the young people from Stark Street Gospel Chapel (now Eastgate Bible Chapel). Colleen was always there. Church involvement was not drudgery but filled with happy times.

The sisters took piano lessons for about five years. The cost was fifty cents a lesson or three lessons for a dollar. Kate purchased an old upright piano for fifteen dollars. She catered meals and did housework for wealthier families to pay for the lessons. Colleen remembered,

> I progressed quite rapidly. One year my teacher encouraged me to enter a city-wide competition. When the day of the

big event finally arrived, I managed to sail through the first half of the assigned composition quite well. But somewhere in the middle my mind suddenly went blank, and I couldn't go on. I turned to face the audience, saying simply, "I forgot." Then, as I turned to bravely start once more, I caught a glimpse of my mother and teacher with their heads bowed, looking very embarrassed and a couple of the judges doubled over with mirth! I got through it okay the second time and managed to get my name in the newspaper as having won third place. I can't be grateful enough to my mother for her sacrifice in giving me those piano lessons because of the large place music has had in our lives and ministry.

Colleen attended Boise Elementary School and was a voracious reader. In those days the public library limited people to one visit every two weeks and three books per visit. That proved frustrating for Colleen, who could never check out enough books.

At Jefferson High School she was an honor student and sang in the seventy-five voice a cappella choir. Several of her classmates referred to her Christian life as an "inspiration." She graduated in June 1946.

Colleen had put her faith in Christ as a young girl in Sunday School. About her younger years she later said,

I dedicated my life to the Lord, because in that time we had many missionaries visiting in the church, and I loved it. I loved to read missionary biographies and also about pioneers. And when the Lord sent us to the jungle, I said, "This is what the Lord has been preparing me to do—to live a simple life. I was very interested and I believe this is why He fixed the vision in me, because I was not the prettiest of young girls. But I liked to be in the open air [for street preaching excursions], and I enjoyed going to the jail [for evangelistic visits]."

3

Love So Divine

It is appropriate that Bert and Colleen's first declaration of love to each other happened at a Bible conference. The Elliot family, with some of the young people from Grace and Truth—including the recently graduated Colleen—attended a Thanksgiving conference in Oakland, California, in 1946. Colleen recalls, "He asked me if I would be willing to marry him. I didn't need to think very long before answering yes to that. From then on we had an 'understanding,' although we weren't officially engaged."

Bert told me, "When I looked for a woman to marry, I looked for a woman who loved God. I began to notice the girls who went to the open-air preaching meetings. I don't know if they noticed, but the good material was there. And furthermore Colleen played the piano, and it was the music that helped our work." Her love for God and commitment to ministry resonated with him.

Colleen had always admired Bert but never thought anyone of his caliber would take an interest in her. Their love for each other was like a rosebud waiting for the light of day so it could quickly come into full blossom. Bert referred to this time as "when our love was new and each kiss an inspiration."

Their courtship would last just over two years—approximately half of it long-distance, communicating through correspondence. More of Bert's letters have been preserved, although it's evident that Colleen's missing letters conveyed reciprocal affection. During these two years the couple focused on fanning the flame of their love and preparing for missionary service.

Following the Oakland conference, Fred and Bert headed east on an itinerant preaching trip while the rest of the group returned to Portland. After a brief visit with Bert's German Brethren friends from the forestry camp they went to Kingman, Arizona. In one of his first love letters to Colleen, Bert waxed eloquent,

> How I wish you were here to share with us just today's joys, both natural and spiritual. By natural I mean the pleasure that comes to one's soul witnessing the sunrise over the vast barren hills run its steady course through the azure skies. And the sunset swathed in crimson and gold, while in the eastern hills the big, silvery moon peeks out ready to quietly take over where the sun left off, transforming the desert into a silver blue paradise. Perhaps this is exaggerating, but really one must see it to appreciate its original enchanting beauty. By spiritual I mean the joy one gets in telling Calvary's love story, the emancipating gospel, to some twenty Hualapai Indians, who for centuries have been bound in heathen darkness, which has stripped them of every vestige of morality and led to depths of sin.

Bert preached in Kingman while Fred preached in nearby Valentine and Peach Springs. Before returning to Portland, they conducted a series of evangelistic meetings with the Navajo in northeastern Arizona for their Christmas celebration. They ministered alongside missionaries who were part of Navajo Gospel Mission, which my parents joined three years later, so I grew up with the same missionaries, Navajo people, and culture. This connection strengthened my bond with Bert. When I visited Peru,

Uncle Bert often referred to my involvement with the Navajo when he introduced me both privately and publicly. He knew it would enhance my credibility among the Peruvian believers.

In April 1947 Fred and Bert took another short preaching trip through south central British Columbia, preaching in towns like Penticton, Westbank, and Kelowna, before ministering in Ellensburg, Washington. This gave Bert opportunities to develop his speaking gift. On this trip he observed, "It seems the devil has people so deluded with his religions that you can't hand out a tract without being branded a Jehovah's Witness or have a street meeting without being branded Pentecostal."

———◆———

Colleen had a genuine interest in missions so when Leonie Soubirou came to Portland in early August 1947 recruiting students for the School of Missionary Medicine at the Bible Institute of Los Angeles (now Biola University), Colleen was all ears. Miss Soubirou had just started a critical program to equip missionaries who lived in remote areas with basic medical skills. Missionaries were often the only people with any medical knowledge among these tribal groups. Otherwise the people sought out the local medicine man or witch doctor. This one-year program trained students in everything from dentistry to tropical medicine. It was exactly what Colleen was looking for.

The problem was that admission to the program required a prior college-level Bible degree. Colleen had just graduated from high school. Miss Soubirou was aware of the quality of Bible teaching Colleen had received through the years at Grace and Truth and was impressed with her spiritual maturity and passion for missions. So, with a letter of endorsement from the church elders, Colleen was accepted into the program. Her transcript indicated she had graduated from the "Brethren Assemblies Bible School."

This was a whirlwind decision, so by the end of August Colleen was on the train to Los Angeles. In her acceptance letter Miss

Soubirou warned, "Possibly I should take this opportunity to say that you will be younger than the other students in the course, and this may be a bit of a handicap unless you are willing to discipline yourself. By this I mean you must assume the attitude of a graduate student." This makes it especially notable that Colleen's fellow students elected her vice president of their class. She found the training fascinating and extremely practical for the situations she would face overseas on a daily basis.

As Colleen was wrestling with the decision to attend Biola, Bert and Fred were off on another preaching trip back to northern Arizona. They drove all night through Utah to avoid the heat, alternating drivers. At about eight a.m. Bert was sleeping in the back seat when he was awakened by the screeching of brakes and the car rolling on its side. Fred had dozed off and lost control. Fortunately neither was injured, and they were able to right the car. It was drivable, so they limped along to Flagstaff, Arizona, where they sold the damaged car and ended up leading the buyer and his wife to faith in Christ.

Their main speaking engagement was at the Southwest Bible and Missionary Conference in Flagstaff, hosted in a camp-style facility in the shadow of Mount Elden. Missionaries to various Native American tribes and their indigenous leaders were encouraged by the high-quality teaching. Charles Fuller, along with some of the Dallas Seminary faculty, spoke there regularly. As a high schooler twenty-five years later, I attended a session where the popular Bible teacher Dr. J. Vernon McGee taught.

The Elliot men taught morning and evening, Fred to the adults and Bert to the young people. Carl Armerding was teaching while they were there. Bert observed that Armerding, as an "educated orator, speaks logically and powerfully but seems to be self-sufficient, while Dad seems to be tender and dependent but not so logical. I was a bit concerned at first thinking Dad wouldn't stand a chance with the big gun preachers they have here, but it seems those who are spiritual think vice versa."

Bert wrote openly to Colleen,

Our love had a little test last week when Louise Warren arrived with the Armerdings. She is a sweet girl whom I met first about ten years ago at our house and again last year coming west at the Oak Park meeting in Chicago. She is a junior at Westmont and a music major. Strange to say, I found myself much drawn to her and enjoyed her company, something that hasn't happened since I've been going with you. Needless to say, it caused me no little wonder and perplexity for a while. Could it be possible that my love for you wasn't real after all? After careful comparison and much thought I can still say, "I love you darling," and even more than before, if that's possible. The Hopi word for love means "to give my heart." I love you in Hopi, too, darling. Perhaps I just should have left this paragraph out, but it's there now, so will let you be the judge.

Bert was getting his taste of the itinerant lifestyle. When the conference concluded, his and his father's destination was "in the Lord's hands." Invitations from Kingman and Lubbock, Texas, came, as well as an encouragement from Clara to return to Portland.

They chose Lubbock, where they handed out tracts during the week and tried to encourage the little local church. Bert wrote, "I hope I learned some lessons. The devil has practically ruined this meeting with just the littlest things. The whole thing could be straightened out in about five minutes with a little grace and forgiveness. And yet a few hearts un-melted by the love of Christ make it impossible. May God keep us from listening to rumors."

After a couple weeks in Lubbock, Bert took the train to Los Angeles for a brief visit with Colleen at Biola and then home to Portland to begin studies at Multnomah School of the Bible. (Fred stayed in Texas for another month, purchased a 1939 Buick for one thousand dollars from a lady in the church, and drove home.)

Although Fred hadn't had any formal Bible training, Bert was focused on preparing himself for missionary service and recognized the need for a firm foundational understanding of the Bible. His taste of preaching may have underlined the importance in his mind. His parents encouraged advanced education, and Bert's three siblings all attended Wheaton College. With Colleen at Biola, Bert saw this as an opportune time to further his education, even though schooling was not his forte.

But the decision to attend Multnomah was spur of the moment. In early September Bert was in Texas, fully engulfed in the preaching tour without a hint of school on his mind. Twelve days later he was back in Portland, sitting in doctrine, synthesis, Bible study methods, and spiritual life classes. While studying came hard for him, he enjoyed the classes. He earned money by cutting hair at fifty cents a person in the basement of one of the school buildings. The school even found an old barber chair for him.

Bert and Colleen found this academic year of separation to be difficult but were confident of the value of the training. Although not officially engaged, they wrote openly about their plans for marriage and their thoughts about their wedding's timing. In one letter Bert lamented, "I wonder how I could support a wife when I can't even muster enough to buy an engagement ring."

From Biola Colleen wrote,

> The Lord has been bringing before my mind so much of late the fact that He is coming again for His own. I found, as I examined my own heart in the light of what He has been showing me from His Word, that I, down deep in my heart, was hoping that He would delay His coming at least until I had had the privilege of being married to you (for a short time anyway). Isn't that awful, darling? But it's the truth, and I had to get down on my knees before the Lord and ask Him to take away that selfish desire and keep me ever looking unto Him and "hasting unto His appearing." Have I an object here below which would defer Thy coming, Lord?[1]

---

1   Scripture quotation paraphrased from 2 Peter 3:12.

Bert continued to have occasional correspondence with Joe Hocking and another missionary, Ed Christensen, in Peru. They were enthusiastic about Bert and Colleen coming to Peru but recommended that they take advantage of Wycliffe's formal language training school—the Summer Institute of Linguistics (SIL).

Cameron Townsend founded SIL in 1934 as an academic training school to prepare prospective linguists to learn and analyze unwritten languages in rural Latin America. Also the founder of Wycliffe Bible Translators, Townsend saw firsthand the value of indigenous people having the Bible in their "heart language." Meeting on the campuses of the University of Oklahoma in Norman and Briercrest Bible Institute in Caronport, Saskatchewan, Canada, SIL was a rigorous two-month course in learning and transcribing a language. Bert and Colleen both wanted to take this training.

The big question was: Would they do it as singles or as a married couple? Christensen offered his perspective:

> I am in favor of being married if possible. There is no advantage that I can see in the wife not learning the language just cause she has a few dishes to wash. She will get you to dry them, you can be sure of that. There is a distinct disadvantage in the husband learning the language first, for it gives the wife an inferiority complex, and they think they will never learn and have their husbands do all the writing, etc.

Except for the gross understatement regarding household responsibilities, the advice that both partners receive language training was good. Bert and Colleen decided in mid-March to pursue attending SIL. The training would begin mid-June. Both of them were deep in the throes of studies—Colleen in Los Angeles, Bert in Portland. Bert wrote, "I told your dad, 'If we went to the same school together, it would be married.' He meekly but wisely replied, 'What will you live on?'"

For Bert and Colleen, marriage was more than their love and commitment to each other. Bert wrote,

It was with keen delight that I noted Hocking's remarks on marriage and mused on your tender words of love; my dizzy heart soared above my unstable brain as I anticipated a hasty wedding on June 18 with a honeymoon at the Canadian Wycliffe. By the next evening the Lord was probing ever so deeply into my heart. Was I really willing to forsake all and follow Him? Content to leave you and go alone if that were His will? What would you do if I did? Make plans and go on your own? Did I really want you if your call weren't definite enough for that? These questions pressed on my

Fred, Clara, Ruby, Bob with daughter Beth, Bert, Jane with cousin Patty, Colleen, Jim

soul with such new force that, for the first time in months, my cold heart took to weeping. Tears have been coming quite easily since then, and along with them a renewed and, I trust, firmer faith in Him who alone is a fit object. Also a deeper realization of the fact that, being dead, I should not henceforth live unto myself. My desires, whether good or bad, I am to reckon dead. This makes the problem of marriage simple. I am neither to seek it nor long for it until His voice speaks clearly, and even then not on the old level of fleshly desire, but because He has willed it for His eternal glory.

Bert raised the question about going to Peru alone. And, if so, would Colleen go on her own? It doesn't appear that he was seriously considering that option. He used the question as an avenue to confirm each of their individual commitments to ministry in Peru. Specifically, was Colleen's commitment deep enough that she would go even it if wasn't with him? In the end, his heart was satisfied that they were in it together.

In contrast several years later his younger brother, Jim, asked the same question regarding his relationship with Elisabeth. He became convinced that remaining single as a missionary, at least initially, would help him avoid distractions and divided loyalties in his pursuit of full obedience to God. Jim was also mindful of the dangers working with the Waodani. So he went to Ecuador as a single man in early 1952 and married Elisabeth more than a year and a half later, when both were fully convinced they could serve God more effectively married than single. The path of obedience is not the same for everyone.

For Bert and Colleen, marrying before SIL was impractical. And it would be too distracting to go to the same school as singles. So the couple made plans for Bert to go to Norman while Colleen would take the same training in Caronport. In the meantime they had to finish their school years at Biola and Multnomah.

Her studies at Biola challenged Colleen. The high points of her week were the hospital rotations, where she especially enjoyed the maternity ward. She excelled in the classroom and saw the irony in one particular assignment for anatomy class. She wrote, "That old 'pelvis paper' is really beginning to haunt me. Each time I even sit down I'm reminded of what I'm sitting on. I can't sit down unconsciously anymore, because I know that I should be writing about the very part that enables me to sit down."

———————

Just before Colleen's June graduation from Biola, Bert visited her for a day, then continued to SIL. His registration day in Norman, Oklahoma, was hot and humid and the stack of books for the course intimidating. "I wondered how I would ever make it and would have turned back had not He given grace." The instructors were so young it was difficult to distinguish them from the students.

Several instructors who were on their way to teach in Caronport, Saskatchewan, attended his get-acquainted session. Every connection with Colleen—and the school she would attend—warmed his heart. In that session Bert met a college acquaintance of his brother Jim from Wheaton College, named Elisabeth Howard. At this point in their relationship Jim and Elisabeth realized their deep love for each other but were uncertain as to where it would lead or God's purpose in it. Consequently, they kept it very much to themselves. Bert—or anyone else in the world for that matter—knew nothing of the seriousness of their relationship. Because of their connection through Jim, Bert and Elisabeth spent time together singing around the piano, talking and sharing spiritual insights—so much that people started to talk, much to Elisabeth's amusement. She enjoyed the friendship, but of Bert she wrote at the time, "He has not the strength of character nor force of personality which Jim has . . . or nearly the self-discipline. In J., I see all that I think of as true, pure manhood."[2] In other words, Bert was no Jim Elliot! Interestingly, Bert would have been the first to agree. He recognized a unique giftedness and commitment to God in his younger brother.

My own parents, Fred and Evelyn Gleason, were also in the same SIL class with Bert, as they were preparing for their forty years of missionary work among the Navajo of northeastern Arizona. At this

---

2 As quoted in Valerie Elliot Shepard, *Devotedly: The Personal Letters and Love Story of Jim and Elisabeth Elliot* (B&H, 2019), 20.

Bert and Colleen's wedding, January 29, 1949

point in its development SIL was concentrating its work on three fields: Mexico, Peru, and the Navajo.

Of the training Bert wrote, "It is so interesting that I don't mind studying. I can hardly wait till we start writing letters phonetically. Like this—/maⁱ vɛri prɛšəs darliŋ aⁱ lʌv iu wɪθ al maⁱ 'hart/—no more spelling problems. It's so much fun." What a godsend for a notoriously poor speller!

Bert and Colleen's correspondence was filled with romance and thoughts of marriage. Bert wrote, "I feel more strongly than ever that we should get married and to the field as soon as possible. School only makes for more soft living and marking time. Though it will be terrifically hard and lonesome on the field, is He not as sufficient for the young and untrained as He is for the old and educated?"

Meanwhile, Colleen had to be in Caronport to begin SIL twelve days after graduation from Biola. Briercrest Bible Institute had just purchased and moved into an abandoned World War II British Commonwealth training base for pilots. Although the accommodations were rustic, the weather with its average temperature in the upper sixties was much more comfortable than Norman's ninety degrees.

Bert's class was a couple weeks ahead of Colleen's, so they enjoyed comparing notes and anticipating the next challenge. She loved the classes and especially enjoyed the friendships she made and the strong sense of community.

After SIL Bert spent a couple weeks in Gentry, Arkansas, encouraging a small group of believers. He met up with his parents in Oakland, California, and then returned home. Colleen traveled directly from SIL to Portland.

In fall 1948 Bert and Colleen enrolled at Multnomah. There was a rule that new students weren't allowed to cultivate relationships, which made their situation awkward since theirs was already well cultivated. Missionary Neil Weir visited Grace and Truth and invited them to join him and his wife in Peru. Neil said to Bert, "You don't need more studies. What you need is a wife!" With the encouragement of their elders, the couple dropped out of school, became officially engaged, and started planning a January 1949 wedding and a departure to Peru as soon as possible. It was at Laurelhurst Park in Portland that Bert asked Colleen to marry him, and he presented her with an engagement ring. Once the date was set, they had three months to plan the wedding.

As the day approached, Jim was in Wheaton finishing up his semester of studies. His professors agreed to let him take his finals early so he could return to Portland for the wedding. His parents sent him the train fare and begged him to come. He responded,

If I do come, may I make one stringent request? That there be no eating engagements planned prior to the wedding—either our going out or anyone's coming in. I should like if possible to get in a time of real quiet with you all and feel that since this may be the last family get-together before Glory, we should make it specially *family* with sufficient time for family prayer and Bible study. If it's to be a week of social hubbub, I refuse to come home. I can have that here on campus with bands and flowers. Promise?[3]

His premonition proved to be true—it was the last gathering for the Elliot family "before Glory."

January 29, 1949—the much anticipated day was bitterly cold, and snow was falling heavily. Some of the guests even left the reception early for fear they wouldn't make it home safely. Grace and Truth Hall at Northeast Sixth and Prescott was simply decorated. Fred, the father of the groom, officiated. The Elliot and Collison siblings were all part of the wedding party. Bert and Colleen sang "May the Mind of Christ My Savior," changing the first-person singular to first-person plural, as an expression of their shared desire:

May the mind of Christ our Savior
Live in us from day to day,
By His love and pow'r controlling
All we do and say.

May the Word of God dwell richly
In our hearts from hour to hour,
So that all may see we triumph
Only through His power.

May the peace of God our Father
Rule our lives in everything,

---

3   Elliot, *Shadow of the Almighty*, 90.

Fred, Clara, Pat, Colleen, Bert

That we may be calm to comfort
Sick and sorrowing.

May the love of Jesus fill us
As the waters fill the sea;
Him exalting, self-abasing—
This is victory.

May we run the race before us
As we seek the lost to win,
And may they forget the channel,
Seeing only Him.[4]

Bert and Colleen always stated that their honeymoon destination
was Peru. Plans for that started immediately. A week and a half after
the wedding they were on their way to the San Francisco Bay area
to tell church groups and friends about their plans to go to Peru.

---

4 Adapted from Katie Barclay Wilkinson (1859–1928), "May the Mind of
Christ My Savior," public domain.

Returning after three weeks, they began in earnest to pack and crate all their needed furniture, appliances, clothing, and other supplies to be shipped.

In early May they traveled once again to San Francisco, this time to board the MS *Grenanger,* bound for Peru. This Norwegian freighter, which also carried their belongings, had cabins on the main deck for eight to ten passengers. The accommodations were quite luxurious and the food scrumptious.

The ship stopped briefly in Los Angeles, where Neil and Genevieve Weir joined the Elliots for the two-week voyage. Fred and Clara, along with Colleen's mother, Kate, were at the dock to say their final farewell.

Elisabeth Elliot dedicated *The Journals of Jim Elliot* to Bert. In it she wrote, "Upon Bert's leaving Jim wrote to his mother: 'Remember we have bargained with Him who bore a cross.... Our silken selves must know denial. Hear Amy Carmichael:

> O Prince of Glory, who dost bring
> Thy sons to glory through the Cross,
> Let us not shrink from suffering,
> Reproach or loss.'"[5]

The voyage was just what Bert and Colleen needed. The past six months had been hectic with the wedding plans, packing, meetings, visiting, and other details. This was relaxing and productive. The crew put up an inflatable swimming pool. The Elliots wrote 133 thank you notes for wedding gifts and other kindnesses extended to them. They enjoyed becoming better acquainted with the Weirs. And the captain gave them permission to pull out their organ and hold services the two Sundays they were onboard.

Next stop, Peru. Finally.

---

5   Elisabeth Elliot, ed., *The Journals of Jim Elliot* (Old Tappan, New Jersey: Revell, 1978), 5.

Aboard the MS Grenanger

4

Honeymoon Accommodations

Bert and Colleen first set foot on Peruvian soil at Salaverry, the port town for Trujillo, on May 28, 1949. Due to the small size of the docks, they anchored off the coast and were ferried in to town. It wasn't until an English company rebuilt the port in the 1960s that it could accommodate ships the size of the MS *Grenanger*. The main commodity offloaded was lumber.

Colleen wrote,

> We had a very interesting two days in Salaverry; it was all so interesting and different. They tell us it's quite typical of most South American towns. The scenery was beautiful after the clouds lifted. There are fairly large sand dunes all along the shore, and then the Andes Mountains start rising in succession, different heights and shapes, but all very rugged and beautiful. It is really a beautiful setting for a city; the beautiful blue ocean on one side and the rugged mountains

rising behind. One is reminded of that hymn, where "every prospect pleases, and only man is vile."[1]

The town itself is quite primitive and very unique. No one is in a hurry to get anywhere, and everyone does pretty much as he pleases. Most of the houses are right on top of each other and made just out of a thin layer of adobe or palms or something of the like. You see people sticking their head out of every nook and cranny and hole, and you wonder how so many people can exist in such a little place. Water is quite scarce, and as a result the people aren't too clean. The town has one city well. You see, at all times of the day, little boys leading their donkeys to the well and then back again with water barrels on their backs. If they don't have a donkey, they carry it in all sorts of conveyances to their homes. The people are quite small. Naturally Bert and I drew quite a bit of attention, not only because we were foreigners, but because we were so big. I guess they had never seen a woman quite my size before.

Bert was six feet two inches, Colleen five feet ten inches.

Bert wrote his initial impression:

This was our first contact with the people. They came on board the ship in the morning, and from then on it was "watch everything." The custom officials are worse than any, for they have nothing to do but swipe things. If you were to rebuke them, they would tie you up in so much red tape, you couldn't move for weeks. We went ashore the first afternoon and presented about as strange a sight to them as they did to us. We were struck immediately with the poverty and filth of the people. Every phase of their life presents its own appeal for the gospel. How we long to be used of God to bring them into eternal joy and blessings. I found one can

1   Quoted hymn lyric from Reginald Heber, "The Missionary Hymn," 1820.

walk down their narrow dusty streets with considerable ease. The tranquility of his stomach may be changed, however, on passing by the terrific odor; but by quickening his pace he will soon pass where the air is somewhat clearer.

Seven miles inland from Salaverry was Trujillo, Peru's third-largest city with a population of about forty-one thousand people. It was founded by the Spanish Conquistadors in 1534, within a generation of Columbus discovering the New World! As soon as Columbus returned to Spain, a flood of explorers ventured west from the shores of Europe. Forty-two years later these explorers had already sailed around the southern tip of South America and inhabited its western shores. Trujillo was strategically located among four Chimú settlements, so the Spaniards could establish an alliance against the Incas.

Colleen wrote,

After we spent all the time we wanted in Salaverry, we boarded a bus to go to Trujillo. That was real funny, too, the way we did that. They have a bus (if you can call it that) running between the two cities. They are supposed to run on a half-hour schedule. When we decided we wanted to go to Trujillo, we just missed the bus, but there was another one waiting there that would be going in another half hour. There were seven of us from the boat who wanted to go. So we started talking to this bus driver to find out how long of a wait it would be. I guess the driver, seeing all us "foreigners," thought it would be a good opportunity to make some money, so he said he would take us all over there right away for twenty soles [$5.71 in 1949]. Neil told him that was too much, so he finally brought it down to ten soles, and we all bounded onto the bus and went bouncing on our way to Trujillo, regardless of the bus schedule. I don't know what the people did who came at the regular time to find the bus.

They just waited for the one that came at the next half hour, I guess. As I said, time doesn't mean much to these folks.

Trujillo is an interesting town, but very noisy. It doesn't have any street signs or signal lights. So the cars come roaring down the narrow streets. When they approach the corner, they just blow their horn for all they are worth to let you know they are coming. When you get several cars doing that, it makes quite a bedlam, I assure you.

We were walking past one of the city schools on Monday. The principal spied us and came out and very politely asked us in to inspect their school. He was a very educated man, well dressed and polite. He took us to every room, explaining what grade this was and everything. And the class would proceed to perform for us in some way. One class sang some national songs for us. I've really never heard anything quite like it. They don't use any instruments, but every boy knows his part perfectly, and they seemed to never miss a note. They really sang beautifully; it made cold chills run up and down my spine, especially when I thought how wonderful it would be to hear boys and girls sing the praises of the Lord Jesus like that. Neil and Gen say that all these Peruvians have wonderful voices, and when they start singing the hymns and choruses, it's really wonderful. Then in another classroom, two of the little boys recited for us. Those little fellows will really make orators if anyone will. They were reciting some kind of an oath to the flag and their country. They used such expression. They really did well. Of course, we couldn't understand their words, but we could almost tell what they were saying by their gestures and all their expressions. The government is doing quite a bit for the education of the children, and all the folks are quite proud of their schools.

A visit to a local restaurant prompted the following response from Bert:

It is the closer contact with the people that calls for the practice of the grace of God. I refer to taking a meal in one of the nicer restaurants in Trujillo. The table cloth was in its third or fourth consecutive day's service; if there ever had been silver on the utensils, it had long since worn off. In fact, a piece of pot metal flew out of my knife handle when the waiter threw it onto the table. Nothing about the place spoke of cleanliness; in fact, nearly everything was quite the reverse. By the time the food arrived, all traces of our appetite (which is mostly psychological anyway) had vanished. But after washing our utensils in the tea, we went through with it anyway, mostly by brute force and determination and because we didn't want to baby ourselves at this stage of the game.

Colleen added, "We know that this kind of life isn't going to be the easiest one, but we are looking forward with real joy to getting into the work, because we believe that this is what the Lord would have us to do. We delight to please Him. We know He will go before us every step of the way; He has proved that already."

While in Trujillo they visited the ruins of the ancient city Chan Chan. It was the largest pre-Columbian city of South America and at one time had thirty thousand residents. This adobe city was built by the Chimor around AD 850 and lasted until it was conquered by the Inca just prior to the arrival of the Spaniards and the founding of Trujillo. Much work has been done recently to restore this archaeological site, but it would have been quite undeveloped in 1949. The Elliots caught a glimpse into the richness of Peruvian history and culture, along with the complexity of the interaction between the Inca, the Spaniards, and the indigenous people with whom they would be working.

After two and a half days in Salaverry and Trujillo, they again boarded the ship and set sail for Lima, the capital of Peru and its largest city. Although right on the coast, it is actually part of the

Sechura Desert. Early June marks the onset of winter in Peru. They found it to be quite cool, and the skies seemed overcast most of the time. It looked like it could rain at any time, but it never did. The humidity was usually high, especially in the mornings.

Colleen wrote,

> Lima is a very beautiful city, and very interesting, too. Some of the most elaborate homes in the States don't begin to compare with some of the homes they have here in the wealthier districts. Their architecture is really exquisite, and the lawns and flowers especially are simply gorgeous. They have lots of bright red geraniums in most of the yards, as well as other colorful and beautiful flowers, shrubs, and trees. One especially is a climbing plant that is vivid red most of the year round. Most of the houses have this climbing on them, which adds to their beauty. But of course not all the homes are like this. I think I can see why they call this the "land of contrasts." Huddled up close to the walls of one of these beautiful homes may be the tiniest hovel made of mud and sticks, where a poor Indian and his family may be living. In the States they wouldn't think of having such contrasting homes in the same district, but here it seems to be quite characteristic.

Making it through customs was a three-day affair for Bert and Colleen. She wrote,

> The Lord brought us through customs with all of our things. You probably would have torn your hair, Dad [Elliot], if you would have seen how they went through and disrupted your very neat job of packing, but I guess that's the way it has to be done in order to really see everything. Most everything will have to be repacked before shipping it over the mountains, but we are so thankful to get it through that

we really don't mind too much. It cost us approximately two hundred dollars [about $2,180 in 2020 currency] as duty on all our articles, but we had planned on that.

About customs Bert remarked, "One has to come to the country to appreciate just how dishonest the government can be. But the Lord delivered us out of the mouth of the lion and will continue to deliver us, for which we give Him unfeigned praise."

They enjoyed the hospitality of the linguistic home run by Wycliffe Translators. On Sunday evening they attended their first authentic Peruvian worship service in one of Lima's largest national churches. It proved to be more of a Spanish lesson than a worship experience, but they were pleased with how much of the message they could understand.

It was now time to press forward to their intended destination— the jungle. Peru divides geographically into three distinct regions. The coastal desert borders the Pacific and stretches along the 1,500-mile western edge of the country. Trujillo and Lima are representative of its climate and culture. The Andes mountain range also runs the entire length of the country from north to south. It offers spectacular views of snow-capped mountains and glaciers with its seventy peaks that rise above eighteen thousand feet, the highest being Mount Huascaran at 22,205 feet. Vehicular travel across the Andes is tediously slow with limited routes. To the east the Amazon Basin transitions from the Andean highlands to the vast reaches of the low jungle. The Amazon River has the largest discharge volume of water and empties the largest drainage basin in the world. From its headwaters in the Peruvian Andes it meanders to the east four thousand miles until it reaches the Atlantic Ocean. Bert and Colleen learned that, not only is the typography distinct in each of these regions, but the culture, languages, religious practices, superstitions, and personality of the people are as well.

The Elliots' plan was to haul their belongings by truck over the Andes to the jungle city of Pucallpa, traveling a road that had been completed only four years previously. They would then travel down the Ucayali River to Iquitos on a river launch. From there they would proceed up the Maranon River to their final destination, which was still uncertain. The total distance was about 1,500 miles.

Transporting the two couples with all their gear over the Andes Mountains down into the jungle was the next challenge. Colleen wrote,

> This morning [Tuesday, June 14, 1949] I had my first plane ride and really enjoyed it. Bert and Neil left Lima last night on the truck with all our "earthly possessions" and should arrive in Pucallpa sometime Friday. Gen and I wanted to go with them in the worst kind of way, but there wasn't enough room on the truck for us, too, and to hire another car would have cost twice as much as going by plane. Just think of it, it took us just a little over two hours by plane, and it will take Bert and Neil something like four days by truck. The trip on the plane was beautiful as we crossed the high Andes Mountains, which at their highest tower about sixteen thousand feet [in this vicinity]. The plane climbed to nineteen or twenty thousand feet, and looking down we could see these rugged peaks with lots of snow on them. It hardly seemed believable to see that here in the tropics. I enjoyed the trip immensely. It almost beats the car; you hardly know you are even moving.

Meanwhile Bert and Neil traveled in the truck, enduring the difficult seven-hundred-mile journey over the 15,807-foot pass. Although it was not stated, it appears the truck rental included a Peruvian driver. Extreme altitudes often cause sickness. Neil succumbed to it, but Bert escaped. Needless to say, the town of Pucallpa and their wives were a welcome sight for the two men after the arduous four-day crossing.

In Pucallpa they enjoyed the hospitality of the Hocking family. Joe and Jeanette had six children ranging in age from fifteen months to twelve years. Theirs was an active household that included a virtual zoo. The entourage encompassed a huge turtle the size of a large dog, lizards, a cute little monkey, dogs, cats, chickens, a variety of birds, and six big snakes, each about six feet long. To Colleen's great relief, the snakes were nonpoisonous and caged! Joe had worked for a snake venom company in the States, so he took a special interest in the jungle snakes.

Colleen wrote,

> I wish you could see the people and the way they live; that is the most interesting of all. The Indians here are known as the Cashibo tribe and are quite primitive. You wonder how the women see, for they let their hair grow a certain way so it hangs right down over their eyes; it's very original if nothing else. Their dress is quite unique, too, with a funny blouse and a narrow wraparound skirt that hangs quite low on their tummies (kind of hard to explain, but perhaps you get the gist). The married women with children are barely more than little girls in their early teens. They choose their wives while very young; I guess they want to train them themselves while they are still trainable. They all have some kind of a silver piece in their nose. Many of them use a lot of paint on their faces, too, just like the Indians at home, only they use blue instead of red coloring and cover a wider area. Their little babies are so cute, but evidently they are not satisfied with the shape of their heads, because, when they are quite small, the mothers press their foreheads.

Peru's population comprises two distinct classes—"Indians" of purely indigenous descent and "Peruvians," or nationals of Spaniard descent. In the jungle, the Indians and Peruvians have mixed quite a bit, so there aren't many pure-blooded Indians left, especially in the larger villages. They are mainly found in remote villages.

Colleen was able to put into practice some of her medical training for the first time. Joe did his medical and dental work before breakfast. The nationals would line up each morning, most commonly for tooth extractions. Colleen gave several intravenous shots, which brought her a sense of fulfillment.

It was also in Pucallpa that Bert and Colleen were introduced to the isango—tiny insects that live in the grass. They are harmless, except their bites cause continual itching. The good news, they were told, was that they would become immune in two to three months.

Adapting to the jungle climate brought an assortment of changes. Colleen wrote, "I did the inevitable yesterday. I put my hair on top of my head in braids, and I think it's there to stay. It may not be so charming this way, but it's a hundred times cooler. It's just too warm to have all that hair dangling on your neck all the time. Bert likes it better anyway, so that's all that matters."

Colleen giving an injection

Loading their possessions onto the boat for the journey to Iquitos was an adventure in its own right. Five Indians carried their belongings down a steep bank over narrow planks to the boat. Bert wrote, "Imagine, if you can, our washing machine crate perched on the back of one man, held only by a strap over his forehead around the crate and hooked under one of the corners. One slip on that bank and it would have crushed him. While one is sometimes amused at their foolhardiness, he is often amazed at their ingenuity. They seem to do so much with so little."

Colleen wrote,

The trip downriver from Pucallpa to Iquitos on the little river boat was most interesting, even more interesting than the trip across the ocean, although not as comfortable. Everything on the boat was made to fit the size of the people here and consequently didn't fit either of us too well. Especially the beds—we hung over the end and the sides. Bert touched the top of the bed even if he bent his knees a little bit. What a time we did have. As a result of this, poor Bert got a kink in his back and leg, and is still walking around with a game leg. He sure wished many times that his mom [a chiropractor] was here to put him back in shape.

It's interesting to see these boats when they are loaded. On the bottom deck are all the third-class passengers plus crew, plus freight and cargo, pigs, chickens, cows, and such like. They don't have refrigeration on board, so they keep meat fresh this way, and just kill it as they go along. The first-class passengers ride on the upper deck, where they sleep in cabins, on hammocks, on benches, or just plain spread out on the deck. There are people of all kinds and descriptions.

We find that the people are really very likeable, and especially the kiddies are so loveable. We had brought some bread along with us in the boat (to eat in case the food on the boat wasn't too good). One place the boat stopped there were seven little kiddies standing on the shore. So we decided to give them each a piece of bread. I wish you could have seen their faces. They never get bread in their house. One hunk of bread is just like a candy to them. They were sure thrilled and grinned at us with great glee. Their father came along and saw what we had given them. The next thing we knew, one of the little boys came running back with two eggs in his hand as a gift for us. These were probably the only two eggs they had in the house, but it was the best they had, and they gave them as a gift to us. So you see, these people aren't unintelligent or heartless or any such thing, but rather very kind and thankful for any kindness shown them.

Receiving no fewer than seven long and interesting letters from home was the highlight of their arrival in Iquitos in early July, following a five-day voyage. The letters reached them through a local missionary. It had been six weeks since they had heard from home, and they were getting pretty homesick. Colleen read the letters out loud. Bert remembered, "In the middle of Bob [Elliot]'s letter Colleen's voice wavered. I chuckled, and we both burst into tears."

Iquitos is nicknamed the capital of the Peruvian Amazon. It is the largest city in the world that cannot be reached by road. Smaller ocean vessels regularly bring freight 2,200 miles up the Amazon River from the Atlantic Ocean. Remarkably it is only 106 feet above sea level. It became a prominent industrial center in the early 1900s due to the rubber boom. The industrial revolution in the northern hemisphere brought a great demand for rubber, found in abundance in the Amazon rain forest. Many young single European men immigrated hoping to make their fortunes. Much of the wealth that was still in Iquitos when the Elliots arrived was money from rubber. The Europeans married Peruvian women and established families. Most of the missionary work, however, was done among the poor and indigenous people groups.

While in Iquitos, the Elliots stayed in the home of Rodimiro and Belmira Lopez, who were not wealthy but of a higher class than most. Rodimiro was a carpenter and had built some beautiful furniture out of mahogany that Neil had delivered to him—a handsome bed and a large wardrobe for the Elliots, and a long chest of drawers for

Genevieve. Bert and Colleen were overwhelmed with this delightful local couple's kindness.

As in other places, Bert and Colleen's height and ethnicity drew a great deal of attention. Colleen wrote,

> I think the hardest thing to get used to down here is the fact that we are so different looking than the rest of the people. They make no bones about letting you know it. When Bert and I walk down the street, one would think we were a parade or something. All the youngsters especially, when they see us coming, run and tell the rest of their little friends. Then they just stand on the curb or in the doorway, with their mouths hanging open so their chin nearly reaches their knees (don't take this too literally), and they just stare. And it's not only the children that do it. Bert said that one time, when he was walking down the street, one woman was so engrossed in staring at him that she forgot to watch where she was going and fell flat on her face. Another woman walked right into a mud puddle. It sure made her mad. So it goes. Well anyway, it surely makes one feel self-conscious. I hope pretty soon either they get used to us or we get used to their staring.
>
> By the way, perhaps you didn't know that I am not Colleen down here but rather am called Norma [her given middle name]. It would be awfully hard for them to say Colleen. They could say *colina*, but in their language it means hill or mountain, and although I may resemble a mountain pretty closely, I'd rather not be called one. Norma or Normita is a very common name here, so Norma I am.[2]

The letters from Iquitos reflect an openness to the Lord's leading as to where they should finally settle. For example, there was a need in the little village of Nauta. But they decided not to go because of the

---

2 In this book I will use Colleen, except in a direct quotation, where I will maintain the name used by the source.

unhealthy team dynamics there. Bert reflects, "We are increasingly thankful to God for keeping us clear of these entanglements." Their priority for the moment was to learn the culture and language.

They chose to join the Weirs in Lagunas. Colleen wrote,

> We arrived here in Lagunas on Monday morning [July 18, 1949, after a three-day upriver boat ride] about eleven after two months and two days of travel. It's good to be here and to be able to unpack your suitcase and know that you will be here for a while. Neil managed to get a horse and cart and some men. They were able to get all our things up from the port by Tuesday noon, and all thirty-six crates and trunks were piled on the porch. A good number of them are still awaiting us to unpack them as we find time. It's been lots of fun to unpack what little we have done and start using our things a little bit. We have unpacked three trunks and a couple of crates and have been thankful in that we have found nothing broken, although there were a lot of glasses and other dishes. Best of all, our big mirror that Uncle Mick and Aunt Ruth gave us came through without a scratch. We had almost given up hope for it. It was packed with the bedspring. When they loaded it on the boats here in Peru, they put it in the hold of the ship and then proceeded to pile the heavy stove on top of it. The men walked all over it, and no one knows what all it went through. But it really packed well and withstood all the bumps.

The Elliots started out sharing the Weirs' house, made of packed earth. Bert said, "When we arrived, the house had cracks in the walls, because the ground was splitting—large cracks where a snake could go through. In the corner the wood for [building] the launch was piled up and full of snakes. We wanted to put up our cots. But Neil said, 'No, sleep on the floor; it's fine.' And since I didn't agree, we had a fight. The following day we looked for the bathroom. It was a hole outside with long grass. It was a shock at the beginning." Bert observed that this was their first disagreement with the Weirs.

Colleen wrote,

> The house was pretty dirty when we arrived (naturally since the Weirs had been away over a year and one-half). The living room was piled half full of lumber for the boat. All the furniture was piled in the bedroom, and everything was rather unfit for living. So we have been busy the past few days cleaning and putting things in their proper place. The fellows have been carrying out the lumber and setting up the stove and washing machine; things are beginning to shape up nicely now. The Weirs are giving us a good portion of the living room for our room (about twelve by fourteen feet). Today Bert and Neil put up a partition, and we brought in some of our things, hung our mirror, hung one of the plastic wardrobes the Majors gave us for our clothes closet, and set up our wardrobe trunks for dressers. We really got nicely settled, comparatively speaking. [Many of the items they brought were wedding gifts anticipating their living in Peru.] All in all, we feel quite cozy in our little room. Bert has been real clever in fixing up a wash stand and other little things to make the room more complete and handy. He even made a wastepaper basket for me today out of cardboard. Now I'm anxious to get busy on the curtains and other little things to brighten up the place a bit.

Bert added,

> The house was pretty discouraging when we arrived. We have worked from dawn till dark ever since then until tonight. We have one little fairly clean corner we can call our own that looks inviting, at least to us. Earth houses may be cool, but earth is earth no matter how you stack it and has

a way of cracking and being dirty. As yet we have no well, no shower, and no outhouse, but we are learning to do just lots of things. I don't know when I've worked so hard, sweated so much, got up so early, accomplished so little, felt so good, and been so happy.

The first order of business was language acquisition, so they began working with Andres, a national believer, for two hours a day, after which they would study on their own. The Spanish lessons were helpful, but they found actually working at it hard to do. Colleen wrote, "Of course they all tell us that we are learning more rapidly than anyone they have ever seen, but they are great ones to flatter, and they tell everyone else the same thing." Eventually they both mastered the language. Bert picked it up more quickly through his constant interactions and working with people. Colleen learned it more slowly and precisely through meticulous study.

They quickly became involved in the church and found that the organ they brought was quite a drawing card. Besides the services on Sunday morning and evening, they also met on Wednesday and Friday nights. Gen also offered the children morning Sunday school and a class on Sunday afternoons. She was a good teacher, and the children thoroughly enjoyed the classes. Simultaneously Neil and Bert held a class for the adults—mostly a Bible reading time. All these classes kept the two couples busy and motivated Bert and Colleen to apply themselves to their Spanish lessons so they could understand their students. Colleen wrote,

Gen and I are having a class for girls on Saturday afternoons now where we teach them to embroider and to sew as well, after which we have a Scripture lesson. All I know about embroidery you could put in your eye, but for the present I take the younger girls and teach them the simple stitches. Gen has the more advanced ones. We have been having between twenty-five and thirty girls each time. That is about all we can really manage in the house. I do enjoy this class so much. It is a good way to reach them, because so many want to learn who wouldn't come at any other time.

The need to get a better handle on the language was evident, as seen in this incident Colleen reported:

We were awakened very early in the morning by a loud knock on the door and a masculine voice calling. There at the door was a prospective father. His wife was trying to have her first child, and things were going a little too slow to suit them,

Bert loved entertaining the children.

so he came after our help. When Bert first went out there, the man tried to explain why he had come. He said, *"Me esposa no puedealumbrar."* *Alumbrar* is the verb that means "to illuminate" or "to give light," but they use it here in the expression that means "to give light to a child," or in other words, "give birth to a child." Bert of course didn't know this expression. All he heard was the verb *alumbrar* and thought surely he must be referring to the eyes of his wife. So Bert promptly replied in Spanish, "Is this the common disease of the eyes?" It is the common disease alright, but I am not sure that it has anything to do with the eyes. I can't help wondering what the poor husband thought. He probably thought he had come to the wrong place for help for sure and that we were a little wacky.

Colleen quickly put her medical skills to work:

I have been doing a little medical work since coming here, although not much—just treating sore eyes, one abrasion on the leg, and such like. The first case I had was a pretty sad one, and I felt pretty bad about it. It was an obstetric case. The girl had been in labor four days before they called us. It was a case where the girl was young (about fourteen or fifteen) and underdeveloped. She should have been a Cesarean case in the first place. She was too far gone when they called us. We tried to help her with Pituitrin shots and other methods, but it was beyond our ability, and we could do nothing. She died the next morning. So it goes, but I surely felt sad about the whole thing.

I got the thrill of my life last Friday when we were awakened early in the morning by a man who came to get us to help his wife, who was trying to have a baby. He thought she wasn't getting along normally, but it was her first baby. She was nervous and thought things should happen right quick. But anyway Gen and I went to see her and reassured her that everything was alright. Then we went back several hours later. By this time things were more ready to happen. We gave her a shot of Pituitrin, and in a very short time she had a nice big baby boy. It was the first case I have ever handled actually by myself, and I surely got a big thrill out of doing it. The Lord is good and certainly gives help at times like these. The fact that I delivered the child and cut the cord and everything makes me the "madrina" or godmother of the boy. I consider it a real honor.

Bert and Colleen found that they preferred the jungle to the desert they had encountered in Trujillo and Lima. It reminded them of Oregon, where everything is green. This area of Peru and a region in India were considered the rainiest places in the world. Although this was supposed to be the dry season, it rained every day. They found that working in the humidity was quite draining.

The humidity and rain also took a toll on their belongings. Bert wrote,

> Here if it is metal, it rusts. My barber equipment has aged terrifically in the past few months. If it is leather or cloth, it will mildew or mold unless constantly cared for. If it is paper or wood, the white ants will be after it. They devoured all my notes on spiritual life last week. I don't think the notes helped them much more than they did me. All my books are sitting in arsenic now. Maybe that will help. The easiest way is to have nothing, like the people here.

He discovered he had to dismantle and repair the organ on a regular basis, because the humidity made the keys stick.

Meal preparation was difficult, because there was little variety. But then again it was simple, because there was little variety! Breakfast was usually coffee with milk (purchased from a local man and then boiled), cereal or eggs, and bread with jam made from a local fruit. The typical lunch was beans, rice or yucca, boiled bananas, and *paichi* (a salted, dried fish), along with a vegetable and a cup of tea. Soup was the mainstay for supper—often the prepackaged variety they brought from the States.

The common vegetables were squash, cucumbers, tomatoes, roasted ears of corn, *chiclayas* (like string beans), *caywas* (a native vegetable that tastes unlike any they had eaten), and eggplant. Gen made "pumpkin" pie out of the squash.

The fruit available to them were bananas, pineapples, papayas, *tapiriba* (a rather tart fruit, but very good), omari (tasted "absolutely ghastly" to Colleen, but was considered a delicacy—something like an avocado with a strong flavor), *gwayaba* (good for jam), *agawje* (not very good, but edible), avocado, and a "washed-out affair" of a watermelon. They didn't have the proper seeds to grow "dandy" watermelons like those they were used to in the States. Colleen also listed "cashews (not the nut)." After the nut matures on the tree, a delicious cashew apple forms attached to it. But the fruit rots within twenty-four hours of picking, so it's only readily accessible in its native region.

The Elliots didn't have meat very often, but available from time to time was beef, pork, chicken, turtle, and a variety of freshwater fish. Gen was a great cook, and Colleen enjoyed learning from her. The Elliots found the diet monotonous and starchy but certainly didn't go hungry.

Besides concentrating on learning Spanish, involvement in the ministry, and medical work, Bert worked with Neil on a couple of building projects to make life a little more comfortable. The first was to put up a four-by-four-by-eight-foot outhouse in the backyard. Previous to that their "latrine" was a bucket in their room, which was emptied into a hole in the backyard.

At the same time they erected a utility structure in the backyard that housed the water pump, shower, washing machine, generator, and work bench. It was twelve by twenty-four feet and built native style, with poles and a palm-leaf roof and walls. The shower was quite an upgrade. Colleen wrote,

> Our bath up to now has consisted of standing in a basin and pouring cold water, or hot water if you care to take the time to heat it, over yourself. When we first came, we thought we could make it seem more like a real bath by sitting on the edge of the basin (a little bit bigger than a dishpan) and washing away. Bert even made a little board affair for us to

sit on, but we soon learned our lesson. It worked fine for Bert, but when it came to me (clumsy one that I am), I was sitting there nonchalantly washing when all of a sudden the bucket went out from under me, water went every which way, and I found myself sprawled all over the dirt floor. I ended up by being dirtier than when I started. All Bert did was stand there and laugh. Ah me, such is life. But I guess it is things like this that keep us from getting old too fast. As I reread this last paragraph, I realize that some of the things written are kind of personal, and maybe I shouldn't include them at all. But somehow I think you would be interested in them, so here they are. If you decide to mimeograph this letter, like you have been doing with all the rest of them, please don't include this part.

These modern conveniences caused quite the stir. Colleen wrote, "I wish you could have seen the number of folks that gathered when Gen and I started up the washing machine. They had never seen such a thing before. It was, and still is, quite an oddity to them. They can't quite get over the fact that we don't have to wash our clothes by hand, but that the machine does the work for us. I think it's a pretty wonderful invention all right." The Peruvians must have wondered what these gringos would think up next!

At this point it's appropriate to consider a question of values. Bert observed, "To seek to maintain a North American existence here is a greater problem than I had anticipated." Missiologists might question whether one should even try to maintain a lifestyle that was noticeably more privileged than the people they worked among. Can you not better identify with and minister to them if you live like them and with them?

Reading between the lines of the Elliots' letters, it appears that the Weirs had lived without some of the amenities that Bert and Colleen provided. They had lived in this house for sixteen years and didn't even have a functioning outhouse. Was this a philosophical decision on their part to "live like the nationals"? Probably not. It seems that it had more to do with a lack of initiative, ingenuity, aptitude, or resources, or a combination of the above.

It is my observation that it is important to live on somewhat the same level as those with whom you minister. If not, you lose touch with their struggles in life and become less able to understand them. The locals can rightly say, "You don't have a clue what life is like for us."

We must remember that even with the few amenities the Elliots had, they were still a long way from a "North American existence." They had dirt floors and walls, no electricity or running water, no indoor plumbing, or many of the conveniences we take for granted. What is more, they were living in a partitioned-off portion of the Weirs' living room with minimal privacy. They often referred to this as their "honeymoon accommodations."

Some improvements were made in the interest of personal hygiene and maintaining proper health. A clean water supply, proper care of sewage, and avoidance of mosquitoes are essential to preventing serious diseases—diseases that constituted much of the illness they had to treat in others. The missionaries needed to stay healthy so they could help others.

Many of the amenities were not just for creature comforts, but to save time. To do daily household tasks in the manner of the nationals was very time consuming. That would rob the missionaries of time to conduct the ministry for which they were sent. The following story from Colleen illustrates this point:

I hadn't washed for two weeks, and one uses so many more clothes down here. Well, I got through the washing about 10:30 and hung all the things nicely on the line, and the sun was shining so nicely, and the sky was so blue. But sure enough, about noontime the clouds began to hover. I didn't know whether to take everything in or not. But the rain coming down soon convinced me. I ran and gathered everything in. It rained really hard for about fifteen minutes, and then out came the sun again. So I went back and hung everything on the lines again. Before long over came the clouds again with the promise of rain. So in came the clothes again. After this happened the third time, I gave up in despair, and we hung a rope in our room, and as much as I could I ironed things dry. What a day! Bert and I have been trying to invent in our minds some kind of slide-on roof for the clothesline so that, when it starts to rain, you can just slide on the roof. But so far we haven't been able to invent anything so practical.

Something as simple as that or a clothes dryer would have freed up time for them to teach, do medical work, and encourage people.

Often missionaries hire domestic help to assist with household chores. When people in the States hear, they are tempted to say, "I wish I could afford a maid." In the missionaries' defense, remember two things: First, domestic help is much less expensive in Third World countries because of the lower standard of living and the lower cost of goods. In 1949 this kind of help cost two to three dollars a month in US money. Adjusted for inflation, that would be about twenty-five dollars a month today.

In addition, most of us in the States have domestic help—called appliances. Microwaves, dishwashers, washing machines, dryers, vacuum cleaners, irons, toasters, and ovens all help with the chores that a maid would be asked to do. Even something as standard in our homes as the refrigerator is an incredible time saver. Without it many missionaries send paid help on a daily basis to the market for fresh meat, fruit, and vegetables that we take for granted as we open the fridge door. That chore itself can easily take an hour a day. In addition, hiring locals provided jobs and was an economic boon to the community.

Bert and Colleen were always very careful with their money both because times were often lean and because they were well aware that the financial gifts they received came from individuals and churches that gave sacrificially. They were generous to a fault for others but frugal about their own comforts. In their later years in Trujillo they lived in a home that would be considered a nice middle-class home by North American standards. They were self-conscious about their "luxurious" accommodations and would jokingly tell visitors from the States not to tell people at home how nice they had it! God provided for them through the years, and they were deeply grateful for that. They used whatever they received to further His kingdom.

5

Dining Room Table

As you can imagine the Elliots were anxious to get into a home of their own. The Weirs had been most gracious, and they seemed to work out the accommodations with little conflict. Not only had Bert and Colleen taken up a portion of the living room, but the two couples had now taken in three children, Hilda (nine), Niria (eleven), and Ricardo (sixteen). Due to their mother's illness, the parents had to leave Lagunas. The children moved in with the Weirs and Elliots for a couple months near the end of 1949 so they could finish the school year. The adults enjoyed them, but the house became cramped.

Bert and Colleen were sensitive to the Lord's leading as to where they should establish their home base and felt peace about staying in Lagunas for the time being. They had fallen in love with the people there, were able to use their gifts in ministry and medical work, and knew they still had much to learn from people like the Weirs before they ventured out on their own.

The Weirs began to take extended river trips, which placed more ministry responsibility on Bert and Colleen's shoulders. In this vast section of the jungle virtually no roads connected villages, so rivers were the major routes for all commerce and personal transportation. The Weirs traveled from village to village sharing the story of Jesus.

After sharing the Weirs' home for about six months, the Elliots looked for a house to purchase. One lady offered to sell them her home, but they suspected she was selling because she thought it was inhabited by an angry demon! While they certainly didn't believe in any of that, the rumor might prove a barrier to the nationals' willingness to come into their home.

"We purchased a home," Colleen wrote in April 1950. "It is not much—native style with grass roof, palm slat walls, dirt floor—but it looked like a palace to us. At the present rate of exchange we figured our house (as is) only cost us about forty dollars" ($417 in 2020). It fit the definition of a fixer-upper. Bert thoroughly relished the challenge of building and creating things. He loved taking things apart, learning how they worked, repairing them, and reassembling them. He and Colleen had spent a great deal of time dreaming over the plans for their home. Bert seized the opportunity to build a lovely home for his dear bride.

Colleen wrote,

Bert has five men working with him now. They are working on the walls on the house making them of the rammed earth construction. It is tedious work. They start by digging trenches about twelve inches deep all along where the wall is to be. In this they set up the form made out of wood about a yard high, a foot or so thick and a yard and one-half long, which they fill with dirt little by little, tamping it as they go until the box is filled (this usually takes two men working steadily all day long). He is well along on the bases and will soon be ready to start in on the second tier of blocks. We can hardly wait until the last row is completed and we can move in. The house when completed will have more or less four rooms. The front part of the house, which is the main part, will be divided into two—to one side the bedroom and to the other side a combined living room and dining room. Both of these rooms will be screened in so as to make them mosquito proof. Along the back of the house runs sort of a porch-like affair, which we will close in partially then divide it in two, making one end the kitchen and on the other end a utility room, where we will keep our washing machine. Bert will have his carpenter bench and the like. From in back of the house you can see the jungle in the near distance with all its silhouettes of different-shaped trees—really pretty we think. To the one side of the house is the village soccer field. On the other side is a large vacant lot, and in the front of it a little shack. But these are not all crowded up around it like so many of the houses here—for that reason we like it.

After a year and half of marriage, it was exciting to finally have a place they could call their own. They enjoyed furnishing and decorating it. To them, the essential piece of furniture was their custom-made dining room table. As Colleen described it,

It's not a real fancy one, has very simple lines—in fact, they made them almost too simple in trying to copy the picture out of the catalog we showed them. But it is nice and has a lovely finish on it—is made of pure mahogany wood, which is really lovely. It has the same extension design as the table the Elliots have. When we pull out the extension on it, the table appears to be positively huge. The folks can hardly understand that here—why two people should want such a big table. But maybe someday the Lord will give us a big family with which to fill it. Anyway we wanted a big table as long as we are getting one. The Weirs have such a tiny one—it will hardly accommodate four after all the food gets on. And then when they want to have anyone in for dinner, they are always lacking for space.

Both the Collison and Elliot homes in Portland had large dining room tables that were often put to full use. They understood the importance of hospitality. Throughout their six decades of ministry, there were very few days when they didn't have guests at their table for at least one of the meals and usually for all of them. To them their table was more than a piece of furniture—it was a ministry tool.

When Bert and Colleen moved out of the Weirs' home, they left the water pump and shower behind. Bert soon replaced the basin bathing system with a bath tub "made by cutting an old gasoline drum in half long-ways, putting a hose in the bottom for the water to drain out, and painting it." It felt luxurious. He also dug a twenty-two-foot-deep well in the kitchen with a pump so they could have access to good water. Colleen wrote,

> We live with dirt under us, around us, and over us, too—for the floors are but of earth and the walls the same. The walls are not plastered but are still in their rather rough stage, but well whitewashed over, so they look quite nice and clean. The roof is made of stripped palm poles with more mud and dirt on top of them. This makes it cooler and also keeps out any stray mosquitoes. It may not be the most elegant house in the world, but to us there could be none better. We are so thankful for it and have been exceedingly happy here. Bert has done a wonderful job, and I love him so much for all his work for me.

———————•+•◆•+•———————

Throughout their first four years in Peru, Bert and Colleen became acquainted with the local customs and holidays. These provide a window into a culture. For through them one can begin to understand a people's worldview. Several of the Peruvian customs are linked to events on the calendar. Colleen wrote,

One such fiesta in mid-February is called the Carnival and is really quite a riotous time. It lasts for three days when anything can happen. Everyone tries to do as much damage as possible to the other person. One is likely to see a girl walking to the well to get water with a *tinaja* (water crock) on her head, when all of a sudden someone will come running up with a bottle of dye water (they have various colors made from roots, etc.) and throw this dye all over her dress, face, anything they can get at. Or they might throw a bucket of muddy water or the like all over a person. Almost

Colleen delighted in making a new friend.

everyone who goes by these days looks a mess. For this reason we stick pretty close in the house. Also at this fiesta the Indians go out into the jungle and cut down a huge palm tree and bring it into the village amidst much drum beating and pomp. Before they put the tree up, they weave the leaves together and form them in sort of a circle at the top of the tree. On the circle they tie fruits, bread, bottles of liquor, and whatever they have. Then they slowly raise the tree into position, where it stands in majesty until the last day of the fiesta, when they have a dance around the tree while one, specially chosen, dances with an axe in his hand, whacking away at the tree until it falls. When it falls, there is a mad scramble to get the goodies. And so continues the beating of the drums, the dancing, the drinking, and the fun making.

Much to-do was made over Holy Week every year, including processions and special bells ringing and all types of rigmarole, beginning on Palm Sunday. Colleen wrote,

On Wednesday they had the procession that they call here the Seven Falls. It's a depiction of the Lord staggering under the load of the cross. They carry along a huge idol of the Lord with His cross, and they make it fall seven times. Also, in every one of these processions, almost every day of the week there is a long stream of people they call "penitents." We couldn't find out just exactly what they expect to gain, but apparently, or so they tell us, some of these people are suffering from some disease, and they hope to be cured by doing penance, or else they have done some wrong and hope to make atonement for their sin in this manner. All these penitents in the procession wear long old robes. Their hair is thrown down over their faces, and they carry a heavy wooden cross through the streets. Those crosses are terribly heavy, some heavier than others, according to how great the sin is, I guess. And they must be almost unbearably heavy after several hours bearing them through the streets, especially for some of the older women one sees in these processions. Poor folks, how they misinterpret that lovely verse "take up thy cross and follow me,"[1] as if it were an external thing. And oh how one longs to be able to impress upon those

---

1   Paraphrased from Matthew 16:24; Mark 8:34; 10:21; Luke 9:23.

folks especially that the redemptive work is finished—the Lord bore the shame of the cross for us, and we are saved by receiving Him in simple faith.

On Thursday they once again carry an idol of the Lord crucified on the cross—with a large crowd following and many women especially wailing because of the dead Christ. On Friday they carry Him through the streets in a coffin with a large figure of Mary draped in black behind Him, mourning His death. Most of the women who follow are also in black, characteristic of their mourning. They say too that they have large doll-like figures all over town representing Pilate, which they spit on or kick and in general abuse to show how mad they are at him for the sentence he pronounced on the Lord.

Today, Saturday, at noon the bells pealed forth, and firecrackers were shot to announce that the Lord has risen—today is known here as "Saturday glory," just a day ahead of the usual time, but I suppose that is considered a minor detail. And now many of the folks are busy dancing, drinking, and making merry. Or if they aren't yet, they will be by nightfall—and so on into the night! How inconsistent it all is.

A couple months later, Colleen wrote about another traditional holiday:

We recently passed the *Fiesta de San Juan* (Holiday of John the Baptist) at the end of June here in Peru. The Catholics have a special day in the year given to each of their saints—every day of the year is filled, and some days have two saints. But some of the days are more important than others, and John the Baptist's day is one of them. On the eve of the holiday they always hold a big dance and always serve plenty of liquor, so the next day not many are fit for anything. It's quite interesting to watch some of their dances—Bert and I are still in the curious state and want to see all we can of anything new. So we usually go for a walk on these nights and peek into the different houses as we go to see how the celebration is coming along and what they do. It was a lovely moonlit night anyway, so we really enjoyed our walk on the eve of San Juan.

There are three distinct types of dancing. First, there is the old Indian group (very few of them are left) who cling to dancing to the music of the drum and a reed instrument, something like a fife but with only five notes. Men and women dance separately, going continually around in a circle in a sort of hopping fashion, keeping time, not only with their feet, but with their whole body. Then there is the younger set of this group who apparently have a dance all their own—they continue to cling to the music of the drum and fife and dance in the same hopping motion as the older set, but they have modernized just enough that they dance girl embracing boy, the same as any dancer at home, I imagine. Then there is the third class, which is apart from the Indian group almost entirely, that dances to the music of the guitar, banjo, etc., and their mode of dancing is like anyone else's at home. Perhaps I shouldn't go into such things, but it is rather interesting to note the differences. At midnight of the eve of San Juan (we didn't stay up to watch this) everyone (every good Catholic, that is) goes to the river or nearest stream to bathe. This is supposed to wash the sins of the past away, and the sooner after midnight that it is done, the more efficacious the bath. On the next day, the actual holiday, they all go on a picnic or excursion of some sort and eat *"Juanes,"* which are made of rice, chicken, eggs, garlic, etc., all cooked together in banana leaves. And thus ends their holiday of San Juan.

94

Halloween is a special Catholic feast day called the Day of the Angels. It presents a very different twist from what is practiced in the States. Colleen described it:

The Day of the Angels is set aside to remember the dead children. The day before, nearly every family gets pineapples or watermelons or bananas or the like from their little farms, and they make up soups and other foods that the youngsters here enjoy. Some of the parents, we are told, even make little clothes for their dead children and set them out. Then on the thirty-first, about 4:30 in the morning, one is awakened by the shouts of children running from house to house yelling, *"Angeles! Angeles!"* And then the folks in the houses give them the fruit and food. They believe the spirits of the dead children are walking around with the living children, and, when they feed the children that come around, they are in reality feeding their dead children, too.

Christmas is a big time of fiesta for the Indians[2]. For three weeks they carry on, beating their drums and carrying on in their drunken manner. Before the fiesta starts, the men go out looking for wild game, and the women cook it up along with other native foods. They have a real time of feasting, drinking, and everything else. How often we have wondered just where they get the endurance to keep going all the time, but I guess it is from the alcohol they keep drinking. What a way to celebrate the birth of the Lord, since they claim that is what they are doing.

They not only celebrate Christmas and New Year's here, but the Friday after New Year's is supposed to have been the day when the three wise men arrived to worship the Christ child, so these folks have a big fiesta then as well.

---

2 There was very little celebration of Christmas among the Peruvians of Spaniard descent who lived in the village.

Besides the celebrations connected to the calendar, Colleen described another custom that is worth mentioning:

> The other night we had an almost complete eclipse of the moon here in Lagunas. We were already dressed for bed when one of the boys came excitedly to our window and called us to come and look at the eclipse. Very shortly after that the village bell started ringing, and the people made all kinds of noise; they even had the drums beating. They have an old belief here that the moon has a certain path it travels each night, and when it is darkened like this, somehow it has gotten off its path and is lost. So they make all the noise they can to help it find its way back to the path again, and they are so happy when it finally is shining brightly again. Not all the folks believe this now, for some of the younger ones have had sufficient education that they know this is not true, but there are still many who believe it and cling to the old practice.

Death is a frightening event for those who have no hope. Bert and Colleen saw evidence of that firsthand as they observed their first wake. A woman with malaria was near death when her family brought her to Neil. Her condition improved in response to a new malaria drug the Weirs had brought from the States. But she came down with diarrhea. This greatly weakened her so that a family member decided she needed a strong purge. She died as a result. Bert described the wake:

> Outside on a small fire some coffee was brewing. Crowded around a table and a little flickering lamp, a group of men played cards. From inside came the mournful strands of half-heathen, half-Catholic songs, or should I say, chants. Their minor-key melodies were sufficient, apart from the shrieks and howls of the mourning family, to send chills up our

backs. We looked in. At the end of the room nearest us, on an elevated slab or table, lay the body covered with a sheet. A sort of bonnet on her head tied under her chin kept her mouth closed, but her eyes weren't quite closed. At her feet several candles burned, giving the room most of its light. On the wall above her head, a black piece of wood with a white cross and other figures carved on it (including her saint) protected the assembled people from the recently departed spirit (especially for the first eight days after death). Bending over her face in a half embrace stood the young husband in a drunken trance. You may think this is exaggerated, but we feel it's impossible to describe. The whole thing made a mark on us. It seemed so diabolical—the weeping, the chanting, the drunken laughter.

As soon as a person dies, the locals believe he becomes a very angry spirit who will try to molest the family. In the case of the girl described earlier, who died in childbirth, it was rumored that her spirit bothered the family so much that they moved out of the house. The purpose of the wake is to help keep the spirit away.

6

Opportunity and Opposition

The passion of Bert and Colleen's heart was to be "a living sacrifice, holy and acceptable to God" (Romans 12:1, ESV). They wanted to devote their lives to the task of loving God and loving people. This commitment was significant in their initial attraction to each other. It motivated their time of training and personal preparation. It was the purpose for going to Peru.

It was a thrill when their language skills improved enough for Bert to lead music and Colleen to teach the girls. To preach in Spanish was challenging at first, but it brought a sense of fulfillment.

The Elliots' hearts were stirred by the filth, drunkenness, poverty, and medical needs of the people. But underneath all those needs they saw lives that needed more than a cosmetic change. One can do his best to clean them up, sober them up, raise their standard of living, and cure all their ailments. But that doesn't touch their heart need. It is the good news of Jesus Christ that changes the heart. That's why they were in Peru. Their burden was to lead people to Him.

Peppered throughout their letters are references to that burden. When they accompanied the Weirs on river trips, Bert and Colleen saw villages that had never heard this message. To them, the outward filth and poverty symbolized souls in need of the cleansing power of the Christ. Watching the empty religious feasts, parties, and wakes highlighted the depravity of man's soul.

Bert and Colleen were impressed by the vastness of the region. How could so few reach so many? They had already been contemplating using a river launch for an itinerant ministry. To settle in a village of a couple hundred people for years of ministry was not going to effectively complete the task ahead.

But building a strong base from which to work was important. The Elliots initially poured their lives into the church in Lagunas. After a couple years, they found they needed a larger facility for church meetings. Everyone pitched in to erect a rammed-earth structure in a couple of months. They ended up with a fine building. But more important than the building was the camaraderie and sense of accomplishment that the whole church realized as they worked together.

As they were finishing this building, the church saw the need to begin a new work in the section of Lagunas known as the Old Village. This rose out of a vision to reach into a different subculture of their community, to a group of people who would not feel at home in the main church. They purchased a home there, and all joined together to renovate it into a meeting room. Soon began a vibrant Bible class for children and a Sunday-evening meeting, and a new church was planted.

Before the Weirs' furlough, Neil had acquired wood to build a boat. When they returned with the Elliots, Neil and Bert spent considerable time planning and building it. But much of the wood had rotted, and the process was frustrating. It was also possible the boat's design might not allow access to some areas. Neil and Bert took a short evangelistic trip up the Chambira River, where they also obtained more wood for the boat. Neil eventually completed the boat, and he and Gen took frequent trips, following up on the river contacts they had made.

In November of their first year, 1949, Bert and Colleen had visited Yurimaguas to see the work there. It had been established by the Burnses, but Mr. Burns had passed away five years previously. Yurimaguas, a twelve-hour boat trip upriver from Lagunas, was strategically located at the confluence of the majestic Huallaga and Paranapura Rivers. Larger in size, Yurimaguas was a commercial center boasting its own airport. The living conditions there were much nicer than in Lagunas, and the work had seen substantial growth. It caused Bert to reflect,

> The contrast between this place and our humble situation in Lagunas represents a contrast in belief between the Burns and Weirs, and perhaps also a difference in financial income through the years. The work here has been numerically much more prosperous than in Lagunas. The population and growth of the town itself probably being largely responsible. Perhaps also Mr. Burns's personality and greater willingness to own nice things and serve the people may have had its influence. We understand the attendance has been dropping steadily since his passing. We ourselves are watching, unable as yet to formulate any definite opinions and yet believing the Lord will use these observations when the time comes for us to be making decisions [regarding the nature of their ministry and where they would live].

It was on this trip that they first met Jerry and Pat Couenhoven, missionaries from Minneapolis, Minnesota, who had also just arrived on the field with their six-month-old boy. The two couples were the same age, with the same passion, and a bond of friendship developed immediately. They also met Ed Christensen, who lived there with his family and had corresponded with them when they were still contemplating coming to Peru. The Elliots had made the trip from Lagunas to Yurimaguas by plane, which prompted Bert's observation:

The early years in Lagunas

The trip was a new challenge to my own soul, to look down on the little huts that dotted the banks of the muddy twisting river—like the view that the Lord had looking down on a world of men living and dying on the banks of the murky river of sin. We would have returned to Lagunas yesterday, but we were overcome with a desire to return by canoe to better acquaint ourselves with the region and people, and also to sow the good seed as the Lord leads.

A year later the Couenhovens visited the Elliots and Weirs in Lagunas. One afternoon Bert and Jerry spent several hours studying a regional map, considering the possibility of a more effective boat-based ministry. Innumerable unreached villages were only accessible by river.

As we read between the lines, it seems Neil was building a larger, self-contained boat designed for extended trips. Jerry thought this was impractical on two accounts, and so was considering building a smaller boat for shorter trips. First, the Huallaga River up from Yurimaguas quickly became unnavigable by larger crafts. A smaller one would be more pragmatic. Second, Jerry was, as Bert put it, "becoming more and more tied down with family responsibilities."

He was recognizing early that a family made an extensive traveling ministry difficult.

Jerry and Bert decided to return to Yurimaguas and embark on a three-week canoe trip up the Huallaga River to follow up on contacts that Jerry had made previously and to get a feel for river work. They soon found that travel even by canoe was difficult as the river narrowed and the current became much faster and more difficult to paddle against. A power motor of some sort was essential.

They met with believers and conducted evangelistic meetings, and Bert pulled teeth. They even put out a house fire for a national who had earlier been inhospitable to them and their work. They trusted that their help in putting out the fire might, in Bert's wording, "subdue" his opposition. Some of the nationals were responsive to the gospel, and Bert and Jerry baptized in the river three who had previously come to faith.

While the Elliots were ministering in the Lagunas church and evaluating the possibility of a strong commitment to river-based ministry, Bob and Grace Finnagan arrived from England and settled in Lagunas in August 1952. They were a delightful couple about a decade older than the Elliots. They jumped right into learning the language and helping with ministry. The Elliots thoroughly enjoyed working with the Finnagans, the support eventually gave Bert and Colleen freedom to consider new ministry directions. In September 1953 they sold their home in Lagunas. Colleen explained,

> I can well imagine that there are lots of questions in all your minds as to why we are pulling up stakes here in Lagunas— and it is not easy to explain on paper. But be assured that we are only doing it because we are convinced it is what the Lord would have us do! It wasn't an easy decision, to sell the only place we can call our own, especially since we don't know when or where we'll have another. But the Lord knows, and we are so glad we can trust Him. It is really the only logical thing to do—we know that we would more than likely be away from Lagunas for a year and a half at least,

since both the Christensens and Couenhovens have asked us to take their place while they are on furlough. (Though we still don't know to which of these places we will go, we would like to help one of them at least.) And during our absence who would take care of our house? With no one in it, it would go to rack and ruin, and everything in it, too, and having nationals in it is sometimes worse than no one at all. The house is badly needing a new roof, and we would have to be here to see to these things, or we would come back to find that the rains had washed away our house.

That is only one small angle. Frankly, after seeing the vastness of the region and traveling over some parts of it, especially the upper Huallaga region, we have seen the tremendous need. It seems rather strange that three families of us should settle in one village, concentrating most of our efforts here while there are so many more nearly the same size without anyone. We don't know, but we feel perhaps the Lord is using these invitations to other parts to stir us up a bit to think about other places, too. These are some of the reasons, and we are happy with the Lord's leading.

The Elliots moved to Yurimaguas and lived with the Couenhovens for a couple months, until the Couenhovens left for the States in February 1953. Bert and Colleen stayed in their home for over a year, assisted in the ministry of the church, and launched much of their river work from there.

When discussing ministry strategy, one aspect of the river work must be emphasized. It provided a hands-on opportunity to train the national believers in discipleship and ministry. Bert never traveled alone, and he and Colleen rarely traveled alone. They took people with them to help with children's classes, visiting, handing out tracts, teaching, and learning firsthand what it means to minister to people. That is a key reason why, six decades later, believers are still traveling up and down those rivers encouraging the churches in those little villages and starting churches where there are none.

Opposition to God's work in the hearts of people is inevitable. Often for Bert and Colleen it came from religious and governmental authorities. In Lagunas the local police, responding to pressure from the Catholic priests, prohibited them from having "cottage meetings"—Bible studies in homes. In the Old Village church on the outskirts of Lagunas, school teachers tried to prohibit their students from attending the Bible classes. Both of those situations were rectified by appealing to higher governmental authorities.

"Have you seen how pretty she is?"

The opposition intensified in some of the upper Huallaga villages. At a certain point the river crossed into a different department (equivalent to a state or province) of Peru. The missionaries' first inkling of the opposition was a report that some believers in one village had been jailed for starting to build a church facility.

On the next river trip, the local police informed the Elliots they had received orders from their superiors to "do what you can to eliminate the propagation of the Protestant Religion." The local churches were forbidden from having religious meetings in private homes and from preaching in the streets. They had to meet in a church building or rent a hall if the village didn't have a church building.

On a trip a full year later, Colleen wrote,

> The guards showed Bert a letter from the bishop of
> Moyobamba (and which letter the chief of police had
> authorized, making it legal in that district at least) forbidding
> us to have meetings in private homes or baptisms in the river,
> so that put an end to our public meetings for a while, but
> they still can't stop us from visiting or people from visiting
> us. Maybe that kind of work is more effective anyway. All the
> [local government] authorities were in sympathy with us,
> but they are scared stiff of the priests and of their position,
> so they had to prohibit us. We also found out that the priest
> had denounced Bert for saying terrible things about the
> Roman Catholic church in his preaching, which is a lie.

On the next trip the formal denouncement had arrived from the
bishop of Moyobamba. Colleen wrote,

> It turned out to be a long series of lies and false rumors. Just
> to give you an example, Bert was charged with blindfolding
> a woman and forcing her to the river to be baptized, also
> running after children in the streets and plazas and carrying
> them to the river against their will to be baptized. He was
> charged with teaching husbands to beat their wives until
> they were willing to join our religion and a whole long list of
> other absurdities. At the time the police were in the process
> of investigating the charges. We are thankful to say that the
> head of the police here is a very just man who had often stood
> outside and listened to our meetings himself. He wrote back
> a very favorable report to Moyobamba, which should put an
> end to the whole business, or at least we trust so.

Another attack on their reputations was mentioned in the context
of a visit to Lagunas by the Couenhovens with their two children.
They were having a great time with "Uncle Bert." Colleen wrote,

It's good for the nationals to see children of *"evangelicos"* around the house. Since we are three childless couples [Weirs, Finnigans, and Elliots] living in Lagunas, weight has been added to the rumor that we are cured so as not to have children. Since this is very definitely against Catholic doctrine, the Roman Catholics capitalize on this a bit. Don't know how to make them think otherwise except that the Lord would give us children someday—that's just a little item for prayer.

On a personal note, I find it ironic that I'm writing about the opposition and attacks from the Catholic priests while I'm enjoying a personal study time at a Catholic monastery's retreat house in Oregon's Willamette Valley. I browsed through their bookstore, attended the communal prayers, and witnessed their devotion to the monastic lifestyle. It's amazing that the simple proclamation of the good news of Jesus Christ could be so threatening to those who claim to be its most ardent defenders.

A highlight of Bert and Colleen's first term on the field was a visit from Bert's parents, Fred and Clara, Bert's sister Jane, and Colleen's sister Joan. They arrived in Peru in October 1954. Fred had come to Ecuador several months earlier to spend time with Bert's brother Jim and his expecting wife, Elisabeth. Then Bert and Colleen met the group from Portland in Lima, and they all traveled to Yurimaguas. Joan stayed about six weeks and returned by herself via Ecuador. Fred, Clara, and Jane didn't return home until late January.

They spent most of their time in Yurimaguas, but also visited Pucallpa, and Jane was able to go on a brief river trip with Bert. Fred was asked to speak several different times. The family gained understanding of the opportunities and challenges that Bert and Colleen faced. The locals loved meeting all four visitors. One lady even named her daughter after Clara.

The visiting family's presence livened up the Christmas celebration. They also experienced a wake and funeral. Colleen wrote,

We sang hymns, Bert spoke, and then they served us coffee and bread. Little by little the less interested ones started home. By midnight there weren't probably any more than twenty-five or thirty still there. The body was beginning to give off quite an odor by then, so they decided to put her in the box and cover it. Prior to this she was just laying on top of the table with a sheet over her. When Bert, along with a couple other brethren, went to pick her up to put her in the box, they saw a great long worm crawling out of her nose—I guess it began to get too cold inside, and it came crawling out looking for a better place to live. Poor Bert. He just about turned green. But not wanting Dad and Jane to miss anything in this land of new and strange experiences, he called them over to see it, too. It was just about more than Dad could take to even think about looking at such a thing, and he thought Bert sure had his nerve calling him over.

After leaving Yurimaguas, Fred, Clara, and Jane spent more time in Pucallpa and Lima prior to traveling through Ecuador to see Jim and Elisabeth (Valerie was born a month later) and returning to the States. As soon as the family left, Bert and Colleen's focus turned to preparing for their upcoming furlough. Their plan was to coordinate their departure with the return of the Couenhovens, so the house would not be left unattended for long. They hoped to spend a couple weeks in Ecuador with Jim's family and then get back to Portland in time for Jane's wedding to Jerry Hawthorne on June 17, 1955.

Bert and Colleen made several trips both up and down the Huallaga River to encourage the churches, in addition to touching base with the believers in Lagunas one more time before leaving.

As their departure date approached, it became evident that the time required in Lima to process their travel paperwork wouldn't allow them to both spend time in Ecuador and make the wedding. They faced a difficult decision. They contemplated going straight to Portland for the wedding and seeing Jim in Ecuador at the end of their furlough. However they sensed that seeing Jim and his family was more important at that time.

As difficult as that decision was, in light of the events that unfolded in the ensuing months, they were so thankful they were able to spend the three weeks with Jim, Elisabeth, and Valerie.

They thoroughly enjoyed their time in Ecuador. It was quite restful, and they felt spoiled. Colleen wrote,

> I don't think Jim has changed a bit. Betty[1] and Valerie look swell, too. The baby is just darling. Her Uncle Bert and Auntie Colleen have been accused of spoiling her badly. But it's such a temptation to pick her up at every opportunity. I have her in my lap right now, having just fed her. It's so much fun; we really miss a lot not having kids, but the Lord knows best, and we have so much more than many in other ways that we mustn't complain.
>
> Betty and Jim sure speak Quechua enviably, and we are picking up a word or two. They are doing a great work. It takes brains like them to do it—translation, schoolwork, etc. It seems funny to us not to be able to talk to the people. They seem like our people in some ways, and so we often rattle off in Spanish and expect them to understand. But of course they don't. Bert spoke in the meeting on Sunday, and Jim translated. It was very good.

Bert and Colleen always counted this time with Jim and his family as a special gift from God. While in Ecuador they were also able to spend time with Ed and Marylou McCully, Pete and Olive Fleming, and Rachel Saint. From there they flew to Mexico City and then home to Portland, arriving in August 1955 with plans to return right after the first of the year. Because of an event in early 1956, they didn't return until May.

---

1   This is the family nickname for Elisabeth Elliot. In this book I will use Elisabeth, except in direct quotations, where I will keep the name used by the source.

Uncle Bert shared with me several times the difficulty of the heartbreaking decision to miss Jerry and Jane's wedding. But Bert and Colleen looked back and recognized God's definite leading in their decision, even though they had no idea of its ramifications at the time.

Colleen, Bert holding Valerie, Jim, Elisabeth

7

Operation Auca

The Christmas of 1955 at 7272 in Portland was a sharp contrast to the previous six Bert and Colleen had celebrated in the Peruvian jungle. The light drizzle and daily high of fifty-two degrees Fahrenheit engendered the couple's feeling of Christmas more than the ninety degrees and oppressive humidity of Yurimaguas. Fred Elliot typically downplayed Christmas, but Clara insisted on celebrating the birth of the Savior, who provided salvation through His death on the cross.

Once again celebrating Christmas with the Elliot and Collison families warmed Bert and Colleen's hearts. December 25 was a Sunday, so they enjoyed the added blessing of fellowship with the church family at Grace and Truth. Then, with the holidays behind them, they concentrated on preparing to return to Peru.

The first week of January 1956 brought a letter from Jim in Ecuador that caused some concern. He had written it two weeks earlier, on December 22:

> Friday morning [December 16] on the radio contact, Ed
> and I were standing by for Marilou in Arajuno, and she

sounded scared. A Quichua who was staying with her had gotten up early and almost ran head-on into a naked Auca[1] standing with a lance in his hand not fifty yards away from Ed's house. So Ed and Nate flew out there [by plane] in a hurry, but nothing more was to be seen of him. The Quichua had wanted to kill [the Auca] on sight, but Marilou took [the Quichua's] gun away from him and went out shouting a phrase that means "I like you" and tried to give him a machete, but he was gone. One lone wet footprint on a board and some smashed grass where he took off into the jungle were all she saw of him. We would like to reach this tribe. They have never had friendly contact either with whites or [other] Indians, but we know where they live and will make a definite effort to reach them soon. This needs two things. The first is secrecy. There are some who, if they got wind of our plan, could wreck the whole deal, so don't tell this to anyone till I write you to do so. The second thing is prayer. These people are killers and have no idea of getting along with outsiders. Our Quichuas are deathly afraid of them, as are the whites, and we will be called fools for our plans. But we believe that God has brought Ed to Arajuno for this contact, and we want to do His will in taking the Gospel to them. They have no word for God in their language, let alone a word for Jesus. There is a [civilized] Auca woman at Ila whom Betty and I have visited, and we are working on their language at present. It is much more difficult than Quichua and will need more work at analyzing, so pray for

---

1 Auca is a pejorative Quichua word meaning "savage." It was later learned that the Aucas call themselves Waodani, which means "the people." I use the term Auca in this chapter and the next to be faithful to the historical context and understanding at the time. The missionaries never used it in a derogatory way and, in fact, usually used it with great love. In subsequent chapters I use the term Waodani to reflect how they identified themselves. As a side note, I grew up among the Navajo, which is a Spanish name given them. They call themselves *Diné*, which means "the people."

us. You will be hearing more of this in a month or two as plans develop.[2]

The history and plight of the Aucas were well known to the Elliot family. Jim first heard of them at the Summer Institute of Linguistics in June 1950 from a missionary to the Ecuadorian Quichua. Elisabeth wrote, "Jim's heart was immediately set on fire. A tribe untouched by civilization? A people who had repulsed every attempt of the white man to contact them? The pioneer spirit in him was kindled at the very thought. Some may say it was his romantic temperament. Very likely it was."[3]

The Aucas had a storied history of contact with the white man and other Indian groups—almost all interactions ending in violence and killing. The white man intruded on their territory first looking for rubber and later for oil. Those encounters painted the jungle red with blood. The local Indians fearfully kept their distance. Killing was even common between different clans within the Auca tribe.

Before deciding on Ecuador, Jim had wrestled over whether God was leading him to India or Latin America. He had corresponded with Bert and Colleen about the possibility of joining them in Peru. Learning about the Aucas tipped the scale. He set aside ten days for concentrated prayer, seeking a definitive direction from God. He came away convinced that God was calling him to Ecuador.

He challenged two of his friends, Ed McCully and Pete Fleming, to consider whether God wanted them to join him in Ecuador, ministering to the Quichua with an eye to possibly reaching the Aucas for Christ. The driving force of Jim's life was obedience to God—in this case to obey His call to present the gospel to every people. These three found kindred spirits in Nate Saint and Roger Youderian, who were already in Ecuador.

When these five men and their wives began to seriously consider initiating contact with the Aucas, each had been in Ecuador between

---

2   As quoted in Elliot, *Shadow of the Almighty*, 242.
3   Ibid, 129.

Jim in Ecuador

three and seven years, working in five different locations among several different tribal groups. They were seasoned missionaries. One of their prayers was that God would open the door to the Aucas.[4]

Back in Portland a phone call from Ecuador to the Elliot home on Monday, January 9, changed everything—five missionaries were missing in the jungles of Ecuador and thought to have been captured by the Aucas. The details were sketchy. A search plane had spotted their small Piper plane, stripped and abandoned on a river bank in the heart of Auca territory. An unidentified body was seen near the wreckage.

---

4 The impact of this story has been well documented. Elisabeth Elliot told the account of Operation Auca in *Through Gates of Splendor*. She wrote more broadly of her husband, Jim, in *Shadow of the Almighty*. Both of these are missionary classics. In addition, Olive (Fleming) Liefeld wrote *Unfinished Destinies* and Ken Fleming wrote *Man of Faith* about Pete Fleming—husband and brother, respectively. Steve Saint wrote about his father, Nate, in *End of the Spear*. Ellen Vaughn told the story in *Becoming Elisabeth Elliot*. All are worth reading.

The news of the missing missionaries spread immediately. HCJB in Quito sent it out over its vast radio network: "Five men are missing in Auca territory." Radio stations and newspapers across the US picked up the story. People around the world prayed for these men and their families. The hours following the initial report were filled with uncertainty and hope.

In the middle of this week of uncertainty, a letter Jim wrote on December 28 arrived at the Elliot home and filled in more details for the family. It was Jim's final letter.

> By the time this reaches you, Ed and Pete and I and another fellow will have attempted with Nate a contact with the Aucas. We have prayed for this and prepared for several months, keeping the whole thing secret (not even our nearby missionary friends know of it yet). Some time ago on survey flights Nate located two groups of their houses, and ever since that time we have made weekly friendship flights, dropping gifts and shouting phrases in their language—which we got from the woman in Ila—from a loudspeaker. Nate has used his drop-cord system to land things right at their doorstep, and we have received several gifts back from them—pets and food and things they make, tied onto this cord. Our plan is to go downriver and land on a beach we have surveyed not far from their place, build a tree house—which I have prefabricated with our power saw here—then invite them over by calling to them from the plane. The contact is planned for Friday or Saturday, January 6 or 7. We may have to wait longer. I don't have to remind you that these are completely naked savages (I saw the first sign of clothes this week—a G-string), who have never had any contact with white men other than killing. They do not have firearms, but kill with long chonta-wood lances. They do not have fire, except what they make from rubbing sticks together on moss. They use bark cloth for carrying their babies, sleep

115

in hammocks, and steal machetes and axes when they kill our Indians. They have no word for God in their language, only for devils and spirits. I know you will pray. Our orders are "the Gospel to every creature." —Your loving son and brother, Jim[5]

The US Air Force Air Rescue Service, the US Navy and Army, and the Ecuadorian Air Force sprang into action. The assembled search team included a doctor, missionaries, Ecuadorian soldiers, and support personnel to make the two-day trek in hopes that one or more of the men were still alive. The search party left on Thursday morning, January 12, and arrived at the site by Friday afternoon. In the meantime a military helicopter flew in on Thursday and found four bodies, which, along with the one seen earlier, confirmed that all five men had been killed.

Fred and Bert spent Thursday afternoon leading a men's Bible study in the backroom of fellow church member Claire Wiley's watch repair shop in Vancouver, Washington. It was there they received the message that Jim's body had been found—he was speared to death. Claire's seven-year-old son, Wally, watched as fifteen grown men wept over the news—a scene similar to another my sister-in-law Beth vividly remembers witnessing during those difficult days.

When Fred and Bert's brother Bob arrived at prayer meeting at Grace and Truth that evening, their faces were ashen. The family and church had been preparing for the eventual possibility, but the finality of the news brought incredible grief.

Bert wrote,

In those dark hours before dawn my parents sat weeping as grief overcame them like waves of the ocean. They would think of those dear men, so prepared and consecrated to God, suddenly gone, and they would weep for them. Then

5   Elliot, *Shadow of the Almighty*, 243.

they were comforted, only to think of the five widows without their husbands, and they would weep again and be comforted again, until another wave would hit them as they remembered the children left fatherless and the mission stations abandoned. My own heart was trying to make sense out of what only seemed tragedy and loss. The question surfaced in my mind, *If we give ourselves to God in obedience to His Word, shouldn't He protect us as we live for Him?* The meaning of Jim's words, "We have bargained for the cross," and Elisabeth's words, "There are worse things than dying," had not yet entered my understanding.

The true cost of obedience became a reality—even for those who stayed home. But their faith was not shaken. Clara was quoted in the local paper: "There is some reason for this—the Lord would not permit it to happen otherwise—and He makes it bearable for us." She added, "Jim felt God's call and he answered."

Fred said, "God so loved the world that He gave His own Son.[6] Could we do less?"

They found comfort in hearing excerpts found in a diary at the murder scene. Fred said, "Their hearts were filled with joy when they saw the Aucas, for they thought they could help them be born again in Christ. It's the poor Aucas I'm sorry for."[7]

For Bert, mingled with the grief and loss was a yet another emotional distress. Why Jim? In Bert's eyes, Jim had an influential ministry, a spiritual fervor, a flair for leadership, and a dynamic walk with God. *Why take Jim and not me? He had so much more to offer God.* In Bert's assessment God wasted Jim's abilities and left the less capable brother. As time passed, Bert submitted to the "right" of God to choose—to take Jim and leave him. By the time Bert and Colleen returned to Peru, that initial distress was completely gone,

6 Paraphrased from John 3:16.
7 All quotations from preceding three paragraphs from "Parents of Port-lander Bear News with Faith," *Oregonian*, circa January 16, 1956.

and Bert had recommitted his life to taking "the gospel to every creature."[8]

Years later, after Elisabeth had successfully begun to live among the Aucas, she learned one of the Auca men had told a lie that led to an intertribal conflict, which they thought would be best remedied by killing the missionaries. Killing was their default method for resolving conflict. It was an unfortunate misunderstanding, and the Aucas later regretted their actions.

The Fleming and Elliot families were close, so the Flemings asked Bert to speak at Pete's memorial service in Seattle. Bert chose to center his remarks on the story of David and Bathsheba from 2 Samuel 11! I must say that, in all the funerals I've officiated through the years, I've never considered using *that* passage. The story tells us that David should have been on the battlefield leading his army to victory. Instead he was enjoying the comforts of palace life. He spotted Bathsheba, called for her, and committed adultery. She discovered she was pregnant. To cover his sin, David brought Bathsheba's husband, Uriah, home from battle for a little rest and relaxation. An honorable man, Uriah denied himself the pleasure of spending a night with his wife while his fellow soldiers were at war. Seeing that his cover-up attempt was thwarted, David sent Uriah back to war with instructions for the general to put him in the fiercest battle and then to abandon him, assuring his death.

Bert continued,

> Uriahs are rare in our day and age. And even we, as missionaries who have come home from the field, find a tendency to settle down in this materialistic age, to surround ourselves with comforts, and to forget those who are there laboring faithfully for God. Jim's last words in his last letter home are a note of confidence. He says, "I know you will pray. Our orders are 'the gospel to every creature.'"

---

8   Mark 16:15, NIV; see also Colossians 1:23.

Jim with his parents before going to Ecuador

But as I examine my own heart in the light of that word, I wonder, *Have we been praying?* I wonder, *Did we pray?* As I see it, my friends, we are very much like David in this day and age here in this country. We're settled down. We leave the battle to others.

And then David tries to cover his own sin by sending Uriah back in the appointed time with the message in his own hand: "Put Uriah in the thickest of the fray, where the battle is the hottest." And while we sometimes permit our young men to go out and push the battle right into the very gates of the enemy's territory, we sit back in our ease and forget them. And we are even too lazy and too tired and too burdened down with material things to pray for them. This is a message to my own heart.

As we think of the problem, we are all prone to ask ourselves, "Why did God permit this thing that seems to us to be a tragedy? Why did He permit it?" The only answer I can come to is this, my friend: Conceivably these men could have gone in and established contact and won the Aucas to the Lord. Conceivably the Aucas could have been won at much lower cost. But I cannot conceive any other way God could have brought this congregation together here today to forget our sectarian feelings, to forget our pride, to sit in self-judgment. I cannot conceive another way God could have shaken the church in this country so greatly, except by the blood of those five men.

Which means exactly this: that instead of laying the bloodguilt at the foot of the Aucas, it comes home to our own doors. It tracks us down. We're guilty. God is speaking to us. Oh, that we might have tender hearts and open ears to the voice of God to hear His message to us in these days. That we might not settle down like David in our wealth and our luxury. That we might be men like Uriah, who has his heart out there in the field. Although his body might be home, his heart and soul are there where the battle is being fought. That we too might press the fray against Satan and against his emissaries in these days. May we not be found guilty of—as Nate said so fittingly—"the charge of not counting the cost."

God help us to act with Uriah's integrity. Let us each one examine our own hearts and find ourselves at the crossroads today. May we not let self have its way. May we hear His voice, to take up our cross today and follow Him.

David Jannsen, one of Jim's boyhood friends, said to me years later, "When I first heard about the death of the men, I said to myself, 'The cause of world missions is going to be set back for an entire generation.' I couldn't have been more wrong." People began to get in line to replace the five men on the mission field.

For instance the watch shop owner, Claire Wiley, and his wife Arlene had been trying to take their family with five children to the mission field. The children remember Nate Saint visiting their home before going to Ecuador. He stood on their kitchen chair to demonstrate the method he discovered to lower a basket from an airplane to deliver gifts to the Auca. The Wileys were frustrated because no missionary organization wanted to take on a family of their size. They came to Bert for advice. In light of the recent events, Bert said, "Claire, take your family and get going. The Lord will use you and provide for your family." For the next forty years they did construction work in Mexico, Brazil, and Ecuador.

As Bert and Colleen returned to Peru after a ten-month furlough, leaving friends and family behind was much more difficult than it had been the first time. The events of the past couple of months had strengthened their bonds with their families and underscored the brevity of life on earth.

8

The Long Journey to Cajamarca

Fred and Clara drove Bert and Colleen to New Orleans, where they would set sail for Peru by way of New Orleans and the Panama Canal, with a stop in Ecuador to visit widowed Elisabeth and Valerie. On their way they stopped at the headquarters of Missionary Aviation Fellowship in Fullerton, California. Colleen wrote, "Saturday we drove out to Fullerton to see the movie the fellows made of their contact with the Aucas on the Friday before they were killed. It certainly was most interesting, but heartbreaking, too, as you can imagine."

Bert's sister, Jane Hawthorne, traveled from Wheaton to New Orleans and joined Fred and Clara in seeing off Bert and Colleen on May 17, 1956. Onboard ship that evening Bert put some perspective on their lives:

> This morning's farewell was the most difficult I've ever experienced. It seems as though the last few months have knit us closer than ever together. As speaking distance grew to shouting distance and shouting to waving, and at last

those three precious people (the most precious on earth) blurred into the New Orleans skyline, I thought my very heart was being torn. I can't remember feeling anything like it the first time. I don't quite understand it, unless since Jim's going we realize more fully what parting may mean. But, as at other difficult times, the holy reasoning of faith soon put to flight all my morbid ponderings and lifted my soul into Glory.

I remember spending some time blessing God for such a spiritual heritage, for a father who towers in spirituality head and shoulders above other men. And for a mother the size of whose heart can never be measured but is hinted at in all she has suffered to bring us all up and then give us back to God. I then began to thank Him for my darling wife and tried to imagine the loneliness that would have been mine were she not with me.

An emotional farewell

My mind flashed to dear Betty, who will have to be doing just that from now on. And then back to the reason for it all, back to Christ who plans it all for our highest good and who giveth grace in increasing measure, always abounding more than our increasing need. Oh, bless God for giving us His Christ. How my soul longs to know Him more in all ways and whatever the cost. "Oh, Christ, He is the fountain, the deep, sweet well of love; the streams on earth I've tasted, more deep I'll drink above; there to an ocean fullness His mercy doth expand, and glory—glory dwelleth in Immanuel's land." I couldn't help being solemnized by it all and singing, as I searched my own heart, Jim's hymn to Betty: "Have I an object, Lord, below, which would divide my heart with Thee; which would divert its even flow in answer to Thy constancy?"[1]

On their stop in Panama Bert and Colleen received a letter from Missionary Aviation Fellowship that included a set of twenty-five colored slides of the Aucas taken by the fellows before they were killed. The Elliots showed the slides and told the Auca story to missionaries in Panama and Colombia. One of the missionaries in Colombia had "been stoned for preaching the gospel, and on one occasion he had a gun leveled at his head and the trigger clicked five times but failed to go off," wrote Colleen.

Their next stop was in Ecuador to visit Elisabeth. Colleen wrote,

Needless to say, it was wonderful to see Betty (who looks real good) and little Val, who is just adorable. Val was exposed to measles a week or so ago, and she has a cough and cold now, so Betty is afraid she is in for a case of measles while we are here. We stayed up late last night talking and looking at some of the pictures Betty had of the Auca incident. It was most interesting. Betty is wonderful, or I should say it

---

1   First quotation is a verse from Anne Ross Cousin, "Oh, Christ, He Is the Fountain," 1854, included also in a different version of the song titled "Immanuel's Land." Second quotation from George West Frazer (1830–1896), "Have I an Object, Lord, Below."

is wonderful to see the grace of God operating in her life. I wish I knew better how to explain it, but her attitude about everything is most Christlike.

They stayed with Elisabeth for two weeks in June. Bert preached several times with Elisabeth translating into Quechua. He also helped with many odd jobs around the house. Colleen assisted in the kitchen and accompanied Elisabeth on several house calls, including the delivery of a baby girl, who the mother named "Colin" (the Quechua version of Colleen). Colleen wrote,

> I sure do admire Betty—she never complains a bit, even though it is very obvious she misses Jim terrifically. Of course she keeps very busy with school work, translation, meetings, letter writing, treating sick Indians, supervising them when they work, and a multitude of other things besides the care of Valerie and the house. On Sunday afternoons she has an instruction class for some of the young fellows giving them a lesson in flannel graph, and then they in turn will go out to Indian houses during the week and hold meetings. How she does it all I don't know! The Lord had given us such a happy time with them and drawn us so very close together that it was hard to say goodbye again. But the Lord gave grace, and we were so very thankful that her brother Tom Howard was there with Betty when we left.

When Bert and Colleen landed in Lima, no one met them at the airport, since the letter announcing their arrival time hadn't been delivered yet. Instead, some Wycliffe missionaries happened to be there and invited them to stay at the Wycliffe house. Colleen wrote,

> So it was real nice, and we could discern the hand of the Lord in it all, because the next day they were to have a luncheon at the house with Cornel Cappa [the *LIFE* photographer who

took the pictures of the Auca project]. Of course they invited us. This is something we wouldn't even have known about if we hadn't met them at the airport and then gone home with them. We sure enjoyed meeting Cappa and hearing a non-Christian who was closely connected with it tell his viewpoint of the happenings on the Curaray River. He was a very nice fellow, in his early forties I would judge, very nice looking. He is Hungarian and speaks with a distinct accent.

We all fired questions at him. His general comments were interesting. He refused to say even that he recognized the hand of God in all of this. But he did say he felt that he had gotten into something real there, and now it was up to him whether he wanted to probe into it deeper or not. He said also that most of their photography experiences are ones they like to forget about as soon as possible, but this was different!

Someone asked him what he considered the most important part of his Ecuadorian experience. Of course he mentioned the attitude of the wives, etc., but he said it was especially wonderful to him to see how things worked out for him to come down. Everything just seemed to dovetail right and get him down here at just the right moment. In the first place, he had just returned from South America in December. It was the last place he wanted to go back to. When *LIFE* called him on Tuesday night and asked him if he would be willing to go down to Ecuador to do the story on the fellows, he was almost sure that by Wednesday morning the news interest would have died down. So he figured he wouldn't have anything to lose, so he accepted, thinking he wouldn't have to go anyway. Then, since he hadn't planned to do any stories for about a month or so, he had sent all his camera equipment out to be repaired and told them to take their time. But on Wednesday morning they just "happened" to call and say his cameras were all ready. Of course he found out the news hadn't died down. They still very much wanted him to go, so he began to make arrangements right away.

Then he got to Guayaquil on Thursday and found there was absolutely no possible way to get down to Shellmera, so he almost turned around and went back after trying for hours to get transportation. But then, too, a naval plane just "happened" to go to Shellmera for fuel instead of Quito, and he was able to get a ride in. There were many other incidents he mentioned, things that he can't understand. He outwardly is inclined to call them coincidences, but we know it was the hand of the Lord, who was interested in getting the story out to the world.

One of the reasons *LIFE* was so interested in getting the story was that a few months before they had decided to do an article on "a bush pilot." Through the influence of Sam Saint [Nate's brother] and one of his friends (who is also a friend of Cappa), they had decided to do the story on Nate. Of course when the killings happened in January, they were interested.

Bert asked Cappa how he would account for the fact that this story had had so much publicity all over the world when other things had happened and been so soon forgotten. I don't remember all the details he gave in answer, but one thing he said was that, first, it was such a terrific story in itself—the fellows had put so much preparation into the project. There was such a wealth of documentary material, diaries, etc. He couldn't understand why it was in such demand all over the world—it was understandable in the States, because of the kind of story it was and the fact that it happened to Americans.

But he also said he was the only photographer who could have sold the story and pictures to foreign magazines because of his affiliation with Magnum Films, and also the fact that he persuaded Sam Saint not to sell the story outright to

Falling in love with the mountain people

LIFE. But it was sold to *LIFE* just to be used once, and then they were to relinquish all rights. Thus he sold it to magazines all over the world. That's how it got around. It sure is hard to explain all this on paper. I hope I am getting some of the thoughts across. He brought out some other things, too, which made us see more clearly than ever the hand of the Lord leading all the way through, even though he wouldn't say so in these words.

While this is a long description of this meeting, it serves to underscore God's intent to use this tragic story for the furtherance of His kingdom throughout the world. The Auca story also stirred in Bert and Colleen's heart a desire to expand their ministry so as to reach more communities in northern Peru that were untouched by the gospel.

Besides the luggage they brought with them from the States, they had also shipped some freight, including a set of kitchen cabinets given by Wil Van Dyk, a cabinetmaker in their home church. The freight was to be delivered to the port at Chiclayo. Instead it was left on board the ship and went on to Chile. While they waited for it to be returned, Mr. Aish, a British missionary, invited them to travel with him to see the work in Cajamarca. Colleen describes it,

> Cajamarca is a lovely spot, situated as it is in the Andes Mountains. It reminds us a lot of Quito, Ecuador. The elevation here is about ten thousand feet. We find we get out of breath easily if we walk or move much. When the sun is out, one feels quite comfortable, but when it goes down, we feel the cold quite a bit. We sure have been thankful for the winter clothing we brought this time. The place is quite picturesque because of the mountain Indians who live here with their typical garb and customs.

They saw a sharp contrast between the mountain people and those in the jungle. Colleen wrote, "They are all equally loveable and wonderful people, but the mountain folks are so very much more alert and wide awake and seem to have such a thirst for the truth. Whereas the people in the jungle are so much more passive and sort of sleepy. I wonder if the climate doesn't have something to do with that, for we sort of feel the same way when we are in the jungle."

The Elliots were impressed with the need and opportunities in this mountainous region. The people and culture were noticeably different from those of the jungle. They fell in love with the people and appreciated their hunger to learn about the Bible. After communicating with the Couenhovens, Colleen wrote,

We were wondering if maybe the Lord had a purpose in allowing us to see the work in Cajamarca before getting settled in Yurimaguas, and maybe we should build our house here instead of in Yurimaguas. If we built here, it would be with the idea of trading off with the Couenhovens. We would spend some months here and then in Yurimaguas, and they would do likewise. Pat and Jerry rather liked the idea, because, as you know, Pat isn't too well in the jungle, and it would be a nice change for her if she could come here for a few months every year. We'll see how everything works out.

The Elliots' freight finally arrived in Chiclayo, and they decided to have it transported up the mountain to Cajamarca. After much prayer and in consultation with the Couenhovens, Bert and Colleen decided to establish a base for ministry to the mountain communities. They rented a couple of rooms from one of the Christians there and began to set up living quarters. They installed the kitchen cabinets, made a table from a sheet of plywood, and bought a four-inch foam rubber mattress for a bed. After spending two months in Cajamarca, they finally flew back to Yurimaguas in September 1956 and reacquainted themselves with the folks there. They had been away for a year and a half.

9

Rivers, Roads, and Family Connections

Bert and Colleen soon found a rhythm, alternating ministry between the jungle and the mountains. The jungle continued to occupy the greater percentage of their time. But during these next six years in Peru, they made nine trips to Cajamarca and its surrounding villages, each lasting between two and five months. The plan to interchange ministry responsibilities with the Couenhovens never materialized, as the Couenhovens soon moved to Lima for their children's education and a better climate for Pat's health.

A blast of stifling hot air welcomed the Elliots as they stepped off the airplane in Yurimaguas in fall 1956. After reconnecting with the Couenhovens and the local believers, they initially looked for a home to rent or a piece of property on which to build, but did not find anything suitable. So, as Colleen wrote,

> Bert has started a small house for us on part of the Couenhoven property. We are excited at the prospect of

having a little place that we can call our own, believe me, even if we don't plan to be here much of the time! The house won't be very big, but plenty of room for us and for any of you that decide to come down and visit us, too. There is to be a small kitchen, a small living room, two bedrooms (one of which we will use as a study when we don't have guests), and a small room at the back for the washing machine and Bert's tools, also a bathroom.

They were thrilled when it was completed and they could finally move in.

In addition, the believers were building a new facility where the church would meet. They had outgrown their current chapel and began organizing workdays. They went into the jungle and harvested the logs themselves, and they collected material for the adobe walls. The progress on the new church building seems to have been left very much in the local believers' hands with the missionaries providing limited hands-on help. It took considerably longer that way, as the nationals had to fit the construction around their farm schedules and other responsibilities, but they took great satisfaction in the end result.

Bert and Jerry had also purchased the shell of a boat they wanted to rebuild. It would serve as a home away from home and a ministry center from which to do their itinerant river work. Fiberglass, a stove, and a generator had been ordered from the States. The boat had to be totally rebuilt because so much of it was rotten. The fiberglass turned out to be an effective covering. Between their regular trips to Cajamarca, multiple trips on the river in the old boat, ongoing ministry responsibilities, and challenges in the rebuilding of the new boat, it took almost a year before the *Maranatha* was launched on its August 1957 maiden voyage, about which Colleen wrote,

We really did have a wonderful trip. For the most part the boat is wonderful and afforded us probably the most restful river trip we have ever taken. We certainly are thankful for the boat; in fact, it would be just about perfect if it had an air conditioning system attached somewhere (it gets pretty hot during certain hours of the day) and room for a refrigerator in some little corner. At times it seems a bit crowded, too, especially when you are trying to cook breakfast on the little stove in back and about half the village has come aboard to buy medicine or get their teeth pulled or something. At times like that one is tempted to yell "Fire!" or something to get people to scatter and leave you with a little space in which to breathe. But seriously, the boat is wonderful, and we really couldn't ask for anything nicer. The fiberglass certainly sealed in the hull nicely, and the inside of the boat was completely dry, until we hit a sunken log up in the swift water, which made a long scratch in the bottom of the boat, and water began to seep in there. Bert was just sick about that when it happened, but it was one of those things that couldn't be helped. Sunken logs are one of the worst hazards of river travel, and you invariably bump up against them sooner or later no matter how careful you are.

In addition to the *Maranatha*, they saw the need for a more agile craft to use for shorter trips. Colleen wrote,

It was felt that a small aluminum boat would be the best buy in the long run and the most suitable for these shorter trips. We finally saved enough money together with the Couenhovens. (It sure is wonderful to have coworkers like this with whom we can share such projects and everything. The Lord has been very good to us!) Bert has made two weekend trips down the river, and it sure is a time saver. Where it took us six hours, at least, in the old dugout from Providencia to Yurimaguas, in the aluminum boat it is only two and a half. Of course one has to limit the number of

135

people you take, otherwise the boat will not plane with our small motor. But it can carry three men and their baggage very well, and that is usually sufficient.

This craft was much more conducive for the Peruvian believers to take for overnight evangelism and teaching trips. It was gratifying to see them catch the vision for the work. But the response in the village of Papa Playa was quite typical. Colleen wrote,

The Maranatha expands the river ministry.

It's a good-sized place, and we always get excellent crowds out to the meetings, both adults and children. The children especially love to come and I wish you could hear them sing—they all but raise the roof with the few choruses and hymns we have taught them. They are so cute. But as yet there are very few believers in this village, and while we have never faced opposition in this village (in fact the opposite is true; the authorities have always been most cooperative and helpful), we have sensed opposition from Satan himself seeking to hold the souls of men in ignorance and darkness.

Saturday night especially, even though there was a large crowd out, the attention in the meeting was terrible, and we felt that we were getting absolutely nowhere. We were much in prayer yesterday, and there was greater liberty in the meeting last night. The general concept of the gospel folks here have is so far from the truth; they think of it and talk of it as merely another "religion." One can talk or preach until he is blue in the face about the "salvation of your souls" or the "forgiveness of sins," or the "good news of God's grace to sinners," etc. Folks will listen and agree and then turn right around and talk about "joining the religion." It just seems that their minds are blinded, and only the Spirit of God can illumine them. Thank God this has happened in many cases in these villages through the years, but we long for more.

The need for medical work was a constant in their jungle travels. It was their open door to touch the deeper issues of life. Colleen wrote,

The worst medical case that was brought to us this time was a man with an infected arm. His arm was swollen twice its normal size from the shoulder right down to the tips of the fingers. Someone had attempted to lance it about a week before with a jackknife and only made matters worse. They had also applied all kinds of home brews, herbs, etc., and in so doing had burned the skin badly around the elbow. The fellow hadn't been able to sleep for I don't know how long. He was just a shadow of his former self. We were almost afraid to touch it for fear of aggravating it anymore, but we knew, if something wasn't done soon, he would undoubtedly die. So Bert broke off a razor blade into a point, disinfected it, and lanced the arm just above the elbow. He had to go quite deep, but when he finally hit the pocket, you should have seen the pus gush out. They held a gourd to catch it.

I think I can safely estimate we got well over a quart that first day. When he had had about all he could take then, we put a drain in and left it. We also put in a penicillin shot and a glucose-vitamin shot to help build him up again. The next day we found him feeling much better, and the swelling had gone down quite a bit. When we removed the drain and applied a bit of pressure, we got another half a gourd of pus. It seemed like we still had not got it all, but we had to head down the river. The pus seemed to have filled the arm from the shoulder on down. It afforded us a wonderful opportunity to speak to him about his soul, because I think he, more than anyone, realized what a close call he had had with death.

Young ladies with Colleen, Barbara Jo, Kate

It's easy for the casual observer to lump all Indians in Peru's jungles into one homogenous people group, but there are distinctions between these groups. The missionaries recognized the significant differences. At one point, Colleen's mother, Kate Collison, visited the Elliots, accompanied by Barbara Jo Marks, a traveling companion from Portland. During that visit, Colleen made a point of taking them from Pucallpa to see the Shipibo Indian colony along the Ucayali River. Colleen wrote, "I wanted them to see some real Indians before they left Peru. By that I mean jungle Indians who look and dress differently from the normal Peruvian." This group is best known for their distinct pottery

During that same visit to Pucallpa, the missionary community joined together for a fun outing. Colleen wrote,

> Saturday afternoon we all donned our swimming suits and went up to the base for a swim in the lake. The water was so warm it was hardly refreshing, but it was still fun. Johnny Hocking and a friend rented a speedboat and were waterskiing. They are really good at it, and it looks so easy. Bert has been wanting to try it for a long time, especially since Francis Ball wrote concerning it that he hadn't had so much fun since his first kiss! But after three tries and three dunkings, Bert thinks maybe he still prefers the kiss! He said it's too much like work to be fun, but he'd like to try it again! He did look funny.

January 1959 brought a much-anticipated visit from Fred, Clara, Elisabeth, and Valerie. When Bert and Colleen had visited Elisabeth in Ecuador in June 1956, she was continuing the work that she and Jim had begun among the Quechua. In 1957 she wrote *Through Gates of Splendor*, which told a brief life story of each of the five martyred men, as well as a detailed account of Operation Auca. The book quickly became highly influential in the evangelical community, as many who read it were motivated for Christian service. The following year she wrote *Shadow of the Almighty: The Life and Testament of Jim Elliot*, which focused on Jim's life and quoted predominantly from his insightful journals. The two books have become classics in Christian literature and have influenced many lives.

While Elisabeth was working among the Quechua, two Waodani (Auca) women lived there as well. From one of them, Dayuma, Elisabeth and Rachel Saint (sister to Nate Saint) learned the Waodani language. Dayuma was able to open a door for the two ladies to visit the tribe and eventually live there. Their initial task was to translate portions of the Bible into their language. Elisabeth and Valerie lived with the Waodani, starting in October 1958, for a total of two years while Rachel spent the rest of her life there. This is a remarkable story of the impact of Christ's forgiveness on this once brutal people group—forgiveness expressed in action by a widow and sister of the men who were killed.

Since Bert and Colleen's communication with the outside world was limited, they received only bits and pieces of the story as it unfolded. Letters from home contributed information the family had heard. Bert and Colleen received Elisabeth's correspondence, but that was limited. Wycliffe planes that came through sometimes had up-to-date news. Sporadically the Elliots were able to catch radio broadcasts from HCJB in Quito with the most recent accounts. There must have been a great deal of apprehension about two ladies and a three-year-old girl going in to live among a group of people who hadn't given a second thought to killing the five young men. Bert and Colleen were anxious to hear the story from Elisabeth firsthand.

On their way to Peru, the senior Elliots had traveled to Quito to visit Elisabeth and Valerie. Then the four of them journeyed together to Lima, where Bert and Colleen met them. Because of the notoriety of the story and the impact of her books, Elisabeth had a sort of celebrity status wherever she went. Colleen wrote,

> Everyone is anxious to meet Betty and hear her story, and I guess they would like to keep her around longer to get a chance. Yesterday the newspaper reporters found out she was in town, and they came out to the house immediately. Her picture was on the front page of the paper today with quite a lengthy write-up. Today some other reporter or radio

man or something came and tried to get her to talk on the radio, but she declined, saying her Spanish was too rusty. (It's not; she speaks very good Spanish.) Friday night we were invited over to the Wycliffe House for supper, after which they invited Betty to speak to the members of their group. It turned out to be quite a crowd, but Betty was excellent. She has a wonderful way of expressing herself.

Fred with Valerie, Clara, Elisabeth, Bert, Colleen in Yurimaguas

Valerie is just as cute as she can be—a beautiful child, really, and very good. Betty has her beautifully trained to be obedient. She is tall for her age, looks a lot like Betty in some ways, but an awful lot like Jim, too. She is definitely an extrovert, makes friends very easily with other children, and has a happy, vivacious personality. We have both fallen completely in love with her, and she in turn seems to have fallen especially in love with her Uncle Bert. She keeps asking him if he will please be her daddy.

After a couple days in Lima, the Elliot crew flew to Yurimaguas. A highlight of the three weeks with Elisabeth was taking her on a brief river trip. Colleen wrote, "So many of the folks on the river speak

Quechua besides Spanish, and Betty was able to talk to them in this, and they sure got a bang out of it. Her Quechua is quite different in many respects, but they were able to understand each other for the most part. Most interesting." Bert and Colleen thoroughly enjoyed their time with Elisabeth. Colleen wrote,

> Betty can be extremely quiet at times, but she can also be highly entertaining, and often she had us literally in stitches with her stories. Bert and I found conversation with her very stimulating, and it usually left us feeling we had better get busy and study a little more so we won't be such ignoramuses. She is blessed with an unusual mind, and one can certainly see how God has prepared her for her task from way back. No one else would have been fit for it.

They were sad to say goodbye to her and Valerie.

Fred and Clara stayed with Bert and Colleen for a full four months. Clara spent much of her time operating the sewing machine, making curtains and mattress and cushion covers for the boat and a dress for Colleen. Bert and his dad spent a great deal of time on the boat, laying Formica on the counters and repainting it inside and out. Colleen wrote,

> Everyone has worked real hard, but it sure is going to look nice; these are jobs that should have been done long ago, but we never had time, and we sure appreciate the help now.
>
> Did anyone tell you about the near catastrophe Dad had with his teeth? I have been concerned about them ever since Dad came. They have a most disconcerting way of dropping down whenever he laughs, and I thought sure he would lose them the day we jumped the waves in Lima. Actually, I don't know which I was worried about the most, his swimming trunks or his teeth. They both seem to have a tendency toward the "falling away" doctrine. Anyway, the other day he

and Bert were working down at the boat, and Dad stopped to clear his throat as he so often does. Bert said he must have gotten enough air pressure up to send the saliva clear across the Huallaga River. The next thing he heard was the clattering of the teeth on the floor and Dad's exclamation, "Praise the Lord, they didn't go in the river!" I guess some fish came pretty close to possessing a slightly used, though still very sturdy, set of upper teeth.

The parents' reward for fixing up the *Maranatha* was a three-week river trip. Such a trip was especially challenging for Clara due to her crippled leg. Climbing the river's muddy banks was out of the question. But the boat was comfortable, and they made certain she had plenty of reading material. They weathered the trip quite well in spite of the cramped quarters, bugs, bites, heat, dysentery, and unique food. Fred preached in many of the villages with Bert translating. Colleen wrote, "I'm sure they will always be glad that they had the experience of the trip, and I know, as well, that the folks upriver will never forget the friendly, plump lady with the third leg (her cane) and the kind old man who spoke such a jumbled language to them (trying to converse in Spanish)."

Bert and Colleen were anxious to introduce the folks to the mountain work as well. They flew into Trujillo, where they inadvertently left Fred's briefcase in the trunk of the taxi that took them from the airport to the hotel. Colleen wrote,

> Poor Dad was just sick, especially over the loss of his Bible, which was irreplaceable as far as he was concerned because of the years of study notes it contained, as well as Mom's Bible, his medicine, and numerous books. Bert went out immediately and was able to trace down the taxi driver, who denied having seen the briefcase. The only other possibility (unless the taxi driver was lying) was that there was another passenger who came from the airport with us and whom the

taxi driver had taken to the bus station, where he boarded a bus for Chiclayo. It seemed like an impossible situation, but after reporting it to the police, we also committed the case into the hands of the God of the impossible and waited to see Him work. To make a long story short, the next afternoon, just a short time before we were to leave Trujillo, the briefcase was returned, intact! To God be all the praise. It had traveled all the way to Chiclayo and back.

Such a recovery in that culture verges on the miraculous!

The group took a detour to Lima to shop for a vehicle. They had saved up the necessary funds and become convinced that having their own transportation would provide much-needed freedom for ministry. After a great deal of shopping they settled on a 1956 GMC Suburban—it was like a station wagon, except on a panel truck body. They purchased it from a missionary linguist who was returning to the States. It sat eight people comfortably but often carried twice that many. The back seats came out, which provided plenty of room to put down beds. This came in handy when they visited the remote mountain villages.

Along with the blessing of the vehicle came the challenge of driving the roads, which became quickly apparent on their first trip. Colleen wrote,

> The first part of the road to Cajamarca was paved, and we made good time, but the last sixty or seventy miles is just a dirt road winding up over the mountains. We found it in terrible shape due to the rains. In one place the bridge was out, so we had to travel up the railroad track a ways, through a tunnel and across the railroad bridge. We inquired before we started out on that stretch. We were assured that nothing was due to come down that track at just that time, but still it gives one kind of an eerie feeling, wondering what you are going to run into when you round those bends. But the Lord

Challenging mountain roads

was good and timed everything just right for us. A little further up we were almost stopped by a landslide. I doubt we would have noticed it, but a truck stopped ahead of us in the road. There were a bunch of Indians ahead of them clearing the road of some loose rock that had fallen. Bert and Dad went up to help them. Just as they got there, the driver of the truck yelled to them to be careful, that it looked like a big boulder was loosened and would come tumbling down any minute. So they all got back and moved the cars back. Sure enough, in a few minutes this huge boulder came down, bounced at the edge of the road and went over into the ravine below. If a car had been passing at that moment, it would have been too bad! The folks will no doubt tell you about the trip when they see you, though they did say that it absolutely defies description. The scenery is absolutely stupendous, and having our own car, we were able to stop whenever we wanted to enjoy the view.

Dangerous road conditions like this were a common occurrence. Many were unpaved and one lane, often hugging the side of a mountain with a thousand-foot drop and no guard rail. Add some rain and mud to the mix and it was a disaster waiting to happen. Then, if you factor in the hazardous way in which the Peruvians drive, it is amazing that the Elliots did not have a serious accident in all those years. They often marveled at the protection of God in all their travels.

Fred especially was impressed with how much dirt there was in Cajamarca. Colleen wrote,

His remarks as we came along the cobblestone street ran something like this, "My, oh my, what dirt! Isn't it a fright! Man, what a country—when you've seen this, you've seen everything! Oops, watch where you're stepping, honey!!" etc. The folks, though, as we, think the believers here are tops. They sure have enjoyed meeting them and vice versa, of course. It is always an encouragement to us to come and find the believers carrying on so well for the most part. There is real growth and understanding of the Scriptures in most of them, and further blessing as well.

Fred and Clara returned to the States with a deeper understanding and appreciation for the work God was doing in Peru and for the challenges Bert and Colleen faced.

Bert and Colleen quickly adapted to their newly acquired mobility. Their letters are peppered with the names of little villages to the east of Cajamarca and then to the north and then to the west as far as Chiclayo on a loop they made. Some villages had never been exposed to the gospel, while others had a couple believers who were meeting together and needed encouragement. They began to develop an interconnected network of believers who shared a common love for the Savior.

The mountain villages provided a unique setting for evangelism. Bert had done his share of open-air preaching on the street corner in downtown Portland, but such activity was prohibited in Peru. This called for creativity. Colleen wrote,

> One of his big ventures in Cajamarca was to sell Bibles each morning in the marketplace. This proved to be a wonderful opportunity, about the closest thing to a legal street meeting one can have in this country. I wish you could have heard him as he stood there on the curb in front of the market, crowded in between a seller of cheap jewelry and an old Indian woman selling fruit or something; he sounded sort of like a professional barker as he stood there with Bible upraised in his hand, shouting words like "Buy this Bible, the most precious book in the world that costs the least. It contains God's way of salvation! Everybody ought to have a Bible! Buy the Bible!" Actually he found he could give a good bit of the real message of the Bible, as long as he prefaced what he said by the words "Buy the Bible." Pretty nearly everyone goes to the market sometime during the morning, so it is an ideal place to reach them. He went down about nine and stayed until just after noon, for those are the busiest hours. He sold quite a few Scripture portions, New Testaments, and some Bibles, too, so it was worthwhile as far as getting the Scriptures into some of the homes, plus the fact that he was able to be there as a witness in the marketplace.

New believers often faced criticism and opposition from family and friends for their newfound faith in Christ. They were turning away from a belief system that combined Catholic doctrine and animistic ideas with their accompanying superstitions. The superstitions often threatened dire consequences. For example, Colleen reported one young believer whose tailor shop was robbed:

Colleen making a friend

The thieves stole I don't know how many cuts of good wool cloth and even some of the suits that were already made up. Anyway it was a loss to him of between three and four thousand soles and a terrific setback for a man with a large family, who is barely able to make ends meet as it is. It was a real trial of his faith, because of course all of his old friends, and even his family, just shook their heads and said that God was chastising him for having erred from the truth! Bert, however, just a few days before, had felt led to speak on suffering and Job and the trial of our faith, etc., and the man seemed prepared for the loss, and took it as from the Lord; it was good to see.

We are often surprised at the superstition of the people over this way. Being so near the coast and modern civilization, we rather expect folks to be more intelligent than those over in the jungle, but I'm not sure it is true. Otilia's sister-in-law has been sickly for quite a while. One day the husband told us he had to go across the river and get a certain *curioso* (a person who is "clever" at curing sicknesses, even though he doesn't have any medical training. Most of them are just plain witchdoctors, I'm convinced, though the term doesn't imply that) to come and cure her. We asked him what her trouble was.

He told us the following story without blinking an eye or even apologizing for believing such foolishness, even though we all practically hee-hawed in his face. A few months ago their house burned, and some days later the woman had a bad scare in the river.

Both of these incidents cause her such fright that she lost her *ánimo* (soul or spirit). This is what is causing her trouble now. If they don't cure it in the proper way, she will get worse, more pale and thin, until she dies. It is of no use at all to treat her with "drugstore remedies," because they would only make her worse. The medical doctors don't understand this illness, only the *curiosos* can treat it. The *curioso* takes a sweet potato and in the middle of the night starts walking around their yard and small farm, calling to the spirit of the woman. If he is a good *curioso*, the spirit of the woman will heed his call and come into the sweet potato, which he carries in his hands. He then takes the sweet potato back to the house, they roast it on the coals, the woman eats it, and that way the woman gets her spirit back! The *curioso* then collects his fee and returns to his house, and the woman supposedly begins to get better from then on. Talk about animists!

I'm not sure all the folks in the jungle would swallow that one, though I assure you they are capable of telling some stories that are almost as good. Fortunately, Otilia seems to see the foolishness in all this, or at least she says she does! She was telling us that her brother's two small kids are always getting sick with what they call *ojo*. This is caused by people showering too much attention on them, cuddling them, etc. In this case the *curioso* takes a whole egg, rubs it all over the child's body, then breaks it, beats it, and gives it to the child to drink. I don't know what the meaning of all the operation is, but anyway it is supposed to cure the sickness. They also have illnesses caused by *pena* (sadness), *colera* (wrath), etc. each with their respective treatment, and against which "drugstore remedies" do absolutely no good. In fact, they can do much harm according to the *curiosos*.

Along with the animism came a fascination with Satan. Colleen wrote,

Monday was apparently one of the many "fiestas" celebrated in these countries. While we were in Cajamarca, we heard the music start up that is so typical of the Indian people here. When we went out, we found them dancing in front of an idol and having quite a hilarious time. Bert went over closer to try to get a picture (they were very colorfully dressed) and then decided to use the opportunity to pass out tracts. The next thing we knew, someone had started a bonfire using the tracts as fuel, and one of the dancers started yelling *"Vive Satanas!"* (Long live Satan!) The whole situation was definitely satanic; we had never experienced anything quite like it before.

While the medical work was a major component of their jungle ministry, it was much less prominent in the mountains. Although some of the villages were just as remote and sometimes far less accessible, professional medical help seemed to be more available. As we have seen, that didn't eliminate the use of home remedies, *curiosos*, and witchdoctors, but Bert and Colleen found that medical care didn't occupy as much of their time. They were able to place a greater emphasis on evangelism, discipleship, church planting, and visitation.

Colleen's story illustrates a typical visit to a home in the mountains:

Walking the hills to visit remote villages

We were invited by one of the couples to accompany them to visit a nephew and his wife, who are interested in the gospel. We left here at 6:20 a.m. and walked steadily until 8:30, when we finally reached the little farm high up in the mountains. They had breakfast ready for us, which consisted of too-sweet cinnamon tea, bread, dried beef soup, and

151

hominy. Afterwards we walked with them to their potato patch on the hillside. Bert helped harvest potatoes all morning, and later I went back to help peel them. I kept telling the women they were peeling too many, but I soon found out I was wrong. About two p.m. we were told lunch was served.

For the first course we were each given a plate (most of their plates were gourds) with about ten boiled potatoes on it. The only seasoning was ground hot pepper. I thought to myself, *I'll never get away with so many potatoes.* But I did, and they were good. Then our plates were removed and again returned piled high with potatoes, only this time the potatoes had a little yellow condiment added. Hominy was served with this, but that was the extent of the meal! I was glad to walk home to walk off some of that starch. Poor folks, I guess that's what they live on most of the time.

I wish you could see the way they live—pretty near everything they have is handmade. The clothes they wear are made from homespun, hand-woven sheep's wool. They had the large handmade loom there in their dark house. It was most interesting. All their pots are handmade, as are their dishes, spoons, jugs, blankets, plows, and what have you. It was an interesting day, and there was opportunity for witness, so it was not wasted either. They insisted I ride a horse partway back to town, but the horse was so emaciated-looking and walked so slow that I felt sorry for him and soon got off and walked. We were tired when we got home, but it had been fun.

Bert and Colleen traveled together as often as possible on river trips, but at times it meant being apart. Upon their reunion after one of Bert's trips, Colleen wrote,

They had been away for two and a half weeks, and it was wonderful to be together again. I guess Jim's death and talking with Betty and all has made us more aware that God hasn't promised us to each other for keeps, and each time since then that we have had a short separation, we both have experienced similar feelings that this could possibly be "it," if you know what I mean. I don't think we are being morbid—we don't feel that way in the slightest. But I do think in the past we have taken too much for granted that we have no right to, and the Lord would have us come to grips with this in His presence. Anyway, that feeling we both experience upon separation turns into a feeling of special joy on being reunited; I can't explain it on paper, but it is just wonderful to be together again.

Bert and Colleen very much wanted children of their own, but they gradually realized that might not happen. They grieved their apparent infertility and considered testing and exploring fertility options, but decided to leave it in the Lord's hands. In reflecting on this years later, they realized they could not have enjoyed the type of ministry God gave them had they had children. Through the years they saw many colleagues come and go. One of the major reasons for going was to care for children. Being childless was not their choice, but they accepted it as part of God's plan for their life and ministry. It led to an interesting conversation, about which Colleen wrote,

Little Susan [Couenhoven] just asked me a little while ago if I had ever had children. When I said no, she said, "Well, why did you get married then if you don't have children!" I didn't know how to answer that one to a six-year-old, but I explained that children are a gift from the Lord, and sometimes He didn't want to give them to us. Her only retort was "Well, how come He gave them to Abraham then and

153

not to you!" I told her that maybe when I was old the Lord would give us children, too, and with that she was satisfied. What a kid!

Indeed, when Bert and Colleen were old, they realized how many children God had given them through the many years.

They returned to Portland in August 1962 for a six-month furlough.

10

New Friends and
New Frustrations

Bert and Colleen's third term in Peru extended from February
1963 to March 1966. It started with another visit to
Elisabeth and Valerie Elliot in Shellmera, Ecuador, and
concluded with a visit to Elisabeth and Valerie, who had since moved
to Franconia, New Hampshire. During those three years Bert and
Colleen used Yurimaguas as their home base for four periods lasting
four to six months each. They also made three extensive ministry
trips into the mountains and coasts of northern Peru, living out of
their little apartment in Cajamarca.

The transition between those two regions usually included
a stopover in Lima, where their social calendar was always filled
with visits among the community of missionaries in and around
the city. These times of rich fellowship provided respite and allowed
the Elliots opportunities to relax. They were able to get caught up
on medical and dental visits, shopping for supplies and clothes not
available in rural areas, outings to the beach, preaching in some of

the local churches, and just visiting until all hours of the night! They always left Lima both tired and refreshed.

They especially enjoyed seeing the ministry of Barbara Jo Marks develop since she came from one of their home churches in Portland. Colleen wrote, "She sure is doing a terrific job with this Emmaus correspondence course work.[1] You should read some of the letters she gets—questions that would stop the best of us. But some of the letters are most encouraging. She sure is cut out for the job." In their travels the Elliots were able to visit some of the students with whom she corresponded.

The Jungle

The Elliots addressed the ongoing need for leadership and ministry training in churches along Peru's jungle rivers. Colleen wrote,

> Right here in Yurimaguas there is a tremendous need for solid teaching, and we have been wondering how we could help the brethren who take active part in the meetings to study more and prepare real food for the flock. They do the best they can. Their preaching (usually repeating the same phraseology, illustrations, and portions of Scripture) comes, it would seem, from a lack of preparation. This isn't entirely their fault—many of them can barely read and certainly have had little, if any, instruction in study methods or sermon preparation. We have been wondering if some special classes along this line might be helpful, and have suggested to some of the brethren that it might be a good thing to invite some outsider, gifted along this line, to come over and give a couple weeks of classes. Or perhaps we are barking up the wrong tree. Maybe what we need is just a fresh outpouring of the Holy Spirit! At any rate we need your prayers and would urge you to pray for the work in this region. It is plenty needy, as it is everywhere, I guess. Maybe our brethren here

---

1   These are Bible correspondence courses developed by Emmaus Worldwide.

study more than we realize, for they certainly come out with some interesting observations at times. The other night, for example, we learned that the name of the Samaritan woman was Mary Magdalene. Obviously there was some connection between the seven demons of the one and the six husbands of the other!

Colleen also pointed out the nationals' awareness of the importance of education:

More and more of the believers from the villages seem to be moving into Yurimaguas for the education of their children. We have been surprised at the number around these days. This makes a large nucleus of Christians here in town but forces a hardship on those left behind in the villages [it reduced the size of these already small, struggling churches]. And somehow I don't think the Christians grow as well here, for they seem to just get lost in the crowd, whereas before they had been the ones who had been forced to take responsibility. [The following incident illustrates the typical situation for these children:] There was a knock at the door and three kids—ten, fourteen, and fourteen—were standing there with a large basket and advising me that they had come to "visit." They are from one of the villages upriver and are here in town going to school this year. The one little girl (fourteen) is here with her six brothers and sisters, and all but two, of varying ages, are in the first grade. The other two (ten and fourteen) are both in the first grade, too. [In the basket was a gift they had brought for Bert and Colleen from home.] It was filled with eating bananas on the bottom and a large bowl of *mazato* on top. *Mazato*, you will remember, is the jungle "chew and spit" drink. They brought me enough mash in that one bowl that, when mixed with sufficient water, would satisfy the needs of a whole Peruvian family. Being alone, and not overly fond of the stuff, I fear most of it will go to waste unless someone happens by to help me out with it. I appreciated their thoughtfulness much more than their gift.

On one of Bert's occasional absences, this time when he attended a two-week conference, Colleen wrote,

It has been good for me to have to do some of the little jobs around the house that I automatically expected Bert to always do—like setting the rat traps each night, for example, and then carrying out the lifeless form of the victim the next morning. Each night, when these horrible creatures seem to

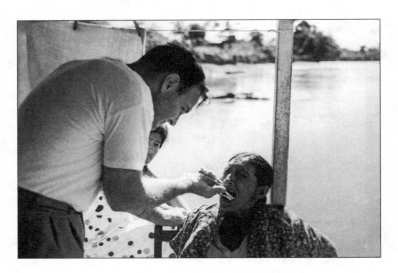

Pulling teeth on the Maranatha

have a rendezvous above my bedroom ceiling, my heart is filled with murder, and I would gladly exterminate them all. But somehow the next morning it is a different story if you happen to catch one and come into the kitchen to find dead, but still sad, eyes looking up at you from the trap. I dislike this job very much. Last Friday I had to kill two chickens, too, and this is another job that Bert has always done for me. I hoped against hope that someone would happen along that

I could draft for the job, but no one came. Since I wanted to get it done early, there was nothing to do but muster up all my courage, pick out my sharpest knife, and then head out to the backyard with two squawking chickens and cut their poor innocent throats. Ugh! One good thing about having Bert away is that it makes me more dependent upon the Lord—instead of yelling "Bert, come . . ." I have had to say, "O Lord, help . . . ." This is good for faith, and I am finding Him very faithful.

One significant type of ministry opportunity was to the "crew" members who traveled with the Elliots on the *Maranatha*. Sometimes they didn't know until the last minute who all would accompany them on a river trip. For example, a lady might catch a ride from her village to Yurimaguas, and the Elliots would put her to work preparing food for other passengers. These often became training opportunities as Bert and Colleen brought along young believers, who thrived under their encouragement and direction. At times their companions presented challenges. Of one Colleen wrote,

The last member of our crew arrived as a complete surprise, and we still haven't made up our minds whether his presence is going to prove a help or a hindrance. I'm inclined to think the latter, but my husband, being a little more broadminded and patient, says we should wait before coming to a hasty conclusion. The crewmember is really from the mountains, but has been in the work of the Lord in and around Lima and is a member of one of the evangelical churches there. He has credentials to prove this, so there is probably no reason to doubt the man, though there is something about him that puts us a bit on guard. He is a rather unsavory-looking character—by that I mean untidy and ill-kempt, however it could be because he is traveling. At any rate he said the Lord had told him in a vision that he was to come over here. His coming has cost him considerable expense, and from the looks of things I would guess he plans to stay awhile. We are not convinced it really was the Lord who sent him, and if He did, why? The only reason we can think He might have sent him is for our own discipline and as a test of our patience and Christian love.

Bert is coming through with flying colors on this particular test, whereas I have failed miserably. I guess the Lord will keep giving me the exam until I do better! This man and those connected with him are great advocates of long fasts to help "destroy the flesh and produce greater humility" in one. The other day, when I was letting off a bit of steam to my longsuffering husband, he said that if I wasn't careful he would put me on a three-week fast to get rid of some of this naughtiness. He was joking, of course, but wouldn't it be nice if something like that would do the job? This man has some rather strange ideas and ways, but Bert is pretty frank with him about them and perhaps will be able to be of some help to him.

Some days [on a particular river trip] we grew pretty discouraged, because it seems like everyone is interested in our medicines and practically no one in our message. Sometimes we wondered if maybe we did wrong by ever starting this business of selling medicines, because in the eyes of the people, at least, their importance has grown out of proportion to the other. In most places we did not have trouble getting a good number out to the meetings. Every night Bert literally preached his heart out, messages that were designed to convert stones, it seemed to me, but if anyone stayed behind, it was not usually because of hunger to know more about God, but rather because they wanted to tell us they would be taking their three children to the boat the next morning for worm medicine, or to have a tooth pulled, or "you did bring shots for rheumatism, didn't you?" Well, when one sees so much physical suffering on every hand, it would be hard not to do something to try and allay it, but there are times . . .

The tension between medicine and message raises a common dilemma for missionaries and mission organizations. Do you put more effort into evangelism, discipleship, and church planting or on needs like medical, literacy, disaster relief, poverty, social justice, and community development? Which do you do first? Missionaries and entire mission organizations must each choose to concentrate on one or the other, or look for a balance between them. Through the years, in their love for the people, the Elliots' ministry addressed many "social action" types of needs. But the proclamation of the gospel of Jesus Christ was their priority. So all their medical and dental care was certainly because they saw the great physical need, but even more to provide avenues to address the spiritual need. The following incident, from the same river trip described in the preceding paragraph, illustrates their priorities. Colleen wrote,

One morning in one of the most degenerated villages, where the conduct of those who at one time professed the name of the Lord is so un-Christlike that we kind of like to sneak past the place whenever we can, we were especially discouraged. We were going to pass it by again, but the Lord seemed to tell us that we should "cultivate" it once more. But, as far as we could tell, it had again been useless. When we finally got to sit down to breakfast after attending to the crowd, we said glumly that it didn't seem like even the Lord was interested in trying to do anything more with these people.

After breakfast there were more patients to take care of. We noticed a young man who kept hanging around long after his tooth had been pulled. Finally Bert was working on the last one (a minor operation removing two bullets that had been in a man's arm for several years and finally worked their way to the surface) and was saying "as soon as I finish this, we will be leaving." I guess this other fellow decided it was now or never, so he sidled over to me while Bert was working and said, "*Senora,* I want to join your religion. I told you this the last time you were here, but you said not yet." I don't remember ever seeing the fellow before, but it is very possible that the way he made his first request threw

Christians leaving for a conference upriver

us off. At any rate, there was something about his sincerity this morning that sent a thrill through us. Or was it just that after all there was at least one in that village who had some inclinations toward God? As soon as Bert was free, we started to talk with him, and he told us he had been listening to the gospel for many years, not only in this village but in other places. He pulled from his shirt pocket a battered-looking gospel of John that he had been given and which he was laboriously spelling his way through. It seemed like the Holy Spirit was definitely working in his heart. A little later we had joy as we kneeled down and heard him stumblingly receive the Lord into his life. Now I am aware, even as I write, that time could prove his profession to be false, like the others in that village, but somehow he seemed real. We were encouraged to believe that the Lord is yet going to bring *life* into that awful scene of *death* there in Tipishca.

A highlight in winter 1965 was the arrival of the "two Annes." Dr. Anne Whittingdale was a medical doctor who was just completing a special course in tropical medicine in Liverpool. Anne Munday was a registered nurse from Victoria, British Columbia. Their plan was to work alongside the Elliots for six months and use the experience to discern where the Lord was leading them. They made a great team and immensely enhanced the medical work. While Dr. Anne dealt with many of the medical problems, Anne M. became quite proficient at pulling teeth, which freed Bert to do visitation in the villages. Colleen wrote, "Apart from all the help they are giving in the medical line, they are both wonderful company and make every day even more pleasurable than usual."

Dr. Anne performed one procedure that would challenge a surgeon in a well-equipped operating room. Be warned that the description is quite graphic. Colleen wrote,

> While they were on a river trip, a woman came running to the boat in tears and told me that her seventeen-year-old son had just been shot in the hand. I can't tell you what a relief it was to be able to holler back into the boat, "Anne, come quick!" knowing that the responsibility for such an emergency was not going to fall on *our* shoulders (Bert's and mine, that is). As we approached the house, we could hear granny, all the brothers and sisters, aunts, etc. wailing. I thought for a moment that we had arrived too late. However, Segundo was still alive, sitting pale and scared. The Annes gave him a shot for pain and antibiotics for infection. Then they unwrapped the hand to have a look. What was left of the hand looked absolutely ghastly. No wonder granny was wailing so hard. The bullet had gone across the back of the hand, leaving it all exposed and taking hunks of bone and finger with it as it went. The index finger was split open all the way up and the end blown off. The middle finger was hanging on by a piece of skin, and the bone at the base of the ring finger was also blown away.

Needless to say, it was a mess, and our first thought was that he ought to be rushed to the hospital in Yurimaguas in the speedboat. However we decided against it for several reasons—(1) it was already too late to get there before dark, and being Saturday night we didn't know where the doctor might be; (2) we didn't have much confidence in the Yurimaguas hospital for a job like that anyway; and (3) he was losing a lot of blood, and immediate attention was pretty urgent. So instead we had them carry him down to the boat in a hammock while we ran ahead to convert the cabin into an impromptu operating room. Dr. Anne did a nerve block on his arm. Then we had to wait twenty minutes for it to take effect, so there was time to get things in order and also drink a cup of hot chocolate [to keep the caregivers hydrated and provide blood sugar for clear thinking through the ordeal after an already demanding day] before the operation began. Finally it was time to begin working, so Bert and I trained three flashlights on the hand as steadily as we could, while Dr. Anne operated and Anne M. efficiently assisted. Really, it was tremendous. Bert and I were completely fascinated watching our first operation of this nature, but also greatly impressed with Dr. Anne's ability. I think what impressed us most was the way she kept so calm right through to the end, despite interruptions, people poking their noses in the door asking questions, poor light and working conditions, blunt needles, insufficient instruments, and what have you.

First she removed the shattered bits of bone and amputated the finger that was just hanging. Then she began little by little sewing things up, starting with the inside soft tissues and then gradually working her way around until the hand began to look like a hand once more. All this took over two hours. The operation seemed to be completely successful. Segundo was a wonderful patient and managed to give us a big grin when it was all over. The local priest took him to the hospital in Yurimaguas the next morning, where he made a full recovery.

The enormity of the task of reaching Peru's many people groups was brought home to them on a river trip outside the Elliots' normal territory. George and Helen Hart of Wycliffe had invited them to visit Chayahuita to teach, baptize, and generally encourage the church. It was an arduous two-and-a-half-day journey into the heart of the jungle. They traveled as far as they could on the *Maranatha* and then completed the last leg by speedboat. Colleen wrote,

That evening the Indians came from all around to the large Indian house for a meeting. It was interesting to hear them all sing in Chayahuita. Then Bert spoke to them and George interpreted. It was most interesting but also a bit frustrating to be in a situation where no one could understand a word you said. Really it is almost unbelievable to see these Indians, almost at the doorstep of Yurimaguas you might say and certainly in contact with Yurimaguas for trading purposes, still living in such primitive conditions.

Most of them—this goes for the men as well as the women—can't understand or speak a word of Spanish. They still retain their own distinctive style of clothing. The women all wear hand-woven, black, tube-like skirts, which they fold over in the front to fit tight, and also brightly colored, highly decorated, short blouses and beads, if they have them. However, the blouses are only worn for decoration or special occasions, so most of the time you see them with just their skirts on. The majority of the little kids don't have anything on at all. Both men and women cut their hair in bangs and wear tight ankle and wrist bands made of lizard skin. They also paint their faces with elaborate designs. Their pottery is different from the other tribes we have seen, and the style of their large houses is also characteristic.

165

What really surprised us was to see the large number of these Indians all along the Paranapura, up the Yanayacu, and apparently along the banks of most other rivers that run into the Paranapura, as well as inland across toward the Maranon. We see a few of these Indians in Yurimaguas at times, but for some reason we had the idea there weren't very many of them. However, there are, and as Indian tribes go, I would say it is a large one. We sure are thankful for what Wycliffe is doing in there, for it's a cinch no one else is doing it except a fringe Christian group that has a couple of settlements among them. Both George and his wife, Helen, speak the language well. They have translated portions of the Scriptures and are working on more all the time. They have a growing church there that carries on by itself most of the time. Praise the Lord!

In one of her creative moments, Anne M. wrote a Violette-style poem:

Our favorite *missionarios*
Are better than *sanitarios*[2]
They sell *remedies varios*
Which always do the trick.

Whatever the disease is
They have a drug which eases
The pain and knocks to pieces
The bug which made them sick.

But this is not their calling
They come to keep from falling
Those who have sins appalling
To God who loves them so.

They tell of sins forgiven
And of the way to heaven

---

2 Peruvian health nurses.

One trip they baptized seven
For this they come and go.

The Coast

Many of the Peruvians up and down the coast lived and worked
on haciendas, which were large tracts of land dominated by a few
landowners. These usually included large plantations of sugar cane,
beets, stock, and other commodities. While the wages and living
conditions were meager, they did provide jobs, which were scarce in
other segments of the economy.

Gathering of believers in Chiclayo

Each hacienda had its own community of laborers, which
provided a wonderful opportunity for the Elliots to visit and share
the gospel. They would take national believers with them into these
communities, have open-air meetings, visit door to door, and see
a small but dedicated network of Christians established. Because
the workers didn't have transportation available, they weren't able to
attend church in nearby cities like Chiclayo, Casa Grande, Sipán,

Paramonga, and Trujillo, so they formed little gatherings in each community.

The gospel changed their lives. Of one hacienda Colleen wrote,

> Bert had a good chance to have a long talk with the engineer in charge of the hacienda. He is not a Christian but seems willing to listen at least. And in the course of the conversation he thanked Bert for the visits up there, saying he saw a big change in some of the Indians who worked for him since their conversion. If thanks are due to anyone, of course, they should go to Chilón [a longtime Peruvian colleague], not us, but Bert explained it was the power of God in their lives.

Bert and Colleen did not endorse the hacienda system, in which owners often functioned as feudal lords. But when President Juan Velasco Alvarado instituted agrarian reforms that dismantled the haciendas and established cooperatives of local farmers, Bert questioned whether the Indians were any better off. The Indians had no experience managing the complexities of a hacienda, so most cooperatives deteriorated quickly.

Summer and fall 1964 brought dark days for the work in Chiclayo, affecting also Casa Grande and Trujillo. Bert and Colleen enjoyed rich fellowship with any who named the name of Christ. They relished the opportunity to meet and have communion with all who were born again and who walked uprightly. Denominationalism and sectarianism were to be rejected. They freely met with and encouraged believers from various mission organizations and churches, such as Baptists and Presbyterians. Bert even accepted invitations to teach several groups with whom he had sharp theological differences, such as Pentecostals and Seventh-Day Adventists. With the Adventists, his teaching and interaction directly addressed those theological differences.[3] Bert and Colleen didn't sacrifice their convictions for the sake of unity.

---

3   Bert questioned whether the Adventists, especially in Peru, understood the biblical teaching that salvation is by grace alone. He saw in their teaching a works-based salvation that cannot be supported by Scripture.

A missionary from Colombia and later a gentleman who operated a Christian publishing house in California exerted a great deal of influence on the church in Chiclayo. They encouraged the believers there to follow what they referred to as "the narrow path with a wide heart." That meant limiting their "circle of friendship" to include only those who fully agreed with them and who associated only with those who fully agreed with them. Bert and Jerry Couenhoven met with these men on several occasions to work out their differences, but without success. These men were convinced that to associate with the Elliots, Couenhovens, and those with them would bring an "evil contamination"[4] into their midst. The bottom line was that the church in Chiclayo was forced to decide with whom they would continue to have fellowship and was pressured to separate from Bert and Colleen.

This divisive sectarian spirit broke the Elliots' hearts. They grieved as they tried to explain it to new believers. They sought counsel from their home church in Portland. Bert wrote to his parents,

> I have solemnly prayed that the Lord take me to Himself before He permits me to make more sad division and confusion among His people. I believe He has heard and will answer, so we must walk softly and humbly before Him. Oh, how we would like to see this error crushed before it takes root in this land. Oh, that we knew better how to use the weapons of our warfare mightily to the tearing down of the devilish strongholds [see 2 Corinthians 10:3–5]. But alas, we are such children, and we feel so alone. Still we pray and wait and rest in the power of His might.

Through the years, Bert and Colleen enjoyed wonderful times of fellowship with two families in Casa Grande—one from China, the other from Germany. The two men also pressured these families to

---

4 This is Bert's phrase to describe how they were being characterized, not that of the two men.

separate from the Elliots. In the midst of all this, Colleen had coffee with the German lady and then wrote,

> She is very upset about all this talk about "separation" since their visit and says she wishes the missionary had never left Colombia! She was telling me a little about their past life today—thirty years ago her husband started working for Casa Grande. She joined him four years later, and they were married, but she was very lonely here and lived for the day when they would return to Germany. But then World War II started, and they couldn't get back, nor was there any mail from there. During that time their first, three-year-old boy died here of meningitis. Six years later they had their

Preaching the good news of Jesus Christ

> second boy, who is now their only child and who has no interest in the things of God. During all these years they had no Christian fellowship until the past few years, when we appeared on the scene. Then they also started having that weekly Bible study with the Chinese couple and a Baptist couple. She said, "I have been so happy of late, and now these brothers come and make us so sad. But I will never separate, never, never!"

The local church leaders at that time decided not to separate from Bert and Colleen, but the problem continued to fester, and soon several church members broke fellowship with the group. Neil and Bert even made a spur-of-the-moment flight from Yurimaguas to bring some resolution, without much success. In subsequent visits the Elliots and their colleagues realized they had to let some go their separate ways and concentrate on those who wanted to maintain unity within the community of true Jesus followers. Among them developed a strong evangelistic zeal.

Meanwhile, the Peruvians faced other challenges, as illustrated by the story of Juan, a seventeen-year-old young man from a nearby hacienda who came to know the Lord. Colleen wrote,

He can't read and has only been saved for about a month and a half, but he gave a clear testimony at one of the open-air meetings. The next morning at breakfast Bert asked him some more questions about his past life and how he happened to get interested in the things of God. The story he told was enough to move the hardest heart, I'm sure. In brief—when he was about five, his father abandoned his mother for another woman, leaving her with two or three small children to raise. It wasn't very long before she took up with another man, who had no love for the children. Instead of sending young Juan to school, he sent him out to the hacienda at the age of eight, to do the job of a man out in the fields. If he didn't get his *tarea* (share) done, he was beaten, and then most of what wages he earned were taken by his stepfather to use for his own personal vice. At the age of ten Juan was taught to drink by some of the local canteen owners, who offered him pop mixed with firewater. By the age of twelve he was drinking and smoking up his own wages every Saturday night and often spent the weekend drunk, with nothing to show for what he had earned the rest of the week. He said that even at that age he often wished for death. Then about two months ago one of the other new believers there began to talk to him about the Lord and invited him to the meetings. It was there that he was saved, and he has been rejoicing in the transformation of the Lord ever since.

On one of their trips down the coast Bert and Colleen stopped in Paramonga to visit a young couple they had known in Yurimaguas, who had moved for better employment. Colleen wrote, "The wife is as sweet as ever. The husband needs our prayers. He is very cold spiritually, is all mixed up in the labor union there on the hacienda, and we noticed a book on communism lying around. So who knows where he will end up." That was a precursor of the coming social unrest that would shake the Peruvian culture and political scene to their foundations, as well as impact the influence the missionaries were allowed to exercise in the society.

The Mountains

At the beginning of one visit to Cajamarca, Colleen wrote,

> One of the things that pleased us in Cajamarca was to hear Chilón tell how the Christians helped him when he was so seriously ill in January. Not only the Christians in Cajamarca helped him, but he also received offerings from Monte Grande and also from that tiny, new group of Indian believers above Cajamarca. When one thinks how poor they are and yet how they got together 110 soles to send to him, it is nothing short of wonderful. You will remember that he, under God, was mostly responsible for bringing that group into existence, and they sure do love him. He seems to have recovered from the operation amazingly, and we are so thankful that the Lord spared him.

Colleen's report illustrates the impact God's grace was having on these new believers as they cared for each other.

172

One of Bert and Colleen's national coworkers was anxious to take them to a mountain village on the far northern border of Peru, where he had some friends who needed to hear the gospel. Colleen's description portrays a typical initial encounter, characteristic of their ministry. They drove up a remote road to its dead end. Colleen continued,

> We were able to contract a burro to carry the things the rest of the way. I thought we would never reach the top of the mountain that afternoon, but after a couple hours we did. Going down the other side, though actually steeper and longer, we found much easier. It took us approximately four hours by foot to make the trip. It was all very beautiful though, and we really enjoyed it, especially once we started down the other side. We found Santa Domingo to be a typical, picturesque mountain town, not too large in itself, but the center of a heavily populated valley with many smaller villages and farms. The valley around Santo Domingo was quite different from any we have worked before. Everything is much greener, and there are scrubby-looking banana trees and fields of sugar cane even at that altitude of six thousand feet. The closer one gets to Ecuador, the more foliage one sees both on the coast and on the mountains close to the coast. The ocean currents must have something to do with this.
>
> I always find it rather difficult going into a new town for the first time, for folks always stare at us as if we were some very strange species recently descended from Mars or something. But fortunately folks here in Peru are easy to make friends with, and it wasn't very long before we had several new friends. Our coworker directed us to the home of his *compadres*—she a rather large, capable woman, he a small, rather mousy but very pleasant man—who ran the only *pensión* (guest house) in town. Here all the visiting teachers, engineers (there are quite a few of these in and

173

out because of the present work on the roads), and what have you receive decent food and lodging for a nominal fee. That evening we had just an informal Bible study with the *compadres* and some friends. Many of the *pensionistas* (guests) gathered around out of curiosity, too, and Bert certainly gave a clear word from the first chapter of John. Our coworker gave a clear testimony, too, but it seemed there were no "ears to hear" that evening. However the Lord knows.

The next morning we paired off in twos and spent the day visiting house to house, leaving a little Scripture booklet in each one and taking time to talk whenever we were given the opportunity. It was kind of hard going, frankly, but perhaps someday there will be fruit from the effort. We did have a good time Sunday morning, though. Marta [a longtime colleague and frequent traveling companion in the mountains and coast] and I went to finish up one street that still lacked a visit. There we found one man and his wife who really seemed hungry to know the Lord. We talked with them for quite a while and then went back to get Bert and the others so they, too, could visit with them.

Then we decided that street would be a good place to hold an open-air meeting. It was one of the entrances into town, and several women had little food stalls set up to sell lunch, etc., to people who come in from the surrounding areas. As soon as we started singing, a large crowd gathered and listened quietly all the time the three fellows preached. I don't think I ever heard Bert any better, and it sure was a wonderful opportunity. Afterwards we sold all the Bibles, Testaments, and portions we had with us, and even though our coworker sold his own personal Bible, we still could have sold more. We feel sure that this written Word will one day produce fruit, even if nothing else does.

I forgot to say that the local priest, an old man with rather a despotic character and certainly not up on modern

Pulling teeth alongside a mountain road

ecumenical trends, had denounced us the day before for selling "heretical" books (the Bible!) and had written to the governor to have us get out of town! Fortunately, the governor and the local police just ignored him and even offered us a guarantee to carry on. The poor priest doesn't have a very good reputation there in town, not having lived a very moral life through the years, but still he held religious sway over the whole area. Since it was the first time the gospel had ever been preached in Santo Domingo, it was not hard to understand why he resented our intrusion. Bert very much wanted to make friends with the man, but was not given the opportunity.

Overnight accommodations could be a particular challenge, as seen in Colleen's letter home regarding a visit to a different village:

The street in front of the man's house is the main Pan-American Highway leading out of town. It's a rather steep up-grade, and all the buses (usually without mufflers) and

175

heavy trucks really made a deafening noise as they slowly roar their way up it all hours of the day and night. We had to spread our bedroll on the floor of their living room. Being right on the street, I'm afraid we didn't get much sleep the two nights we were there. They say one gets used to the noise after a while.

When we first arrived, they apologized for the fact that they didn't have the kind of bathroom we were used to. But they assured us there was a suitable enclosure out in the backyard, in which they had placed a white, clean enamel "pot." The only hitch was that they had a ferocious watchdog, who shared the same enclosure and who attacked anyone who was not a member of the immediate family. Therefore we were warned never ever to venture out there alone. Consequently, what would normally be a very simple, very personal procedure became a complicated family enterprise! I would normally whisper my need into the wife's ear. Then she in turn would yell it out to the rest of the family and alert them to their posts. Following this we were ushered into one of the rooms where the door was carefully shut and guarded by one family member. Then another family member would go get the dog and lead him snarling past our door into another room, where the door was carefully shut and guarded. Then we were released and told to proceed. By the time all this had transpired, however, I was usually so embarrassed that all desire had fled. But one didn't dare lose the opportunity. So I would go out and try to "meditate." However this was very difficult, too, because I was overly conscious of the fact that the activities of most of the family were at a standstill until I got back into the house and the dog could get back out. Believe me, we learned to think twice before asking for bathroom privileges.

Despite the challenges, they loved staying with this mountain family and returned on numerous occasions.

Bert and Colleen returned to the States for a four-month furlough beginning in March 1966. Elisabeth Elliot met them in New York for sightseeing and shopping, then took them to her home in Franconia, New Hampshire, where she now lived after two years in a Waodani village in the Ecuadorian jungle, translating the Bible into their language.

From there the Elliots flew to Wheaton for a visit with Bert's sister, Jane, and her family; to Seattle to see Colleen's sister Joan and her family; and then finally to Portland in mid-April. As usual, details of their furlough are sketchy, except that it could not be classified as a vacation. They had numerous meetings, social invitations, and opportunities to share about their ministry.

Training disciples

One significant event during this furlough was a visit from Neil Weir and an elder from his home church in San Francisco related to doctrinal issues among the believers in northern Peru. They and Bert met with about eighteen leaders of three of the Portland churches who sent the Elliots. Neil charged that Bert was bringing confusion and doctrinal error into the missionary community and the Peruvian churches through the people with whom he associated.

He did not accuse Bert of teaching false doctrine but of failing to see and denounce it in these other teachers. Neil was pressed for details, but had difficulty identifying exactly what the doctrinal issues were. He challenged the men to read these teachers' books and see the errors for themselves. The implication was that, if they didn't see the error—in Bert's words—"it's either due to our ignorance, or more likely to our rebellion and unwillingness to understand."

Bert wrote,

It is obvious that we have lost confidence in each other. He in me, because my position in relation to all believers is wider than he can stand, and I in him, because of his habitual condemning of everyone but himself. Obviously, we have been able to reach no solution, so we just wait. I'm sure the Portland church leaders' feelings are mixed. They are impartial, I think, and would like me to be as sharp and sure on doctrinal issues as Neil is. They, however, know something of his work and conduct on the field and cannot fully endorse him on that score.

As we look into the future, we are trusting the Lord to overrule our imperfections and frustrate Satan's attempt to bring division into the work in northern Peru.

This situation was similar to the problem the Elliots faced in Chiclayo, involving different people, different doctrines, different associations, but the same fundamental question: How wide do you draw your circle of fellowship? Do you only associate with those who are in 100 percent agreement with you? Two years earlier Colleen had written a passing comment regarding a new missionary coming to work with Neil: "And so another young missionary goes to school in Lagunas! Just hope he makes better grades than we did!"

Bert and Colleen wanted to love and serve God's people regardless of the label that might be attached to them.

11

"Please Do Not Share . . ."

The Elliots' fourth term in Peru lasted two and a half years—spanning from mid-1966 to November 1968. It was shorter than usual, as they considered it important to return to Portland to help honor Bert's parents for their fiftieth wedding anniversary. Bert and Colleen continued the pattern of spending half the year in the jungle and half in the mountains and coastal region. A significant encouragement was the addition of two key families to the missionary team—Bill and Ruth Conard, who took up residence in coastal Chiclayo, and Ray and Eunice Cawston, who settled in Cajamarca.

A major impact on the work in both the jungle and mountain/coast was the Evangelism-in-Depth training. It was developed by Kenneth Strachan and pioneered by the Latin American Mission. A number of evangelical churches across Latin America participated in the training, which emphasized mobilization of individuals for evangelism, teaching each to give a verbal testimony of their faith in Christ. Believers were empowered, which resulted in house-to-house visitation in connection with local crusades. This approach

Working with teams

dovetailed wonderfully with the Elliots' methodology. On most of their river trips they took a team of national believers along and would drop off two or three each at various villages to do visitation and share the gospel. On the way back Bert and Colleen picked them up, and each individual shared what God had done. In the mountain and coastal towns they would go door to door by twos before conducting a meeting in the public square.

Coincidentally, at the time Peru's churches were doing this training, Elisabeth Elliot had just completed *Who Shall Ascend: The*

Life of R. Kenneth Strachan and sent it to the publisher. Strachan had headed up the Latin American Mission, but died in 1965 at the age of fifty-five.

Scattered throughout the Elliots' letters are references to the effectiveness of relying on nationals for as much of the ministry as possible. Colleen wrote,

> We began to leave a team of two or three brethren in each place. They always looked a bit lonesome and uncertain as we pulled away, leaving a couple of them to face a strange village. When we picked them up three days later, it was sort of like "homecoming" aboard the *Maranatha,* with much back slapping, hugging, and recounting of experiences.

In another letter Colleen observed that the villagers appreciated their visits more when they brought along some Peruvian believers:

> Spiritually we have felt much encouraged with the work in this area. Despite the infrequency and brevity of our visits made through the years, the believers for the most part carry on faithfully. Since our last visit up this way last June, the brethren in Yurimaguas have been taking greater interest in the work here. Isidro from Achinamisa goes down to Yarina occasionally on Sunday to lend a hand. Manuel from here also visits up there occasionally and to Pucallpa, Tipishca, and also to a place five hours walk from here called Leche. As for ourselves, we feel more and more like mere onlookers. It seems like most of the real work is done before we ever arrive. I don't know what we do accomplish exactly, except to love them up a bit (Bert's rather special gift, I think), listen to their problems, give a bit of teaching, repair their smoky lamps and rusty old shotguns, take care of their rotten teeth and wormy kids—and I guess that's about it. Anyway, we're grateful to be able to share a little in the work here.

On another occasion Colleen wrote, "Often we dream about being able to settle down in Yurimaguas for more-prolonged periods. But I don't suppose that would be the best thing for the believers themselves, so we'd better quit dreaming and keep moving."

Trying to trace the journeys of Bert and Colleen is dizzying, but they sensed they were gifted and called to this itinerant church planting ministry. Colleen wrote,

> Sometimes Bert remarks that he wishes that we could just keep on opening up new places and that someone who knows more about teaching and establishing churches could carry on from here in these old ones. In some ways it almost seems easier to get things started than to see them carry on and function happily and properly. Probably we just don't know enough about waiting on God for the necessary wisdom and power.

That wisdom and power were often needed in abundance as they dealt with problems in these little churches. Colleen wrote,

> As we entered the village, we began to hear rumors that a leading brother was again guilty of adultery. This fell like a bombshell, as you can imagine. We didn't want to believe it was true, but when Bert charged him with it, he confessed that it was. His confession was a terrible shock to his wife, and she just cried. He had denied the rumors to her previously, and she hadn't let herself believe they were true. We were in a dilemma as to what to do and felt more like running than anything else, but we decided we must stick it out there until the situation was straightened out a bit. A meeting of just the adult believers was called for four a.m. the next morning so we could have prayer and go into the whole business without a bunch of little kids hanging around. M. confessed his sin to all of them at the meeting. There were accusations

against some of the others, too, and confessions. How they managed to carry on with orderly worship services became more and more a mystery. Well, nothing was decided in that meeting, and another was called for the next morning, though not quite so early. In the meeting on Friday evening, in obedience to 1 Timothy 5:20, Bert rebuked M. publicly for his sin. Since this was his second offense (in other words, he was persisting in his sin), we felt the verse applied. Also, since the thing was so generally known in the town, we felt something of that nature should be done in order to clear the church's testimony. It was a difficult thing to do, but the Lord gave Bert very special help. He really spoke hard

Open-air meeting

against this sin of unfaithfulness that is so common here. He told M. he hadn't learned thus from Christ. You could have heard a pin drop on that dirt floor, I think. There was such utter silence while Bert was speaking. We all felt something of the terrible shame of the occasion. At the same time I don't think there was any doubt in folks' minds but that it was done in love.

183

[On a different occasion] another one of the newer believers, who frankly confesses to having a difficult time leaving the habit of drink, told of an interesting experience he had the Sunday we were there. After a full morning of meetings he took off in the afternoon to the woods with his shotgun to see if he could shoot a bird or something for supper. A short distance out he came upon a couple of his drunk, former cronies with a bottle half full of firewater, which they tried to force him to drink. He said, "No, I can't. I had a [medical] shot put in today, and I mustn't drink alcohol." They replied, "Oh no, that's not it. It's because you're an *evangelista*, and you're going to drink with us!" With that they rammed the bottle into his lips, hurting them a bit, and he took off on a run. (He had probably never heard of the Scripture "Flee youthful lusts," but it was a smart thing to do nevertheless.) Well, the drunks took off after him. When Roberto came to a small stream, over which a round log served as a bridge, he leaped across nimbly. But the drunk carrying the bottle didn't quite make it. Both he and the bottle flew off the "bridge" into the mud and water. The last Roberto saw of them, both drunks were feeling around in the muck to try and find the bottle, the contents of which were undoubtedly by then well diluted! What a riot! This served as a vivid example of the verse Bert was trying to teach them in an early morning session on Monday, "God will with the temptation provide a way of escape."[1]

Empowering new believers for ministry was not without its risks. Colleen wrote,

If ever we are tempted to think that the assembly here in Yurimaguas has "arrived," so to speak, the meeting last

---

1 Scripture quotations are from 2 Timothy 2:22 and 1 Corinthians 10:13, both paraphrased from KJV.

Wednesday night would have been sufficient to show us otherwise! I don't know *what* happened, but practically none of the men showed up. It had drizzled a bit about 6:30, but not enough to keep folks away. It seemed too much of a coincidence that they would *all* have emergency situations requiring their presence at home that evening. I think *maybe* they were afraid of the chapter up for study! As you may know, they have been going through the Scriptures in order and have now reached Song of Solomon. It was chapter 7 last Wednesday: "How beautiful are thy feet . . . O prince's daughter! The joints of thy thighs are like jewels . . . . Thy navel is like a round goblet . . . . Thy two breasts are like two young roes" . . . etc., etc. [7:1–3, KJV]. The young fellow who had been elected to open up the study stood up, read the chapter, said he hadn't been able to get anything out of it, and sat down again. From then on it was more less up to Wensi, for he was about the only one present who ever takes part. Poor Wensi. Obviously he hadn't studied and didn't know what it was all about either. He kept wiggling his head, shuffling his feet, and adjusting his glasses (as if *that* would help), sometimes peering over them at the back entrance, muttering, "Where is everyone? *Que barbaridad!*" or else, "Breasts, breasts . . . now what significance could *that* have?" and so on!!! Occasionally he got some light on a verse and passed it on to us, but most of the time we sat in embarrassed silence while he thumbed through his Bible looking for some references, which apparently he never found. We finally sang a closing hymn and went out. Thankfully this is a rare exception rather than the rule. Perhaps things like this have to happen once in a while to keep us good and humble.

Some of the meetings did have their comic relief, sometimes at an esteemed missionary's expense, as Colleen shared:

I was sitting at the end of a very narrow, low bench along with about eight other women. Since I was wearing the accordion, when Juan suggested that the meeting be opened with prayer and that we all rise, I decided to stay seated, because it was too much effort to get up from that low seat

Cajamarca

with the accordion. That was the wrong decision, because of course everyone else on the bench obediently got up. As they did, my weight on the one end sent the other end of the bench into the air, and I went sprawling onto the dirt floor, accordion and all, sounding off with a blast of discordant notes as it hit the dust. Dear old Juan, like a disciplined soldier, even though ten thousand fall at his side, carried on anyway, and was well on with his prayer before I got myself picked up and shushed up the folks around me who were trying to help. Bert said later he had heard this musical crash and opened his eyes to see his wife stretched out on the floor in a most undignified manner, just as he heard Juan use one of his favorite phrases in prayer: "Thank You for this precious manifestation." I guess Bert almost choked!

186

One of the distinguishing features of Bert and Colleen's correspondence was the absence of any mention of their financial needs. They went to Peru without a salary or a designated financial commitment from individuals or churches. They regularly took needs to the Lord and trusted Him to lay the burden on people's hearts. Frequently in their letters they acknowledged God's faithfulness for supplying their needs, but were careful not to ask for money or even to refer to needs or financial shortfalls. Dropping hints was not their practice. Note the doubly repeated "Please do not share this" in Colleen's personal letter to her sister Joan:

I want to tell you what a tremendous encouragement your card and gift were to us. Actually "encouragement" is hardly the word. It was a downright, honest-to-goodness answer to prayer. Let me tell you a few details; though please do not share this with anyone else. Your card arrived the day before we left Cajamarca. Previous to that we had been doing a little more fervent praying about our needs than usual. Before leaving for San Pablo two weeks ago, we had cleaned out both our bank accounts (dollar and Peruvian sol accounts). Then we returned to Cajamarca after that trip needing to buy a battery and a couple new tires, fix the gear shift, and what have you—all fairly big items—plus, of course, our pending trip to Lima! When we returned from San Pablo on Thursday evening, we found quite a stack of interesting letters but practically no money. "Well," we said, "there's always Friday and Tuesday's mail before we have to leave." Bert continued to believe, and I began to doubt! In the meantime he bought a battery with what *had* come in and patched the tires. Friday's mail brought nothing, and we decided then that we couldn't take the car to Lima and that maybe I would have to stay home, too, though I sure didn't like the idea. But there was still Tuesday's mail to look forward to! I went ahead and made plans to go anyway, though it was with plenty of trepidation. The mail was delivered about five p.m. on Tuesday. There were just two letters, an air form from Betty and your card. I said to myself, "Well, that's *that*!" Then I opened your card and just about fell flat when that check for one hundred dollars fell out! I started to cry—and bawled the rest of the way home till I could get on my knees to say "thanks," ask for forgiveness for all the doubts, and tell Him to please see to it that you were properly "thanked," too, right then and there. A little later on that evening the assembly treasurer came over with a generous gift for us. When we reached Chiclayo, a brother, who had owed us money for a long time, unexpectedly paid us nine hundred soles of it. So there wasn't any doubt about my going to Lima, and I feel more grateful than usual to be here this time. As I said at the beginning, *please* do not share this with others, especially Mom and Dad, who might get the impression we're in desperate straits, and we're not. I think this is the first time we have ever been so low. During the eighteen years we have been here we have known only abundance, and I'm sure it is necessary for us to have some times like this so we learn, among other things, not to take so much for granted. Well, I wouldn't have told you all this except that I wanted you to know how the Lord had used you to answer our prayers.

A highlight of this term was the month and a half they spent in the mountain town Chulucanas, which is located in far northern Peru, near the Ecuadorian border. With three Peruvians and the Conards, they rented a home and then held meetings there and in about twenty surrounding towns. Most of these had never received an evangelical witness. Colleen described this region as

heat, dust, desert, desolation, goats, burros, matchstick-like houses, impossible roads, but people and more people at every turn of the road.

Our trip up to Ayabaca proved a memorable one, one that we'd not care to ever repeat (at this time of the year at least), nor would we have missed it! All day long on the road we kept passing pilgrims on their way on foot to pay a vow to the image of the "Captive Lord" in Ayabaca.

The culmination of this pilgrimage to the image of *Señor Cautivo* (Captive Lord) takes place in mid-October every year. The wooden sculpture of Jesus with his hands crossed is considered the work of angels and represents Christ when His disciples abandoned Him in the Garden of Gethsemane. The statue is draped in purple and gold and decorated with gold ornaments. After walking for weeks and sometimes months, many pilgrims crawl the final thousand feet on their elbows and knees in penance or in hopes of receiving a miracle for themselves or a family member. Many miracles have been attributed to the Captive.

Colleen using her accordian to draw people

Colleen's letter continued,

These pilgrims were usually identified by a wide purple band tied from their waist across their shoulders and embroidered in gold with the words "Pilgrim of the Captive Lord" and then the name of their hometown. They usually carried just one blanket rolled up, maybe a change of clothes in it, and a water bottle of some kind, though one elderly woman was carrying a banner with the image on it. Going into town, we saw one man carrying a fair-sized wooden cross on his shoulders as well. This is the first time we have seen anything like this, and it was pathetic. Some of them had already walked for days across the hot desert. They still had the worst part of the trip (the steep ascent) ahead of them. Many of them were already hobbling and having to use a stick for a cane. The feet of one man were bleeding. One woman had a baby on her back. A good majority were intelligent-looking men, who looked as if they should know better. Some appeared sick, but all wore a look of determination on their faces that defied anyone to offer them a ride. Bert did offer a lift to the man whose feet were bleeding, and he refused! We calculated that we passed approximately two hundred of these pilgrims during the five or six hours it took us to make the drive. Of course this was only a small percentage of the total. We read in the newspaper afterwards that this had been a record year for Ayabaca. Their estimate of the total number of visitors for the fiesta was twenty thousand. Most of these traveled by car, but also a good number on foot. Since the town itself probably boasts a population of eight or nine thousand, you can imagine what it was like! People were sleeping on sidewalks, in the schools, anywhere!

Bert took the opportunity to proclaim that the Lord was not captive but gives freedom to all.

The missionary team was thrilled to see the gospel begin to take root in the hearts of some genuine believers. Some were baptized in four of the towns. It was refreshing to know the Conards would revisit the area periodically.

Shortly after that trip the Elliots flew from Lima to Miami and then bused the 3,300-mile trip across the States, arriving in Portland to join the joyous celebration of Bert's parents' golden anniversary. Bert and Colleen had deliberated about whether to make the trip, but were thankful they did. They considered themselves privileged to honor Bert's parents.

12

Earth-Shattering Events

During Bert and Colleen's furlough some friends in Portland provided a Ford pickup with a cab-over camper for the Elliots to take back to Peru. Being able to take their "home" with them would facilitate their extensive itinerant ministry on the coast and in the mountains. It was the *Maranatha* on wheels! Fixing meals on the run and sleeping in their own bed every night became more than just a luxury—it saved money and allowed them to travel without imposing on people for hospitality. After using the vehicle for a year, Colleen commented, "We still feel like plutocrats with our truck and camper. When we think of all the love that went into the buying and outfitting of it and which has surrounded our lives in increasing measure through the years, then we feel *really* rich."

To get the pickup to Peru, the Elliots drove to Texas, where they had to wait for the right timing to cross into Mexico. They decided to use the delay to make a quick air trip to Wheaton to visit Jane and Jerry Hawthorne, Bert's sister and brother-in-law. Upon hearing about this impromptu family reunion, Elisabeth Elliot with her daughter and new husband, Dr. Addison Leitch, took an overnight train from New Hampshire to join them. Colleen wrote,

Before she knew all the rest of us were going to be there, Jane had invited the David Howard (Betty's brother) and Paul Little families for that Sunday dinner. So it made quite a crowd. Paul, Add, Dave, and Jerry are all so sharp. They kept the conversation plenty lively. The rest of us didn't have to say much of anything, and it's probably a good thing, because we didn't have much of anything to say. Bert and I always feel just a bit stupid (maybe that's not the word I want) when with such a crowd of sharpies. Something inside keeps warning, "Better just keep your mouth shut, and maybe the rest of them won't realize how uninformed you are." So that's what we did, mostly, and thoroughly enjoyed listening, even though I had to have some of the jokes explained afterwards.

Bert and Colleen always felt a bit intimidated in settings like this, in this instance conversing with college and seminary professors, authors, and an international mission executive. They were much more at ease with earnest Peruvian believers.

Upon returning to Texas, they drove through Mexico to Panama City, where they loaded the pickup on a cargo vessel for the remainder of the trip. They and their niece Jean Elliot, who spent five months with them, boarded the same ship for their passage to Lima. The further south they sailed, the more at home they felt.

This term in Peru encompassed 1969–1971 and began with an abbreviated visit to Cajamarca and Chiclayo to register and equip the pickup. Soon after Bert and Colleen arrived in Peru, Jim Dryden and his fifteen-year-old son Jack came for a visit from Portland and were encouraged seeing the work firsthand. Colleen wrote, "Since they are both so outgoing, they have no problem making friends, even though with Jim especially there is the barrier of the language. But his contagious smile and sincere friendliness make up for an awful lot of words." (As an aside, Uncle Bert pointed out to me on several occasions the impact that Jim's father, Tom Dryden, had on him as a young man. Tom had that same infectious personality, genuine friendliness, and encouraging spirit. Bert said, "That's the kind of man I want to be.")

The Elliots then spent eight months in the jungle. Significant cultural differences existed, not only between different regions, but also between tribal groups. Mark Sirag invited Bert to participate in a baptism among the river people where Mark worked. Colleen wrote, "They had baptized sixty Chayahuita Indians from that Rucoba family group. Apparently these Indians sort of 'follow the leader' in their religious convictions, so that, when the leader of a particular group makes a decision to follow Christ, most of the rest of the group almost automatically make the same decision. Time will tell just how this will work out in practice." This reminds one of Paul's experience with the Philippian jailer (see Acts 16:33). Missiologists study this phenomenon, called household conversions or people movements.

On the international scene this was the time of the moon landing. Bert was away, and Colleen followed the events by radio. It made her

proud to be an American.... Lots of folks here in Yurimaguas have stopped me to shake my hand and congratulate me for the landing on the moon (as if *I* had anything to do with it). Others don't believe it happened at all. Still others are scared that we Americans are going to bring down God's judgment on the whole world with our foolish exploits (like the tower of Babel). Many folks here, after discussing the lunar triumph, ask me in all sincerity, "And now do they plan to go to the *sun*????"

Bert and Colleen were delighted to learn that Keith and Dorothy Ward felt led to move to Yurimaguas and help with the work there. They were from England and had been working for a time with the Finnagans in Puerto Maldonado, in southeastern Peru. Colleen wrote that they sensed their "sphere of service in and around

Maldonado was severely restricted and wrote to inquire about the work in Yurimaguas." Dorothy had a year and a half of nursing training, which was a great help. They moved into the house next to the Elliots and immediately put their shoulders to the ministry task.

Baptizing in the river

Throughout the years, Bert and Colleen frequently expressed their thankfulness for safety in their extensive travels—amazing in light of the countless miles they put on their vehicles, the poor road conditions, the frequent washouts and landslides, the hairpin turns without guardrails on steep mountain roads, and the daredevil Peruvian drivers. But they did experience one accident. Ironically, it was close to home. Colleen was writing a family letter on September 11, 1969, when she received word of the mishap.

Bert had borrowed Julio's motorcycle and was showing Keith around town on Thursday morning. They were coming back from the port to the house about 11:30. Bert saw ahead of him a Ford truck (F-600), which seemed to be traveling in the same direction. But instead it was in the process of turning around, and as Bert swung out to pass it, the truck suddenly backed right across the road without giving any indication. Even though Bert swung to try to get away from the truck, it was coming too fast, and they were caught under the wheels. The back dual wheels went over Keith's chest and stomach (tire marks are still visible across his upper shoulders and chest) and came to stop on Bert's hips. Bert hollered for the truck driver to pull ahead, which he did enough to unpin Bert, and he was able to pull himself out. But he saw Keith was still under the wheels, bearing the full weight of the truck on his stomach and chest. Bert screamed again, and the driver pulled forward once more and freed Keith. The shock at this moment was terrible, and Bert still can't get the picture of Keith lying under those wheels out of his mind. He was sure Keith couldn't possibly survive, because the wheels had gone over him twice. Fortunately the truck was empty, or they would have both been crushed. It still seems a miracle they are both alive.

Another car was going by and got them to the hospital right away. Neither of them ever lost consciousness. During the first little while Bert was able to stand and walk but couldn't lift any weight. He supervised the lifting of Keith into the car, so as not to bend his back in case of spinal injury, and held his head in his lap as they drove. I learned about it maybe ten to fifteen minutes after it happened and called Dorothy. Perhaps you can know what a scare it was. A taxi took us to the hospital in nothing flat. When we walked into emergency, Bert was lying on a stretcher looking as white as a sheet. He said, "I'm all right, but oh, poor Keith, poor Keith." So I went with Dorothy and found him looking very blue. He managed a smile for Dorothy. She was wonderful— so composed and calm and assuring to him. He turned and gripped my hand and begged me to take care of Dorothy. I thought sure he was dying, and I guess he did, too.

About that time they put us out of the room to take x-rays. Dorothy and I had a prayer in the hall. Neither of us was crying. After x-rays Bert and Keith were put in separate rooms (Yurimaguas standard). They kept checking Keith's blood pressure every half hour. The head nun was very sweet. She urged us to get them out to a bigger hospital as soon as possible. They soon got the results of the x-rays. We could hardly believe it when the doctors came in and told us neither had any broken bones. [Eventually they discovered Keith had a broken arm, which was put in a cast.] But there was the real danger of Keith, especially, having internal hemorrhaging. If his blood pressure should suddenly have gone down, indicating bleeding, they would have had to operate. The head nun told us they weren't set up properly (especially anesthetic-wise) to do it. The doctors kept assuring us the men were "lucky" and that with a few days rest they would be all right. But then the nurses would make faces at me behind their back or call me out in the hall and tell me I'd better act quickly and get them out of there.

We all felt we should sit tight until the next morning, when we could get the plane back to Lima. They gave both Bert and Keith shots to make them sleep, but they still had a miserable night. It was hot, and the beds were uncomfortable, and so much noise. At six a.m. Dorothy and I rushed home to pack suitcases, and by nine we were at the airport when the two-motor Satco plane arrived from Iquitos. We got the fellows aboard the plane comfortably. Keith was having trouble breathing. We were worried about his traveling on an unpressurized plane, but he took it beautifully. I had the pilot radio ahead for an ambulance. By four p.m. Friday afternoon we had them settled in this beautiful American clinic. What a contrast to the Yurimaguas hospital!

Several more x-rays confirmed there were no broken bones, ruptured disks, or any internal bleeding that they can tell. Keith is in worse shape than Bert, but as far as we can tell, he will get better. They were sent home to Yurimaguas with instructions to take several weeks off. Keith actually recuperated more quickly than Bert, who had to use crutches for several weeks. How thankful they were to the Lord for their health after experiencing such a close brush with death!

During this season the missionaries were excited to watch the national believers initiate new ministries. Colleen wrote,

We arrived home this time [from a river trip] to find that some of the Christians had launched a weekly fifteen-minute radio program *(La Voz del Evangelio)* over the local radio station using local talent. They are an intrepid bunch, and we can't help admiring them for their courage, even though we cringe at the quality of some productions. Fools rush in where angels fear to tread, I guess. But since they are definitely "in," we want to try to help them as much as we can, especially with their special musical numbers. So there will be some extra meetings this week for practicing hymns, and I *do* hope it helps. Yesterday they spent a little time here practicing and also asked me to please accompany with the accordion. So last night at 6:45 p.m. I had my first experience on the radio! I wasn't really sure I wanted to face the townsfolk afterwards, but at least the message was good! On one of the hymns the tenor really blared out his part about half a note above the pitch of the accordion. Everyone else was about half a note below. Oh dear, it was awful. Some of you might like to add *La Voz del Evangelio* to your prayer lists. It can use lots of prayer, believe me. It has lots of possibilities, actually, for lots of folks here in town and on the outskirts have their radios tuned to this station. And strangely enough, according to the reports so far, the program seems to be better received than the more polished one put on by the Adventists using tapes from Argentina. Corny as ours is, folks seem to appreciate hearing something from their own people.

After a time the Catholic priests even broadcast the program over their sound system out onto the main city plaza. Bert and Colleen knew well that the production quality suffered, not because of some innate cultural inferiority, but because of disadvantages, such as lack of education and other resources that we in the US can access in abundance. They were proud of the Peruvians for serving wholeheartedly with what they had.

Bert and Colleen returned to the mountains and coast for nine months. One of their practical and much-needed responsibilities among the many scattered churches was to help choose elders. Colleen's account from one mountain church illustrates the challenge of this procedure:

Bert opened up the Scriptures simply on the subject, and then some concrete suggestions were made as to who might be the men who were doing the work of elders in that congregation. Of the four suggested, none are legally married as yet. Two are held up by former entanglements and are at present working with lawyers trying to get them straightened out. The other two could have their civil marriages taken care of tomorrow if they wanted to, but have been careless. When Bert asked these two men, one by one, what they were waiting for, the one stood up and expressed doubts about getting legally tied up to a woman who seemed to have so many defects and be so hard to get along with as was his "companion" (the poor companion sat stony-faced through his little speech and apparently was unmoved by his observations). The other man stood up and said his "companion" (a young girl at least twenty years younger) didn't have any defects, but they had just been too busy to take care of this little matter of marriage! It was rather difficult to keep a straight face throughout their frank expressions, but at the same time we felt sobered as we were made aware in a new way of the very real problems involved in seeing that little group established (?) as a functioning church.

About this time, on a Sunday afternoon, Bert and Colleen were literally shaken by another event, as Colleen related:

We were still a couple thousand feet above Chilete, bumping and bouncing our way along (travel on some of these mountain roads is like a continual earthquake, and obviously this is why we didn't feel the real thing) when all of a sudden it looked as if a hundred bombs were exploding in the valley below us. The dust just billowed up like white smoke from all the nooks and crannies and settled like a fog across the whole area. At first we couldn't figure out what it was, but the folks traveling with us said right away, "An earthquake!"

On May 31, 1970, a 7.9-magnitude earthquake jolted central Peru. The epicenter was fifteen miles off the coast, and it caused extensive destruction. It was the deadliest natural disaster ever to strike the American hemispheres. The earthquake claimed nearly eighty thousand lives and destroyed the homes of close to a million people. It triggered a combination avalanche-landslide that unleashed millions of tons of snow, ice, rocks, and mud from Mount Huascaran, the 22,205-foot mountain that is Peru's highest peak. This mass of debris shot down the slopes at speeds exceeding 150 miles per hour. It buried entire villages.

The hardest-hit region was to the south of the Elliots' ministry focal point, but even those not in the devastation's direct path were affected by it. The churches in Chiclayo and Cajamarca took up sizeable relief offerings. Bill Conard and Ray Cawston immediately began buying food, medicine, used clothing, blankets, and the like and organizing a crew to travel and help wherever needed.

Colleen wrote,

> They all went to the town of Jimbe, where they set up a medical base with the two doctors from Cajamarca. Then the rest started out on foot to the surrounding towns and villages. I think they were able to reach eight or ten of them in all, most at least four or five hours by foot from Jimbe up steep, treacherous paths. Ray said that, if we thought conditions in Chimbote were bad, conditions in those isolated mountain villages were just twice as bad. Not only are their houses gone, but their farms as well, most of their animals, their irrigation ditches, and just about all their hope of living, it seems. Many of them were severely injured. Ray and Chilón have hardly ever done any medical work, but they went around putting in injections and cleaning and bandaging up wounds and doing a really fantastic job. They saw some terrible things—a thirteen-year-old boy with his left foot severed off, a little deaf boy with a huge gaping wound on his leg, which was threatening gangrene and which Chilón cleaned up—and saved his life, I'm sure—a little four-year-old girl with the side of her face cut and her left eye just dangling from the socket, others with deep skull wounds, etc. Probably most of these would have died if Ray and the others hadn't been willing to walk out to them.
>
> Monday [following the earthquake] was an exciting day here in Huaraz. About two p.m. [US First Lady Pat] Nixon arrived accompanied by Mrs. Velasco (president of Peru's wife) and a whole host of newspaper reporters, photographers, TV men, secret service men—what have you. The fellows found out in the morning that she was to visit one of the Peace Corps workers camps, so we headed out there to await her arrival and were not disappointed.

There didn't seem to be as many people around as we expected. We were able to practically rub shoulders with her. Once when she passed close by where Barb and I were standing, she smiled and said, "Hi. How are you?" to us! What a harassing experience for a woman, though, to have all those long microphones stuck in your face to catch your every word and any number and kind of camera aimed your way to catch your every pose. No wonder she looked so tired and older than we had imagined her to be. No wonder, too, that she keeps her visits short! Following her around just those few minutes makes us glad we are not celebrities! We stood on the street as we watched her car pull away. As she drove slowly by, Bert called out, "God bless you, Pat!" She responded to this with a smile and something like a wink. Bert was pleased, though I think Ray [an Englishman] was somewhat shocked at such familiarity! Imagine addressing a member of the ruling party by their first name!!

Colleen and Ray appeared on the US nightly news, standing behind Mrs. Nixon during an interview. That was their brush with fame!

After treating the acute medical needs, the missionaries shifted focus to rebuilding. The pressing need was temporary shelters from rain and snow, common in these communities at twelve thousand feet. Bill made multiple trips to purchase corrugated iron sheets for roofing. The team concentrated on a village with a large Quechua-speaking population a half-mile walk off the main highway. Colleen wrote,

Bert seems to have spent a lot of his time the past few days trying to track down engineers and local authorities for final permission to build and instructions on just where to build the little town of Atipayán. We won't actually rebuild the town. The idea is be sure that it is located in the safest spot possible, then give each family a lot and see that some kind of a rainproof shelter (that can later serve as their kitchen) is built on the back of each lot so the family has a small place to live during the rainy season. It's going to be a big job. Atipayán is just one village among so many that need this kind of help. Some more Peace Corps volunteers are supposed to come in this week. One of their engineers has agreed to help us get more roofing. Bill and Keith arrived, so we had a crew of five men [including John Taylor, Bert, and Chilón], and I'm chief cook. I really enjoy this, and you'll never know what a haven this camper is to all of us. It's amazing how many people we manage to get around its table—six or eight or more. Close fellowship, but no one minds in this climate. The temperature usually goes down to forty degrees [Fahrenheit] here in the camper at night, though it's warmer during the day. It's colder of course in the tents. I sure do feel sorry for the people who have to sleep in them. It's a good thing they seem to be hardy. The snowcapped mountains all around Huaraz are simply beautiful, but I guess they're pretty treacherous. We continue to feel tremors here of varying degrees nearly every day.

Saw a sad thing yesterday. We had gone out to Atipayán to get a list of the people whose houses had suffered the worst damage. I was in the camper making lunch. Some of the Quechua women had been so friendly and brought me eggs and a bucket of water and seemed so glad we had come. All of a sudden Chilón came rushing to the door saying a house was burning. I gave him a dishpan full of water I had handy, and he rushed off with it. Then John went with a kettle full, and I just ran. Met a three-year-old girl running down the road screaming for all she was worth. She held out her little arms to me. I picked her up, and she held on for dear life and just sobbed and trembled. After the earthquake had destroyed their homes, these people made shelters out of eucalyptus branches and leaves. There was a strong wind yesterday that whipped one of the cooking fires, and in less than five minutes time three of these shelters and everything in them had gone up in smoke. The women wailed, and I cried with them. Immediately following the excitement the fellows got some of the men organized, and they put up a little better shelter for these women using some of our sheet iron. Bert and Chilón drove to town to buy some blankets and this morning got quite a bit of nice used clothing, more blankets, and some food from the Red Cross. Life is certainly hard here. In another nearby shelter I was called to see a woman who was starting labor pains. I urged her to let us take her down to the hospital, but she said, "Who will take care of my children?" I do hope both she and the baby made out all right in that eleven-thousand-foot cold. One of the Red Cross tents also burned yesterday. I really fear for these camps. The tents are so close together, and many are cooking with open fires or pressure kerosene primus.

The Elliots were thankful for Bill and Ray's leadership in this effort and that they could participate. In all this team received over $14,000 from ten countries for relief. Much of that went toward the corrugated iron sheets that were so useful in building temporary shelters.

Colleen wrote,

We really have met some wonderful characters during our stay in Huaraz. I don't think we shall soon forget, for example, the solo we heard one night in a meeting in Marcará by a simple but sincere Indian brother with a rather pointed head and a rather permanent dent around his shaggy head from the rim of his hat. Right before Bert spoke that particular night, the man hopped to his feet and said he wanted to sing a solo in gratitude for what the Lord had done in his life. There was quite a long pause while he laboriously thumbed through the hymnbook looking for just the right number. Finally he found it, and, looking both pleased and scared, he straightened himself, hymnbook held firmly in both hands. He gulped, cleared his throat several times. Then out it came. Four verses of "How Great Thou Art" sung on one single note! Only on the chorus did he add a couple notes to make the tune almost recognizable. Occasionally as he was singing, he would misread a line, stop short, say "No," pull the hymnbook closer to his eyes, and back up to take another stab at it. As Bert said afterwards, "Folks at home just wouldn't believe it!" I sat watching the man's wife throughout the performance. She looked like she was quite enjoying it. Apparently he was a terrible drunk before, and she is so thankful to have him changed that even his singing sounds acceptable to her. One should write a book about all the fascinating personages we have met and continue to meet during our time in this country.

I can envision the angels giving this brother a standing ovation, because they heard his heart.

On September 4, 1970, Bert and Colleen received the news that Dad Elliot, age eighty-five, had gone home to be with the Lord. Colleen wrote,

It came as somewhat of a shock, as you can imagine, for we had no idea that the trouble he was having with his foot [an ongoing consequence of his diabetes] would lead to anything so serious. And, of course, we hadn't even received any of the letters telling of his hospitalization [it happened so quickly]. Bert's immediate reaction was to rejoice with Dad; my own was a bit more selfish as I thought how *much* he would be missed by all of us. Still, after talking to Portland by phone and receiving your different letters, when we could piece together in our minds just what had happened, we certainly have been made to be thankful to the Lord for all the mercies that surrounded his going. It's wonderful just to think that, a couple weeks before going, he was still able to drive his car and make that trip to Vancouver, BC, to visit his relatives. We're so thankful his suffering wasn't prolonged. He certainly had a long, full life and influenced lots and lots of people for good. Our own memories of him are so pleasant. We speak often of them these days, recalling incidents that tend to either bring tears or a chuckle. It's fun to remember his atrocious attempts at quoting Scripture in Spanish and the postscript he added to one of Mom's recent letters, *Mi madra escribo mucho mala!* [My mother I writes quite poorly!] It wasn't many years ago that we remember gasping as we watched him hobble onto the high board at one of the Portland swimming pools and do a back dive into the water. Our reaction was similar the last time we were home as we watched him hobble to clean snow off the driveway, cane in one hand and shovel in the other! When we remember two winters ago how he nightly descended the basement stairs after the rest of us had gone to bed to bang on the furnace with his cane to get it to shut off. It responded at the first bang (not quite so readily for Bert when he tried the same trick). We are not surprised to hear that the Cadillac stopped short after September 3, and the lawnmower refused to budge. Dad had a special way, it seemed, not only with people but with things. We will *all* miss him. I guess the memory that tends to crop up most frequently in my mind, at least, is that of Dad in the nook at 7272 following a late breakfast, McIntyre on the radio, the reading, interruptions, phone calls, visitors, and then the mail would be brought up, and the contents of each letter shared with great interest. Then he would bow his wonderful head to lead all those present in talking to the Lord about both the problems and joys of those who had written and many others as well. It was this scene that often inspired me as I wrote this letter and which often gave us a lift when times were tough. We knew we could count on Dad's prayers and his very real love for us. We loved him, too, and therefore can't do anything else but rejoice that he is now where it is *far* better.

The Elliots were not able, because of logistics and expense, to return in time for Dad's funeral. But they wrapped up as quickly as possible with a short stay in the jungle so they could return by early February 1971 to spend extra time supporting Bert's mom.

13

More Medical and Another *Maranatha*

The Elliots returned from their six-month furlough in August 1971. Their initial task in Peru was to replace the *Maranatha*. She had served them well, but maintaining her was taking too much time and money. On their return trip they had shopped for boats in Miami, Florida. They determined that having the new boat built there and shipped to Yurimaguas would be too expensive and wasn't quite what they wanted. But they picked up some ideas to incorporate into their final design and were able to purchase some much-needed boat equipment.

Their second option was to have a boat custom built in Pucallpa. They considered a houseboat style but eventually decided the conventional cruiser type was better suited for their travel needs. They debated whether to order a thirty-two-foot fiberglass boat kit from the US or have a Peruvian ship builder build a boat from scratch. They abandoned those options due to cost and logistics.

Colleen described another, unexpected option that surfaced:

The big news of the week is the cable we received yesterday from Keith and Dorothy advising us that the brethren in England had offered several thousand pounds for the construction of a boat in England (to be shipped out), and they asked us to give them a yes-or-no answer by return cable as to whether or not we were in agreement. When forming the reply, I asked Bert what to say, and he told me to just write, "Yes, yes, yes, yes, yes, yes . . ." He was only kidding, of course, but it reflected something of the relief he felt at being able to turn this whole project over to competent builders rather than spending months and months of his own time having to worry his way through it. It is like a big load lifted to know we are now free to think about other things. We have been praising and thanking the Lord ever since the cable arrived.

A letter received from Keith last week told of the chat he had had with one of the top small boat designers in Britain and his offer to design a boat for us that would more adequately meet our needs. This man recommended steel or aluminum construction over fiberglass, the former of course being the least expensive. Bert has written Keith now our suggestions regarding design and also offered to send him the money we have been saving for the boat to add for shipping. Whether they will be able to send it fully equipped and ready to go, or whether they will plan to furnish the interior here, we don't as yet know. It really doesn't matter either way, though the more they can get done over there, where things are much handier, the easier it will be for Bert and Keith here. The things we brought from the States for furnishing a boat could easily be put to use in other ways or sold, *if* they are able to just go ahead and furnish it there. Bert already last week had set up the gas stove and fridge (that we brought) in our kitchen here. They both work beautifully. I had been reduced to just one burner that still worked on my old kerosene range. So it's like a dream having a stove in which all three burners work and which light at just the flick of a match, to say nothing of the automatically controlled stove.

Bert and Keith made the final decision in November 1971 to have the boat built in England, but it did not finally arrive in Iquitos until June 1973. The delay was due to a dock strike in England, the long trip across the Atlantic, the four-thousand-mile journey up the Amazon River, and the inevitable challenges of Peruvian customs.

About its arrival Colleen wrote,

The *Maranatha II*, from that distance [while still on the freighter as it arrived in Iquitos], looked like a pretty, white toy boat on the deck of that large ship. Perhaps you can imagine how fervent the praise was that ascended to the Lord from the bow of the *Maranatha II* as soon as we got her safely to land. We just didn't know how to thank the Lord enough for all His goodness to us. The boat is very nice and has a roomy, airy, light forward cabin, a good-sized space over the motor where we can do our medical work, and then a roomy back cabin with two extra bunks and place for another bed if necessary. We especially like the back cabin and think it will be very useful to have a separate bedroom. Most of the boat is done in pale blue and white. It came complete with a small, two-burner gas stove with oven and a tiny gas Electrolux refrigerator. It goes without saying, I guess, that there would be certain features of design and decoration where our tastes and ideas differed from Keith's and those who built it, but for the most part we really like it and are very pleased and just very, very grateful.

211

Maranatha II arrives.

In a subsequent letter Colleen added an additional comment about the *Maranatha*.[1]

> The boat is really nice, and we daily thanked the Lord for it and for the depth finder and for the small refrigerator (what a *big* difference that makes in living!) and for the separate cabins and even for the tiny shower! Small as it is, it *is* nice to be able to bathe in private and away from the bugs. This boat is much more spacious than the old one. That is a big help, especially this trip, when we were so well accompanied.

While the medical work was a significant aspect of their ministry to the people and opened many doors to share the gospel, the Elliots didn't have any official authorization to practice medicine in Peru. During the same trip to Iquitos to welcome the *Maranatha*, Colleen wrote,

---

1 To be consistent with the Elliots' practice, the *Maranatha II* will subsequently be referred to as the *Maranatha*.

A fellow missionary shared with Bert how he received a letter of authorization to pull teeth in rural areas where there are no dentists (practically the whole jungle!) after completing two hundred hours in the dental section of the Iquitos hospital. He introduced Bert to the dentists there, and so Bert started to work on his two hundred hours! He is finding the experience fascinating and says he is learning a whole lot he never knew before. One morning he was invited into the operating theater to observe and assist in setting a fractured jaw, done by wiring the teeth together, as I understand it. (We will not be practicing this ourselves on the boat, I don't *think*, but it was interesting to see nevertheless.)

Some mornings he would come home especially happy because he had been able to talk to some dentist or nurse or doctor about their spiritual needs. One of the dentists, though excellent in his work, is a very immoral man, another has a foul tongue, almost all of them feed their minds on filthy literature and have domestic problems, etc. Bert seems to have the knack of pointing these things out to them without offending. The head dentist thanked him one day for having come and for having served as a "fount of good counsel" to all of them.

At the same time he started in the dental section, Dorothy and I received permission to go to work in the hospital proper. We, too, are learning a lot. We spent three days this week in the vaccination section, where we vaccinated for small pox, TB, whooping cough, tetanus, diphtheria, measles, yellow fever, etc. It was most interesting. Then I went into emergency, where I will be until Wednesday. In emergency I am learning more about making stitches, dressing wounds, ulcers, lancing abscesses, and even removing fingernails! Most helpful. Following emergency I will go into maternity for a week and a couple days in pediatrics. We are certainly grateful for all we're learning and also for the prospect of some legal recognition, which would only serve as protection in case anything ever happened.

Immediately following the training, Bert and Colleen welcomed from the States Bert's brother Bob with his wife Ruby, daughter Beth, and good friend Jack Mackie. In their ten days together the extended family traveled to Chosica, Chiclayo, Cajamarca, and then on to Yurimaguas. Colleen wrote,

> Let me say at the outset that I am going to lack both ability and adjectives to describe what it has meant to us to have this visit from Portland, but it sure has been wonderful, and we don't know how to thank the Lord enough.
>
> On Sunday evening following communion there were a couple special numbers with guitar, and then Bob and Jack spoke a bit by interpretation, and that was fun. Bert usually had some cute remarks to make about Bob and their childhood together when he introduced him, which the folks enjoyed. Then Bob would follow with some choice remark, too, which Bert tried to faithfully translate. It always thrilled me to see them standing up together.
>
> Ruby brought me a nice pair of double-knit slacks from the States with matching top and a nice White Stag jacket. And so for the first time in Peru I sallied forth in pants, and almost for the first time anywhere. Bert whispered some real sweet words in my ear about my appearance. That helped a lot to give me confidence. I must say I really found them comfortable and warm. I even wore them to the meeting that night. Now how about that!!!

With Bob's able assistance, Jack did his usual job of repairing anything that didn't work or needed sprucing up. Bob, a chiropractor, gave advice on some medical situations that came up. Ruby baked pies and made drapes for the Elliots' living room while Beth kept them well supplied with homemade bread.

This was midsummer 1973, and the *Maranatha* was cruising up from Iquitos with a Peruvian brother at the helm. Bert and the visiting men took a speedboat trip downriver to meet it. Colleen wrote, "Saturday night they spent in Lagunas, where Bert and Bob spent until four a.m. talking with Neil, trying to straighten out Bert and Neil's conflict over doctrinal and fellowship differences. They seem to have been somewhat successful, with the end result that they all sat down at the Lord's table together Sunday morning, for which we praise the Lord." That encounter proved to be significant, because three months later the Weirs announced their permanent return to the US. Colleen wrote,

> They seemed to come to the decision very suddenly, and no one knows the exact reasons for their leaving, except that they told the believers in Lagunas that, as the Lord led them to Peru forty years ago, He was now leading them back to the States to rest.
>
> We can't praise our guests enough, not only for all that they meant to us and did for us, but also for their attitudes toward the people and the different circumstances thrown at them in rapid succession. The language was a frustrating barrier (I have never before seen Bob at a loss for words!), but this was overcome considerably by *love* and a big friendly smile, so it didn't really matter if folks happened to be greeted by a lusty *buenas dias* even at eight at night. We were amused at times by the way some of the Peruvians, after an initial attempt in vain to communicate, would raise the volume of their voices on the second round, thinking that surely that would help. It didn't.

The Elliots continued to encounter opportunities and challenges, as Bert recorded in a letter to his mother:

The work on the river is growing all around, and it's good to know that it is the Lord's and He will direct it, as it is more than we can effectively visit. We had with us on Sunday a Lutheran man Robert Engwall, who is teaching extension courses to a few of the younger brothers. This is a movement around Latin America to upgrade the learning of Christian workers who cannot leave their responsibilities to go away to Bible schools. It is more than just a correspondence course in that the professors make periodic visits to help the students. [This was known as theological education by extension, a major development in training national workers.]

One of the new believers upriver just a week after his baptism was shot and killed by a man who wanted to rob his wife. The robber made her clean up the blood while he buried her husband then forced her to go with him to escape downriver. She finally managed to escape in the dark to a neighbor, and now the man is in jail here in Yurimaguas. The Christians say the dead man was so bright, and they thought he would be a leader in that new village. But it was not to be.

Colleen related stories that illustrate the fervor and commitment of the Peruvians to communicate the gospel:

Juan Bernal from Chiclayo spent three days with us in Monte Grande, and we were glad for that. He is getting close to seventy now, but is still very active. Although he breaks most of the rules any of us were taught on how to lead a soul to the Lord, he has probably influenced more folks for Christ than any of the rest of us will ever hope to do. He *is* a dear, and we don't know many others as wholly given to the Lord and to His work as he is.

In Morropón we would have hated to miss the very original program the believers there had been getting up for Christmas Eve, directed and produced mostly by our sister Eda. What fun!

216

The program was to be held outside. On Sunday morning a couple of the brothers built a cane-and-straw manger under the eaves of Eda's house. The program was scheduled to start about nine p.m., after we had finished a meeting on the plaza. But it was late getting started, because the believers were having a bit of difficulty rounding up all the animals that were props for the program. The burros were proving especially uncooperative, but they were all finally gotten together—a sheep, young cow, rooster, pigs, and burros. Two goats tied to a rope arrived during the middle of the first number, leading Eda behind them. They were both crying and making an awful commotion. It was a bit difficult to concentrate on Gabriel's proclamation to Zachariah. Eda's brother Duber was Gabriel and was replete with white, paper-padded wings!

Churches planted

They took us through the birth of John the Baptist. "Elizabeth" had a real live little baby in her arms as her friends gathered around to ask her what the baby was going to be named. Before this the virgin Mary had come to Elizabeth dressed in a white dress that belonged to Eda and covered her with a sheet. She had pulled this down right over her face, so in the middle of the scene Eda rushed up and yanked it back to where it belonged.

Finally came the birth of Jesus. The young virgin, who was looking a bit sleepy at this point, was placed in the manger, along with the same cute baby, with Joseph standing at her side. Then four little girls dressed in the castoff clothes and bandanas, who were supposed to represent the shepherds, came up and sang two Christmas songs, and each recited a poem to the baby with much arm waving and expression. It was very well done and real cute. About this time the little baby in the manger did what comes quite naturally to babies, and young Joseph's vigil at the entrance to the manger was interrupted by the virgin handing him some very wet rags (diapers) to hang on a nearby line. I held my breath all through the program for fear the cow, who was tied to the post near the manger and who had her rump toward the audience, might also do "what comes naturally" and mortify us all. But she was an unusually well-behaved cow and only concentrated her efforts straining at the rope, trying to get away from the post.

About this time the three wise men put in an appearance, traveling from afar on their donkeys and following a large white star, which had been tied to a line and which was slowly pulled along in front of them with a flashlight shined upon it. After that the teenage girls sang a special song, and then an impromptu scene was arranged by Bert to get Joseph and Mary and the baby gracefully out of the manger: Bert read the Scripture about the angel appearing to Joseph and telling him to take Mary and the baby to Egypt because of Herod's plan to kill.

And so they walked off, making it convenient to do the last number they had prepared. It was an enactment of the prodigal son, pigs and all. They got the story across with much loud prompting from the believers section of the audience. Following, Bert spoke for about fifteen minutes, and then as many as wanted to stay were invited for a midnight supper.

Bert and Colleen returned to the US in fall 1974, after a three-year term in which they spent about two-thirds in the jungle and the remainder on the coast and in the mountains. The furlough was in part to celebrate Colleen's parent's fiftieth wedding anniversary. Their aging parents' needs and various illnesses were constantly on Bert and Colleen's minds. Bob had moved his chiropractic office out of the 7272 basement, providing a place of their own for Bert and Colleen while stateside.

14

Life and Death, Near and Far

Following an eight-month furlough the Elliots returned to Peru in spring 1975, eager to connect once again with their missionary colleagues and national workers. They were pleased to welcome Bob and Mary Marsh, who arrived in Chiclayo to work with the Conards as printers. After a brief visit on the coast, Bert and Colleen headed to the jungle, where things seemed little changed. After a five-week river trip, Colleen highlighted the challenges they faced regularly:

> We had meetings every evening, of course, and that's quite a strain on Bert to find time for preparation and to know just what is needed in each place. I think I could write a book on the interruptions and distractions one has to put up with in these meetings. I'm often amazed that Bert is able to continue on his train of thought and that the Lord apparently does His work in the midst of such confusion. Sometimes it's a drunk who interrupts or an animal who distracts. One Sunday we remembered the Lord to the

accompaniment of a grunting sow and a litter of piglets directly under the floor of the house where we were holding the meeting. The believers would try to shoo them away, and in a few minutes they were back. All this while on the other end of the house a hen was very excited about an egg she either was about to lay or already had laid! Then there were the bugs, which seemed worse this time because of the recent floods. And the *children!* who come en mass because they like the singing, but as soon as it stops they begin to squirm and play around and talk and go in and out and generally add to the confusion. Most of them seemed to be coughing this trip, too, and there's always some small child willing to throw a temper tantrum right at an inappropriate time, while the mother or older brother or sister watches helplessly. Our lamp gave us an awful time this trip, too. Bert often would have to stop to pump it up or try to clean it. We were thrilled on a few occasions by professions of faith that seemed genuine.

In another village four of the brothers had to be disciplined (about half of the male membership of the congregation), and my mind still feels contaminated at having heard the account of one brother's (?) immoral conduct (he is now in jail), provided by his unsaved mother-in-law. The work generally is pretty weak. While there are some gems among the believers scattered around, I would sure hate to count the number of churches along this section of the river.

One of the reasons for the trip downriver was to take part in a wedding in Lagunas, but when we arrived there, we found that it had just been discovered the week before that the bride's fifteen-year-old sister was pregnant by the bridegroom. The bride (just a young girl herself) insisted she still wanted to marry the fellow. They had already gone ahead with the civil ceremony before we arrived. Of course there could be no church wedding or fiesta. Instead of joy there was sadness, discipline, shame, criticism—a blow to the little church there. How that girl could possibly go ahead and marry the man in the face of it all, I guess I will never understand. Is it perhaps that love is really blind, or do these people look at such things a little differently than we do???

Bert has spent a lot of time in visitation and counseling after meetings and at odd times, dealing with the problems of the church, of which there always seem to be an abundance— moral problems requiring discipline, misunderstandings, marital difficulties, dabbling in witchcraft (especially among some of the older women who should know better), carelessness of all kinds, and what-have-you. Being a pastor in Yurimaguas is a full-time job.

Another current case needing attention is that of R., who tried to commit suicide about ten days ago by mutilating his body (he completely severed his penis with a machete). We wonder if this is demon activity.

After working through several of these situations, on top of the cumulative disappointments while ministering to these struggling scattered churches for twenty-seven years, one might doubt one's effectiveness. Colleen wrote,

Jerry Couenhoven and Bert had a part in starting the work in Barranquita, but for many years it has been under the direction of the RBMU [Regions Beyond Missionary Union] mission of San Martín. It was interesting for us to visit again after such a long absence and observe the church's growth. In many ways, and probably for many reasons, they seem ahead of the believers on the Huallaga. This has us asking ourselves lots of questions.

Colleen did not elaborate on the nature of their questions. But the Elliots consistently evaluated their methods. They sought to remain simply obedient to the Lord on a daily basis and trusted Him to guide them. They recognized that the church was the Lord's and not theirs. They investigated and sometimes tried new ideas and strategies. They relied on the Lord as they dealt with each situation, trusting He was ultimately doing His work in the church. He called them to be faithful to His leading. Bert wrote,

Visitation in the village

> Pray for us. There are so many groups to visit, and they need visitation and teaching. We feel so poor when it comes to helping them. Pray that the Lord will guide us each day to those who are most needy and give us the refreshing waters of His Spirit and the green pastures of His Word so that, strengthened ourselves, we might strengthen others.

During a four-month trip in the mountains the Elliots received a bombshell in October 1975. Bert's brother Bob had been diagnosed with lymphatic cancer. The news cast a shadow on the remainder of what became a one-year term. Bert responded in a letter to his mother:

Colleen and I have just come from our knees, praying for you after receiving your letter about Bob a few minutes ago. How our hearts sympathize and hurt with you all, and still how thankful we are for the presence of the God of peace. I have just started studying James 1, and verse 2 [KJV] has been in mind this morning: "My brethren, count it all joy when ye fall into divers temptations." These are not temptations from the evil one, but testing from God. And I hope and pray that the Lord will so fill you with His grace that you may be able to rejoice knowing that His *love* for us is unmeasurable, His *power* unlimited, and His *wisdom* past finding out. We will come when you need us, Lord willing, but we do hope that won't be necessary and you will all see the mercy of the Lord in Bob's health that you have cried for.

Colleen wrote, "Bob's sudden illness was a terrible shock, and we can hardly think of anything else. It's hard to imagine him down— he has always been so strong, and I'm sure we all relied on him much more than we realized. Our hearts are heavy, but we can't doubt the Lord's wisdom and love in allowing this. We continue to trust Him to work it all out for the good of all concerned."

Bert and Colleen went back to the jungle after hearing the news and being assured they didn't need to return to the States immediately. They kept up to date on Bob's condition and sought the Lord's leading about when to return to Portland. They decided to join the family in March 1976. Bob died in May at age fifty-six.

Bert felt deeply the loss of his brother, as did many others. Bob was a godly leader, who impacted all around him. He was a successful chiropractor, served as the president of Western States Chiropractic College for seventeen years, was the key elder at Grace and Truth Chapel, helped launch Eagle Fern Camp, and was a mentor and example to many.

This is when Uncle Bert and Aunt Colleen's story became personal to me. Rich Malcolm and I rented the basement apartment at 7272 when we came to Portland in fall 1975 to attend Western Seminary. Clara asked me to call her "Gram" from day one, and we became good friends. I ventured upstairs most evenings for a visit after classes, work, and studying. She did not have a "crisis of faith" as she faced the possible loss of Bob, but she certainly had difficulty understanding God's purpose in taking him home when He did. Jim, Fred, and Bob were exemplary servants for the Lord. She couldn't understand why they were taken, yet she remained. At this point she was confined to a wheel chair and feeling pretty useless. She didn't grasp that she was still impacting countless lives—including mine.

Rich and I were asked to move out of the apartment at the end of the school year in May so Bert and Colleen could have their own place. This was when I first met them. They came alongside Bob and the family in his final months and participated in his memorial service. They remained in Portland the rest of 1976 to support the family and care for Clara.

Bert and Colleen were thankful for the special time they had shared with Bob and Ruby in Peru. On a number of occasions Uncle Bert shared with me his struggle with Bob's passing so young. Bert reflected on the promise in Exodus 20:12: "Honor your father and your mother, that your days may be prolonged in the land which the LORD your God gives you," and he told me he knew no one who honored his parents more than Bob did. He didn't understand Bob's "premature" death. But, as with Jim's death, he came to peace with God's sovereign choices.

It was during this furlough they first met Jorge Osorio. The twenty-seven-year-old Guatemalan had come to Portland to further his education. At thirteen he had run away from home to work on the Caribbean docks. He studied construction in a private trade high school. He attended university in Guatemala, which was involved in a civil war between the military, right-wing vigilante groups, and Marxist rebels. He and a friend were arrested by the Guatemalan army for alleged Marxist involvement, and after being tortured for a week, Jorge contracted malaria. He had never prayed before, but he asked God to spare him and offered to serve Him. Upon his release he worked on a ship flying the Cuban flag. Now embittered toward his own government, he considered joining the Cuban revolution. He was paraded around communist meetings in Cuba as a victim of a corrupt government. He sailed to various communist countries but quickly became disillusioned by the hatred he saw in North Korea, the alcoholism in Poland, and the lack of opportunity in other countries.

Jorge rejected Marxism and set his sights on furthering his education in the United States. When he asked his mother's advice for his course of study, she said, "I don't care what you study. I want you to give your life to Jesus Christ!" He said, "I'm serious," to which she responded, "So am I." That was his last visit with her. She died a few months later in a car accident.

Jorge came to Portland in 1974. Stan Pense, a fellow student at Portland State University, asked him point blank if he was a Christian and subsequently led him to give his life to Jesus Christ. Through Stan, during Bert and Colleen's 1976 furlough, Jorge became acquainted with the Elliots. Bert recognized the potential in Jorge and challenged him to consider coming to Peru to help. Jorge prepared at Multnomah School of the Bible, while living with and caring for Bert's mother, Clara. She took him under her wing and taught him how to pray and study the Bible.

Bert and Colleen returned to Peru shortly after Christmas for what turned out to be an abbreviated time—basically the year 1977—again due to family needs back in Portland. They spent most of this year in the jungle with a brief time in Cajamarca and Chiclayo.

The trip to the jungle included a scene new to the Elliots. Colleen wrote,

> We had an interesting flight on Tuesday. The plane was loaded with a bunch of mountain Indians moving lock,

stock, and barrel over to the jungle side of the Andes to buy cheap land available for farming. The women were all dressed still in their numerous thick, homespun, wool skirts, which is hardly fitting attire for the jungle. Their luggage was an interesting assortment of all kinds of paraphernalia, including several live sheep and some dogs. The sheep were *baa*ing loudly. You can't imagine the racket in the airport that morning and on the plane a little later when some of the small children, not used to air travel and sucking an oxygen tube, began to protest—pretty loudly, too. When we reached their destination, and the sheep were contentedly eating grass by the airstrip, the pilot laughingly told us, "Our planes are just like Noah's ark"!

Welcome to Peru!

The Elliots' ministry had been focused on lower-income and indigenous "jungle" people. The obvious cultural distinction between this group and the professional class was difficult to bridge. But doors began to open to this professional class. Colleen wrote,

Bert has had some nice chats with the man, Winston, who bought our house and has been encouraged by several opportunities to discuss the Scriptures with some of the wealthier folks of our little town. Salvation is definitely a miracle of God. One is especially conscious of that when trying to deal with this particular class. But it does seem that many more of them are reading the Bible now than ever before, and who knows what will come of it? The other night we were walking home at dusk from some visits and stopped to chat with a schoolteacher and her husband, who were sitting outside their house, which is custom here. We ended up having a dish of ice cream together at a nearby shop, and then I excused myself to go to a women's meeting. I thought they would both continue chatting with Bert, but she asked if she could go along with me instead, which was an unexpected and pleasant surprise. I don't know what she thought of the meeting, but at least she went, which in itself is something of a triumph for some of these folks.

In another letter Colleen wrote,

You can tell how happy Bert has been here in Yurimaguas (so have I). There have been days when I thought he would just plain burst with joy. Now I know that feelings are very erratic and unstable things. It could be tomorrow we'll feel like singing the blues, but we do thank the Lord for the happy time He has given us, especially these past two weeks. Much of the joy we have experienced has centered around the contact the Lord has given with the man who bought our home and will be our future neighbor. He has been down here nearly every day to discuss with Bert the portion of Scripture he is currently reading. It has been very exciting to see his perception and the changes beginning to take place in his life through the Word and the power of the Holy Spirit. And we are excited, too, to think that the Lord is definitely beginning to work among some of the upper crust of our little town, among whom we are having greater opportunities.

From Chiclayo Colleen wrote,

We received another letter from our neighbor in Yurimaguas this week that filled us with joy. He affirms that he has made a very definite decision to follow the Lord. He has not only been going to the meetings there quite regularly (something we scarcely had faith he would do), but is having Bible studies on his own with some of his friends. Even his wife, Yolanda, has gone with him to some of the meetings. He says she is learning how to handle her Bible. So praise the Lord and continue to pray for them.

Later Colleen wrote,

We ourselves arrived back in Yurimaguas and almost right away began to get involved in different activities with some of the upper-class people. It really is thrilling to see the opportunities there are present with them. It makes us want to sit tight here for a while to see what God is going to do. Tonight we are having our third Bible study here in the home with a group of eight. One of the men who comes is a communist school teacher who agreed to come with his wife to study the Bible from a "poetic point of view." Another woman who comes told us she accepted the Lord beside her radio about two and one-half years ago when listening to Luis Palau on HCJB. She bought a Bible at the time, began reading it and praying. Her life was changed. But it was just two weeks ago that she got up the courage to go to one of our meetings at the chapel for the first time. She has been attending faithfully on Sundays ever since, as well as the meeting in our house on Mondays.

Winston seems to be really growing and influencing lots of people. Yolanda talks to a lot of her friends, too, and it is through her that several come to our house on Monday nights. But I think the last couple of months since her baptism have been pretty rough for her, with personal problems in the drugstore [which they owned], having to be here while her two girls are in Lima for school, plus difficult adjustments to life in the church here. She can't go to the meetings very regularly because of the work at the drugstore, but when she does go, she finds the Sunday meetings very long, the messages not too edifying, and the common cup at the Lord's Supper hard to take. When she heard that some of the brethren were upset because she went to church once with pants on, that was just about the last straw! Bert had a meeting with some of the brethren on this issue (and a couple others). He didn't get home until two a.m. He said it ended on a happy note. Well, I think Yolanda will probably be good for the church in the long run and I hope the church will be good for her. We do need your prayers.

———◦—◦•◦—◦———

The Elliots' eighth trip to Portland came rather abruptly. They had just returned from a Bible conference thirty miles outside Yurimaguas when they received word that Colleen's mother had taken ill and passed away suddenly. In September her folks had made their annual trip to the family farm in Missouri. Kate was

Bert and Colleen with their loving parents.
Back: George, Colleen, Bert. Front: Kate, Fred, Clara.

completely exhausted following the trip and never fully regained her strength. She was hospitalized shortly before Thanksgiving and died on November 25, 1977, at age seventy-six, from congestive heart failure. Bert and Colleen returned to Portland immediately.

Within two months of Kate's passing, Colleen's father, George, had his prostate removed. His recovery was difficult. Bert and Colleen lived with him and cared for him, and two months later George was diagnosed with colon cancer. He missed Kate terribly and didn't want to live without her, so he declined any treatment that would prolong his life.

George's spiritual condition was a major concern for the family and had been the subject of prayer for years. Along the way Bert and Colleen wrote George several letters communicating their love and their desire that he come to know Jesus Christ as his Savior. Joan said of her dad, "He was the kindest and most honest man I have ever known." But virtue didn't satisfy his spiritual need.

He had asked Bert not to preach to him. Bert honored that request. Upon learning of his terminal illness, George questioned Bert about salvation and made a clear decision to accept Jesus Christ as his Savior. Bert baptized him there in the hospital room with his three daughters by his side. What a day of rejoicing!

George was transferred to a nursing home, where Bert and Colleen faithfully visited three times a day to feed him—he ate very slowly and said the nurses shoved food down his mouth! Joan came down every weekend from Seattle to relieve Bert and Colleen. They enjoyed this precious time with Dad. He went home to his Lord on July 8, 1978, at age seventy-nine.

Just three weeks later they sang and spoke at the funeral service for Barbara Jo Marks, looking back on more than a decade that their beloved Portland colleague had served alongside them in Peru. She died of cancer at age forty-one. She had excelled at working with students, using the Emmaus Correspondence courses. As Barb was a meticulously clean person, the Elliots marveled at her grace adapting to Peru's pervasive unsanitary conditions. When God calls someone to a place, He gives the grace necessary to live there. When visiting her in Peru, Bert and Colleen always felt they had shared a taste of home—Portland style.

It was during this furlough that my relationship with Bert and Colleen became formal—I became their niece's fiancé. Sue and I had first met in the kitchen nook at 7272 in February 1976, when I was still renting the downstairs apartment with Rich. She dropped by to visit her grandmother one evening and found us sharing a pie with Gram to celebrate my birthday. We developed a friendship over a couple years, then began dating, which led to our engagement. We married on June 16, 1979.

The Elliots' return to Peru in November 1978 felt very different this time, because they had lost a valued coworker and both of Colleen's parents. George and Kate had played a key supporting role in their missionary endeavors. Even though George didn't share their faith until the end, he was proud of his daughter and her work. He wrote letters and sacrificially supported Bert and Colleen through the years. Kate was one of their most faithful letter writers and handled all their banking and practical affairs stateside. Bert and Colleen missed the Collisons and their loving care through the years.

In their absence, Colleen's sister Joan took over Bert and Colleen's stateside affairs and managed them faithfully for the remainder of their lives. The Elliots were very aware of the sacrifices of many on their behalf, allowing them to serve the Lord in Peru. They often expressed genuine appreciation.

The Elliots' ninth term in Peru continued for one and one-half years to May 1980. They spent two stints of roughly three months each traversing the northern mountain and coast regions. They devoted the remainder of their time, in two segments, to the jungle. They marveled that they could never predict what a new day would bring.

They thought constantly about Bert's mother's need for ongoing care. She continued to live at 7272, but experienced declining health. Bob's widow, Ruby, and her family looked after Clara wonderfully, but Bert and Jane (in Wheaton) keenly felt the responsibility. When should Bert and Colleen come back to Portland to look after her?

The Elliots had returned to Peru with funds from the Collison memorials. Colleen wrote,

> We decided against using the memorial money for an organized "cattle project," like we were thinking about when we were in the States. Some of the Peruvian believers whose opinions we highly respect counseled us against this because of the danger of confusing the issues of the kingdom of God—from a spiritual standpoint—with a material standpoint. We still plan to buy a pair of cows for a few especially needy families on a very confidential basis and with no strings attached. We will also use the money for housing, food, or medicines—as well as to help support some of the workers.

This decision process demonstrated an important development in the Elliots' ministry. They were no longer the "authoritative missionaries." They treated the national church leaders as equals and even submitted their own plans to their wisdom. Many missionaries have difficulty making that transition, but it's vital to the national church's health and growth. Bert and Colleen trusted their Peruvian colleagues.

This situation also exposed a misunderstanding of God's kingdom. It doesn't address only the spiritual at the expense of the material, but considers the two interconnected. The purchase of income-producing cows and other resources for farmers and workers is an integral part of God's kingdom work.

The following two accounts illustrate some of the Elliots' ongoing challenges. The first, a mountain story, brings to light the continuing drama of travel. Bert and Colleen were constantly aware of their need for traveling mercies, as Colleen explained:

Because of the rain, the trip down to Chilete from San Pablo was very scary. The road, which is just a shelf cut in the edge of the mountain, proved to be extremely muddy and slippery. The first part had been recently graveled, and we thought we were all right. But a little further down Bert found he didn't have much control of the car. We stopped and prayed and debated what to do. When we first noticed it, we were in a very awkward spot to park, so Bert just kept inching the truck down in compound low gear. Zenaida and I got out and walked most of the way down. Bert kept going until, after a couple of hours, we reached a level where the rains hadn't been so hard, and the road was dry and firm. It was the kind of experience we would not want to repeat. (On one of the curves the truck turned halfway around and started going down sideways.) Bert was completely drained by the time we reached Chilete. I slept so good that night from all the extra exercise that Bert thinks I ought to trot behind the camper for a little while every day!!!

While the Peruvian government at this time was favorable to missionary activity, communists tried to hinder their work wherever and however they could. Colleen's jungle story reveals the growing influence of communism:

After a run-in with a nest of red ants in a village above Lagunas, we encountered a different kind of Reds, who also tried to give us a bad time. A group of communists from the coast have gone in there, formed a community cooperative, and started a sawmill. And they are really trying to influence the town toward communism and atheism. They resented our visit very much. As soon as we started our open-air meeting, they came around, stood right in front of us, and started making fun, contradicting what was said, laughing, and shouting loudly, calling to the people to join with them and trying every means they could think of to interrupt and disturb. I think most of the villagers who have known us for years were ashamed and embarrassed. Instead of joining them, they seemed to rally around us and listen more seriously than ever before. Had it been otherwise, we might have been in trouble. We just learned about some missionary friends in the mountains [Fred and Ruth Webb] who recently were beaten and injured somewhat in a similar situation.

After Jorge Osorio graduated from Multnomah, he joined the Elliots in Yurimaguas to help in the ministry and explore the possibility of his permanent involvement. He quickly proved invaluable for both his encouragement to people and his practical skills. While at Multnomah he had met and fallen in love with Donna Orcutt. He invited her to visit Peru for a taste for life in the jungle. This presented some opportunities and challenges, as Colleen wrote:

Donna really is a lovely girl, and she has a happy personality and is a good sport. Last week she buckled down and worked on the language. She made several friends with the young girls in the chapel, and they just loved the attention she gave them. Marta and I had a real frank talk with her one day about what is discreet for "lovers" in this culture and what is not discreet. She and Jorge have *not* been very discreet up to this point, according to Peruvian standards. I think it was helpful for Donna to hear it straight from Marta. She accepted it very graciously. I just hope they can follow through. I know it's not easy for them. They keep saying that there is no place or opportunity to be alone. We knew they would find this hard and had tried to warn Donna about this in a letter before she came. But one has to be *so* careful. Yurimaguas is a very gossipy town. It is also quite an immoral town. Any overt display of affection is looked upon with suspicion, and then guess what the tongues start doing! The brethren in the church don't even like it when engaged couples sit together in the meetings, much less any other open display of affection. We really have feared for their reputation—and ours, too. And please, when I say that, I hope you won't get the impression that there has been anything incorrect in their conduct—not at all. It's just that they are much freer with each other than folks here are used to seeing. Donna is a very affectionate, demonstrative person, and Jorge obviously eats it up! Oh well! They are both such good kids. Jorge is a terrific worker and willing to tackle almost anything—he undertook cleaning out the fuel tanks on the boat. I'm sure he must have smelled and tasted diesel for days afterwards. We appreciate so much all he had done—he painted my house, too. I know we are fast developing the "Neil Weir" image in their eyes. And there are days when I feel (and act) just like Mr. Weir. Help!

Regarding the ongoing spiritual need among Yurimaguas's professional community Colleen wrote,

The Lord continues to give us good opportunities with the "upper crust." Last week we had the American wife of one of the wealthier businessmen of Yurimaguas over for lunch. She and her husband are having serious problems adjusting. Bert had her read 1 Corinthians 13 out loud, and she started to cry as she read those beautiful words for the first time. It led into a marvelous discussion and opportunity to present the gospel. Sometimes, when listening to some of these wealthier people tell us of the problems in their lives, it sounds like a soap opera! Wow!

On a lighter note . . . we got a good laugh from a paragraph in Anne Munday's last letter. Talking about her son Herbert John, she wrote, "Yesterday John brought home the first composition he has written alone at school, and I felt that Herbert was a good name for him. (Please don't hate me. I really do love you, but I had to chuckle.) It was about a catplr (caterpillar) that went for a woc (walk) and found a leef to eet. After hetheood (chewed) the leef he made a coon (cocoon)." Bert sympathizes with his namesake and wishes his teachers success.

Another letter included a related account:

Bert is sitting here trying to write a letter. He asked me if the word "letter" has one t or two. I told him two. He said, "How come, then, does 'water' have just one?" I didn't know how to answer him. He usually spells "water" with two. I have been drilling him on that point. Poor Bert!

As the Elliots traveled to remote villages, they never knew what to expect of the local churches' health. Colleen wrote,

A little further down the road we were met by another brother who showed us where to leave the car and then guided us on foot up the mountain to where he lives and where they also have a tiny chapel. It's a fairly steep climb from the river to his house, but much easier than some of the walks around Cajamarca because of the lower altitude and, for me, therefore, more enjoyable. There is just a handful of believers there (four men, I think, and their wives and children). But they have been quite faithful in the face of lots of discouragement. There is evidence of some real maturing in the Lord. We were amazed at the knowledge of Scripture a couple of them have and at their ability to refute some of the false teachers who have come in trying to get a foothold there. They are busy communicating the Scriptures to others, too, so that there is now another little group of believers forming higher up the mountain. We returned to the car just before sundown feeling happy and encouraged. I don't know whether our visit did very much for them, but it certainly did *us* lots of good.

But a couple hours down the road they encountered a contrasting scene, about which Colleen wrote,

We stopped to visit in Pacasmayo, where they have the makings of quite a nice little chapel, but no Christians to use it! Some of the believers who formed the group there have followed unbiblical teaching, and some have even been rebaptized! Mr. and Mrs. Quispe lament the departure of the others and, to all appearances at least, are faithful themselves to the Lord, but that's as far as it goes. Bert still holds out hope for a future reviving, but I'm afraid I lack faith.

We personally find our time increasingly taken up in conferences of varying sizes in diverse places. In August

[1979] it was in a desert community in the state of Piura, in October the beautiful mountains of Cajamarca, in December in the fruitful valley on the coast and later on the majestic Huallaga River, in January and February in the neighboring state of Piura with its delightful combination of jungle and mountains. These meetings may lead to slightly more efficient use of time, as they pull together believers from several places at a time for teaching and fellowship. Nevertheless, we feel the solid work is done when we are able to settle down to the day-to-day battles of life in our little town with the big name of Yurimaguas. Here we cry to the Lord for fresh ministry, that there may be true bread to nourish His people. We listen to the problems and hear the sobs of parents for rebellious children. We pray and counsel and wait until the Lord is pleased to send a balm to this Gilead. Here we try to learn patience, along with the rest of the town folks, when the city water is turned off so frequently and at inopportune times and when flights are cancelled and mail doesn't come in or go out when it should. Here we work and sweat, trying to keep the material things the Lord has given from rusting, rotting, or molding into oblivion. After two months of pumping the bilge daily, we finally got the launch beached last week and a patch welded onto the keel. If the rains hold off and the river stays down another twenty-four hours, we may even get a coat of paint on it. If not, it will rust under the dark waters until we get another chance. Here, too, we often have the privilege of alleviating physical suffering and economic pressures. While this goes on, we search our motives and too often find our wicked pride at the bottom of things. Hence, we request your prayers, that we might live *today* in such a way as not to be ashamed when the Day comes to make known the secrets of men's hearts, when we stand before His judgment seat and receive our recompense for the deeds done in the body, whether good or bad.[1]

The Elliots decided to return to the States in May 1980 to help care for Bert's mother, Clara. Several people had lived with her, including Jorge and Donna after their wedding in May 1979, but they returned to Peru permanently. Sue and I were living in the downstairs apartment but were not able to provide the care Clara needed, as we were both working full-time. Jane took Clara to Wheaton to live with her family during winter 1979–80. Bert and Colleen traveled there in May in time to celebrate Clara's eighty-fifth birthday. They brought her back to Portland and lovingly cared for her until she went home to the Lord in February 1981. They counted it a privilege to spend that time giving back to her after she had poured so much love into their lives for all those years.

Bert had also been invited as keynote speaker to Congress West, a missionary conference organized by the Brethren churches in Portland.

While Bert and Colleen were home, they ministered in various churches in the Pacific Northwest but spent most of their time at Grace and Truth, their home church. It was the church in which Sue grew up and where we were fellowshipping. We had been taking an increasingly active part in the ministry, and the elders recognized the church's need for someone who could devote full-time to the work. So Bert and Tim Malyon, one of the elders, visited Sue and me and asked that we take on the pastoral role in June 1981. We have been privileged to serve in that capacity since then. One of the joys of our ministry has been the close bond with Uncle Bert and Aunt Colleen and growing from their impact on us.

---

1 See 1 Corinthians 4:5; 2 Corinthians 5:10.

15

Shining Path

When Bert and Colleen returned to Peru in May 1981, they did so feeling less encumbered by family responsibilities stateside. For the past decade and a half the length of each term overseas had been cut short by concerns for their parents' care. With all four now in glory, they experienced freedom to concentrate wholeheartedly on ministry. This term lasted a full five years and included six extended stays each in the jungle and the mountain/coastal regions. They spent about two-thirds of the time in the jungle.

Immediately upon arriving in Lima, they were reintroduced to the uniqueness of the Peruvian culture, as Colleen explained:

> Sunday afternoon we had an experience we had never had before. Apparently there is a movement of the Spirit of God among gypsy people going on all over the world. A group of these gypsy Christians are using one of the chapels here for their meetings. We were invited to join them to remember the Lord and for Bert to give them some teaching on the

Lord's Supper. What a moving, interesting experience that was with those colorful people. They used a tambourine and guitar for their singing. A woman with a beautiful voice got up and sang a solo with a lot of pathos just before the bread was passed. When Bert had finished speaking, they broke immediately into spontaneous, loud applause. Somehow it seemed right, just part of their very real worship. They used a flat crispy bread for the remembrance and a rather thick grape juice made from freshly crushed grapes. Our own hearts were full of praise to the Lord as we finished the meeting.

While still in Lima, the Elliots also quickly received a sense of their longevity in Peru. Colleen wrote,

Saturday night we had a visit from Peruvian friends we had known in Lagunas, where we lived when we first came to Peru over thirty years ago. In fact the husband was the first baby I had ever delivered. He is now a grown man with children of his own—an engineer, in fact, and quite well off. He came with his wife, children, parents, and sister to see us. It was nice to establish contact with them once again.

Shortly after arriving back in the jungle, they welcomed their niece Lynn Hawthorne, daughter of Bert's sister, Jane. Colleen wrote,

She does amazingly well with Spanish, and her sweet, friendly way with people makes her a great hit with everyone. I realized yesterday, though, that we definitely belong to a different generation, because she said she had never in her lifetime seen a wringer-type washing machine in operation or had to hang clothes out to dry on a clothesline! Lynn commented this morning that so much of our time seems to be taken up with just "living"—housework, cooking, and all—and that may be disappointing to her, but it's the way it is nevertheless. It's especially that way since our arrival back. This jungle climate seems to take a toll on *everything*. On a road trip, a couple times we almost got stuck, but Lynn and I helped Bert pray the car through. A large poisonous snake even crossed the road in front of the car, so she got a little glimpse of the things that creep around in the woods here and which we occasionally see—but seldom when we have visitors. So it was nice of the snake to come out just then.

The Elliots were very aware of the amount of their time that was taken up with just living. They also knew of tools and appliances that could be useful for those tasks. They put a great deal of thought into weighing the cost verses the usefulness of such appliances. Colleen wrote to her sister Joan,

We were very naughty and splurged to purchase a new refrigerator and washing machine. I think we both feel guilty about it, and we don't intend to write home about it yet *except to you*. Probably we feel that way because we seem to be given so many new things this year, and the folks at home have sacrificed so much to get us this new [to them] truck, and then we buy a fridge and washing machine, too! But it seemed an ideal time now to buy. Because of the depressed economy, things are not moving, and therefore folks were anxious to sell. We were able to get very good deals on these two items. Both, of course, are imported from the States, and that's another reason why it seemed an ideal time to buy. Because it is only this present government that has opened up the country to imports (the jungle is a low-duty zone), and, of course, any change of government could close that all down again. Also, Iquitos is definitely the place to buy, and having the boat there to transport them back to Yurimaguas also influenced our decision. I have been using Aunt Tillie's old Maytag washing machine for at least twenty-five years now, and, even though it leaks oil badly, it still works—but I am finding that standing for hours, especially with all the company we have, wringing and rinsing and emptying washtubs, then refilling them, has become very exhausting. Washing this week in the new machine is like a dream— and the clothes are almost dry when you take them out of the machine, so it seems to take about a quarter of the time to dry once they are on the lines. The fridge we had is one we inherited from Diane Tonkyn when she left the country. It was getting so I had to defrost it at least every two or three weeks, or the ice build-up on the freezer compartment would be so bad I couldn't get the door open. This new fridge has automatic defrosting, and that, too, seems like a dream, besides having so much space in the freezer compartment. Well, guilty feelings or not, the purchases are made now, and we have thanked the Lord for them and also given them back to Him, because we know everything we possess is very vulnerable, and we have to learn to hold our possessions lightly.

Did you get that? Bert and Colleen squeezed twenty-five more years out of a washing machine that was already used when they brought it to Peru! What for many people would be routine purchases, they rightly considered an exercise in stewardship of the time, energy, and finances God had entrusted to them. These new appliances were tools essential for their ministry because of the time freed up to care for people.

This tenth term marked the arrival of coworkers Jorge and Donna Osorio in Yurimaguas. The couple had been there briefly before their marriage and now returned with two boys, a one-year-old and an infant. Their impact was immediate. Jorge was a hard worker and a gifted administrator. He helped with repair and maintenance of the *Maranatha*. And he initiated the "Mini-cap" leadership training program. Colleen wrote,

> In one of the villages upriver we held the first of a series of training courses for Christian leaders in that area. Jorge purchased the courses, which were prepared in Honduras. They are short and simple. We taught four of them and gave out two others for the believers to study on their own during the next three months. Representatives came from nine churches—twenty men—and they returned home to put into practice what they learned. Jorge will travel up in a month or so to check their assignments. The second course is scheduled for three months down the road. We hope to have one every three months for the next four years and take them through basic material that they would get in a Bible institute, and are hoping to do this in two other areas around Yurimaguas.

Jorge and Donna opened a Christian bookstore. Jorge organized a Bible reading marathon in the city plaza. He put a "sports court" in next to the chapel to attract young people. With the aid of Dr. Scott Walt, he learned to fit eyeglasses, so he brought his own expertise to the medical team on river trips. Donna helped with the ever-present need for hospitality. She and Colleen formed a choir and presented several Christmas and Easter cantatas in both the city plaza and the chapel. However, within their first year in the jungle, Donna suffered several severe asthma attacks, and it became clear that the jungle climate was the cause. After exploring several options, they relocated to Trujillo in late 1985 to work with the churches on the coast. Organizing *Capacitación Bíblica* was to be one of Jorge's responsibilities.

Capacitación Bíblica was an annual conference for Peruvian leaders, started by Ray Cawston and Bill Conard, lasting three weeks in late January. It was initially held in Chiclayo and later moved to

Trujillo. The keynote speaker was usually from outside Peru. Each session offered teachings on books of the Bible, key doctrines, and practical ministry skills, often with sessions planned specifically for women. Following is a report from Bert about a particular lesson's ongoing impact:

Church in Yurimaguas

Most of this week here in Yurimaguas we have been meeting together as elders and workers, trying to practice what we learned in the conference and to communicate to the assembly the principle of *authority, fellowship,* and *growth.* This has been a time of heart searching and weeping together as the Spirit brought to light hidden offenses that had produced murmuring and darkness among the leaders. Learning to walk in light is not an easy task, as most of you will know. It's easier to cover small offenses and let them produce their bitter fruits of murmuring and criticism so long as we can hold the latter to what we consider tolerable levels. But slowly the power of our witness and the authority of God in our preaching make their stealthy exit from our lives. No communion . . . no authority! Please keep praying for us. I have reached my sixtieth year and am conscious of the increasing need for the mercy and grace of God each day.

On a trip up the Huallaga River in March 1982, in the dark drizzly night, Colleen slipped in the mud and fractured her wrist. Bert and the team gave her a shot to ease the pain and made her as comfortable as possible for the night. Bert later said, "Those of you who have been through similar things well know something of how we prayed that night in that faraway place, searching our hearts to see if something is not pleasing to the Lord and then finally committing ourselves to trust Him, knowing He loves us and is working all things together for good."

The next morning Bert took Colleen by speedboat to Yurimaguas and then decided to fly her for treatment to Lima. According to Bert, doctors found that "both of the bones were broken as they entered the wrist, and one was twisted badly behind the other. When they brought her back from the operating room, she was in a rather strangely shaped cast from her fingers to above the elbow, but the doctor assures us that everything is perfectly lined up, and there is nothing else to do but take his word for it."

About the incident Colleen wrote, "The Peruvians were most solicitous, too, and full of ideas about how to take care of it—in fact, I'm still getting those. Last night several told me that, if I left the cast on, it would never be right. As soon as I got back to the jungle, I should remove the cast and apply the lard of a boa constrictor and, if possible, wrap the arm in the fresh skin of a boa. That was guaranteed to make it heal properly!" She declined to follow their advice, and eventually her wrist fully healed.

Bert and Colleen hosted several SPRINT teams—Special PRojects IN the Tribes was a ministry out of Orlando, Florida—which paid great dividends through the years. That organization focused on giving young people an opportunity to experience missions for four to five weeks in the summer. They sent teams all over the world, including several to help with construction projects in Cajamarca and Yurimaguas and to encourage believers in area churches, large and small. One of the SPRINT teams organized a soccer team to play local city teams. This coincided with a visit from Bert and Colleen's Seattle nephews, Steve and Kevin Benz—both experienced soccer players who enhanced the team.

During this term several doctors from the Pacific Northwest came down for two visits each: Drs. Dan Hayden (general medicine), Dave Walt (optometry), Tom Fisher (dentistry), and Scott Walt (optometry). They worked long hours and treated many patients, also providing spiritual encouragement to the believers. Their visits were a shot in the arm to Bert and Colleen. (Pardon the pun.)

During this time the Plymouth Brethren missionaries in Peru began an annual conference for spiritual refreshment and strategic planning. They all found encouragement in meeting together. On the third of these, Jerry and Jane Hawthorne (Bert's sister) were invited from Wheaton to bring the devotionals. Colleen wrote, "After breakfast Jerry shared with us passages from 1 Peter and in the evenings some concepts that had changed his life. The messages were excellent, challenging our minds and touching our hearts as Jerry himself was often moved to tears." The Elliots and Hawthornes spent three wonderful weeks together in Tarapoto, Iquitos, and Yurimaguas.

Another highlight was a 1983 visit from Colleen's sister Joan and her husband, Ray Benz, from Seattle, which included an excursion to Cuzco, Machu Picchu, and the Sacred Valley of the Kings. After thirty-four years in Peru, Bert and Colleen finally slowed down long enough to see the country's premiere tourist attractions. The experience was a dream come true. They thoroughly enjoyed it and their month traveling with the Benzes to various ministry sites. Although Bert wrote of their drive through the Andes, "I think the narrow roads on the brink of nothingness got to Joan the second day out, but by then it was too late to turn back. So she braved those thirty-some hours of bumping and twisting all the way to Yurimaguas. We hope by now that her nerves have fully recovered."

One of Bert's life quests was to discover, as he put it, "what God made me for." Colleen inadvertently addressed that search as she reminisced following one river trip:

I am often amazed as I watch Bert work on these trips—pulling thirty, forty, fifty teeth in a morning, patiently removing a deeply embedded splinter from a girl's leg, counseling, encouraging, exhorting, taking time to stop and look up some family of believers who have grown cold, getting folks together who are offended, fixing the kerosene lamps of the small churches that always seem to be in disrepair, making a part for the broken-down electricity-generating plant in one of the towns, managing the boat through difficult waters, and constantly making little improvements here and there on it, and then somehow, I don't know how, coming up with an appropriate message for the meeting each evening, as well as teaching in the training session for the leaders. I probably shouldn't be the one to extol Bert's virtues like this, but perhaps I was extra aware of all he does for the people on the river because it was constantly in my mind that this *might* be our last trip upriver in the *Maranatha*!

That last sentence requires explanation. While the *Maranatha* was a wonderful tool for ministry for over a decade, it required an incredible amount of time and money to maintain. Bert realized he could no longer keep it up. So they took it to Iquitos and put it up for sale, without success. Taking that as a sign from the Lord, they moved it back to Yurimaguas, where several of the national church leaders volunteered to maintain it and continue its use in visiting the many villages on the river. Colleen wrote,

The *Maranatha* has been out all this month with our young Peruvian coworkers Rider and Norma Rengifo and their three children, visiting the villages downriver. During the month of December [1984] Rider took charge of scraping and painting the hull above the waterline. It looked real nice when they left. This is the first time we have had so much participation from our local brethren on the maintenance of the launch.

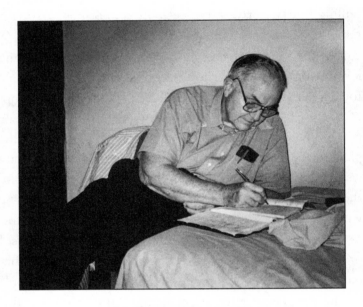

Constant sermon preparation

On the river trips I really felt for Bert before every meeting when he sometimes said he felt more like running than preaching and would cry out to God for just the right message to meet the need of that particular village or church. Considering all the things against him—the lack of much opportunity for preparation beforehand, the very noisy children and easily distracted audience, and the millions of flying insects that so often managed a perfect hole-in-one in one's throat, nose, or ears at most inopportune moments—I am always amazed at the forceful messages that came out. It was my prayer that some sinners would be trembling for their sins as I sometimes trembled for our well-being when Bert, like a prophet of old, would lash out against some of the current evils, especially the planting and trafficking of cocaine, which is very much on the increase in that area. Being possessed of a somewhat suspicious nature, I could easily imagine that some unscrupulous drug trafficker might take a pretty dim view of our presence. But again the Lord was greater than all my fears and graciously protected us from all the real dangers, as well as any imagined one.

While the Elliots were always aware of the inherent dangers of missionary life, two new threats appeared at this time. The first was the introduction of coca (from which cocaine can be made) as a cash crop for the jungle farmers—an exceptionally lucrative temptation for these families, who struggled for bare essentials. Bert openly preached against the drug, highlighting its illegality and damaging effect. The drug traffickers did not take kindly to interference and were known to respond violently.

The second threat came from the communist influence the Elliots had witnessed since the mid-sixties. But recently they had heard of terrorist attacks on the coast. Life mostly went on as usual, but then the danger hit close to home. Bert and Colleen were aware that they, foreign missionaries, might be specifically targeted. Colleen wrote,

These have been strange days for us in Yurimaguas. It all started on June 29 [1985] at eleven p.m., when a group of Maoist guerrillas who call themselves Shining Path made a surprise attack about one hundred miles downriver from here in the village of Lagunas. Three civilians (and perhaps some terrorists) were killed, some injured, and a bank and the police station were partially burned. Two of the victims were from Yurimaguas, and their bodies were flown into town late

253

Sunday afternoon, just before we arrived with the Barnabas team [from Portland] from a four-day trip upriver. Rumors began to fly that Yurimaguas was next in line for an attack. This was verified as they began to capture a few terrorists and find in their possessions detailed plans with specific targets. Special combat police and soldiers were sent in to reinforce the town police force. They made sure the streets were cleared of people by a certain hour every night. For a while the attendance at our meetings dropped by about half, and the atmosphere here in town was understandably very tense. I noticed that even Bert was not averse to my making sure our doors were all double locked at night! About a week later the police surprised the group of terrorists responsible for the Lagunas attack as they were resting in a banana farm in an area closer to Yurimaguas and killed seven of them, including the medical doctor who was their leader. Their bodies were buried in a common grave here in Yurimaguas. Since then there have been no more incidents. Life has gradually taken on a semblance of normalcy, though we continue to hear of armed gangs in the surrounding areas who appear periodically to plunder farms and terrify the farmers. Just this week a man downriver refused to give them the cattle and food they asked for, and they burned his place to the ground. There is lots of speculation about whether these insurgents will carry out their threats and plans for Yurimaguas. Some think they have backed off, but their record in other parts of the country would not indicate that is too likely, unless of course God intervenes and answers the pleas of His people for help in the same way he answered King Jehoshaphat's (2 Chronicles 20) by confusing and frustrating them. Those Old Testament stories and the command, "Do not be afraid. . . . Stand firm and see the deliverance of the LORD," are very exciting and challenging to us. Could He? . . . Would He—in this twentieth century, in answer to the imperfect prayers of some very imperfect Christians in the small town of Yurimaguas—do a similar miracle?? We know He could and have been praying in that way, realizing at the same time that He may choose to be glorified in allowing us to suffer violence. May we be found faithful in whatever He chooses for us.[1]

With the Elliots' much-needed furlough in spring 1986 came the opportunity of a lifetime. Jerry and Jane Hawthorne were in Cambridge, England, for a six-month sabbatical from his teaching Greek at Wheaton College. They invited Bert and Colleen to join them. So for a glorious two months the two couples toured England, Wales, and Scotland and then crossed the English Channel to the mainland, where they enjoyed France, Switzerland (where they connected with their Luginbuhl and Berney roots), Italy, Austria, West Germany, Denmark, Sweden, and Belgium. During their time in Great Britain, Ray Cawston had scheduled several speaking engagements for the Elliots. They also visited the Finnagans, Wards, and other former colleagues from Peru.

From there the Elliots went to Spring Lake, New Jersey, where they spoke at a missionary conference for Christian Missions in Many Lands. After a stop in Wheaton to visit the Hawthornes, they headed for the West Coast. This furlough lasted eight months.

---

1   Scripture quotation paraphrased from 2 Chronicles 20:15, 17, NIV.

16

Trujillo

This five-and-a-half-year term (December 1986 to May 1992) included a major transition for the Elliots as they exchanged their seminomadic rural lifestyle for "city life." Through the years they had "homes" set up in Yurimaguas, on the *Maranatha* for river work, in Cajamarca and Chiclayo, and in the camper they used traversing rugged northern Peru. For the term's first two years they continued dividing their time between jungle and coast/mountains.

Colleen wrote,

> Shortly after returning from our furlough, Bert drove a few of us down to Chiclayo for a women's retreat planned by the ladies of the three assemblies [local Plymouth Brethren churches] there. It was their first experience at this, and they had arranged to have the three-day retreat at a large farmhouse about an hour's drive from Chiclayo. But at the very *last* minute the new owners of the place suddenly decided not to let us use it. Other arrangements were hastily

made by a few who had driven out ahead of the bus. The leaders were told, as we took off from Chiclayo, that we were going to an unknown spot in the center of the town of Chongoyape rather than to the farmhouse. It turned out to be a huge, empty rice warehouse! Can you imagine arriving at about eight p.m. with a busload of fifty tired, hungry, thirsty women (plus a few children!) to an empty warehouse with no lights, no water, no bathroom, no furniture, no kitchen, no *anything* except some foam pads that had been brought out for sleeping and a kerosene stove that they set up the next day? I'm sure in the States we would just have called the whole thing off, but not here! We explained to the women what had happened, decided together to accept the circumstances as from the Lord, ate some dry bread and cheese before stretching out for the night (and took advantage of the darkness for bathroom privileges), and proceeded to have a perfectly wonderful retreat. In fact, they want to make it an annual affair and next time prolong it to *five* days. I should add that we did get the use of one bathroom (?) the next day. We also had water during certain hours each day.

We visited, after being away for several years, the churches in Tambo Grande and Morropón in the northern state of Piura. It's amazing how they continue on with so little help. The Tambo Grande church is more or less status quo, but Morropón is growing and reaching out to other places. It was a real joy to be with them.

Jorge organized the first Mini-cap session in San Pablo, in which leaders from some eleven assemblies participated. It was great to be with them. Five brothers from one of the churches arrived late. They had been engaged in a five-day, fruitful, evangelistic effort in a new area and then walked ten hours across the mountains to join us in San Pablo. Returning to Cajamarca on Sunday afternoon, we came across about ten weary brothers and sisters from Pariamarca who had also been out evangelizing for almost a week— walking long, strenuous hours across the mountains and seeing a number turn to the Lord. Witnessing the sacrificial, spontaneous outreach of these dear believers is one of the most encouraging aspects of our ministry.

The encouraging signs they observed in the coastal and mountain regions were also evident when they returned to the jungle. The nationals continued to make trips up the river to encourage the small churches and to reach into villages previously unreached. Colleen wrote,

We have come back to a church that is alive and growing, but they are making changes that we are observing and wondering about. They are giving more generously than before, but they are taking collections at almost every meeting, something that breaks with our distinctives and is hard to take. The Breaking of Bread is now very structured with a leader of the meeting who only allows for about seven minutes of free participation by others. We feel that it would be an easy step to cut the free time altogether. We are seeking wisdom from the Lord as to just how to give the right guidance to an assembly that is obviously come of age and is a pace setter for many smaller groups. We need your prayers for wisdom.

Bert and Colleen were watching the development of an indigenous church growth movement. Peruvian evangelists and church planters were effectively reaching communities that Bert and Colleen had never even visited. They planned their own conferences for leaders, women, and Bible learning. The missionaries would be invited and sometimes asked to speak, but Peru's own gifted men did much of the preaching. The tension in the preceding excerpt reflects the outgrowth of such a movement. The national church begins to make its own decisions. The missionaries need extra wisdom in guiding a church, which has come of age, to remain true to Scripture while discovering its own identity. Part of that is wrestling with the difference between scriptural truth, denominational traditions, and cultural practice.

Home Bible study

While the nationals were taking a more active role in evangelism and church planting, the aging Elliots were increasingly feeling the demands of itinerant ministry and life in the jungle. Living in the camper for weeks at a time, constantly maintaining the *Maranatha*, climbing up and down muddy river banks, and simply keeping one's balance on the launch were taxing and unnerving.

They found themselves spending quite a bit of time in Trujillo, helping the Osorios in their work. While Trujillo was the first place the Elliots had touched Peruvian soil thirty-nine years earlier, and they frequently traveled through there and often stayed with friends in town, they were seeing it from a new perspective. Through the years the church they visited in Trujillo was in La Esperanza, a poorer outlying section. But the Osorios felt burdened for the largely unreached middle class. These people don't respond to medical/dental clinics or open-air preaching in the central plaza. Nor are they attracted to churches designed for a more rural people with lower economic status. The Elliots had discovered the same phenomenon in Yurimaguas. For years they conducted a Bible study in their home where middle-class friends felt more freedom to ask questions and invite their friends. Some of these came to faith in Christ, but they felt awkward when they attended the church filled with the poor. They weren't guilty of class superiority; overcoming deep cultural differences is a difficult task, especially for those in the minority.

Through friendship evangelism, Jorge and Donna developed a series of home Bible studies that ministered to this middle-class population. Almost all had been raised in the Roman Catholic Church, but their religion had minimal impact on their lives.

The Osorios invited the Elliots to housesit their apartment for two months in early 1988 to sample life in Trujillo. Colleen wrote,

Life and work in a coastal city *is* different than in the smaller towns and rural areas we are used to. We are really enjoying some of the extra conveniences of city life—Osorios' pleasant home and yard, the direct-dial telephone system and daily mail delivery, the nicer stores and market, etc. We especially enjoy the wonderful friends and Monday night Bible study with them here in the home. But how to see them incorporated into a vibrant, functioning church and how to make *more* friends and more contacts—that's the hard part. I'm sure people here are no different than the poorer folk we are used to working with; we just don't feel quite as relaxed with them as yet. Also I think the cultural and religious pressures are stronger perhaps. We felt that a little last Sunday evening when we were invited to the home of one of the ophthalmologists who had visited us in Yurimaguas in November. They asked us over for *cafecito* (coffee), which turned out to be a steak dinner. When we got there, we found that some other friends had dropped in unexpectedly, one of whom was celebrating a birthday and was quite high! They apparently had brought along their own beer to celebrate. As we watched them pass the bottle one to the other and share a common glass as a symbol, I suppose, of comradery [sic] (is that a word?), we felt very much like fish out of water. And I'm sure they were wondering, too, about the two strange fish that had dropped into *their* waters. Later some relatives of the family dropped in, and I began to ask myself what would happen if this doctor and his lovely Japanese wife were to make an open commitment to the Lord. How would it affect all these people and all these customs that are so much a part of their life? It seems like there are so many odds against that happening and against the building of a church among this class of people. Only God . . . !

One aspect of city life we *don't* like is that we always have to be on the alert for thieves and always distrusting anyone we don't know. Some apparently needy person comes to the door for help, and you are warned not to have anything to do with them. Every time you leave the house for a few minutes, you either have to call the caretaker or lock all the doors, set the alarm, and advise the neighbors. Even to walk a few blocks to the corner store, it is best to remove watches and jewelry and carry only the bare essentials. Last week while I was walking to a nearby drugstore, two thieves suddenly came up behind me and snatched the money purse in my hand. A spurt of anger-produced adrenalin (I guess) enabled me to take off after him yelling, "Thief! Thief!" I don't know whether it was the sight of me lumbering around the corner or the fear of what the people on the street might do in response, but he suddenly dropped the purse and took off. I was *very* thankful, because all of the house keys were in it.

Attending a river conference

After much deliberation and prayer, Bert and Colleen decided to move and establish their base of operations in Trujillo by the end of 1988. They returned to Yurimaguas for several months to wrap up their affairs there and say goodbye to the people. Colleen shared how encouraged they were about the Peruvian leaders' initiative:

> We attended a conference in Pelejo that proved to be a very happy and encouraging time. The conference was well organized, well attended by believers from at least ten of the villages, and financed by them as well. They even gave an honorarium to each of the speakers, which included one for Bert and me, too. "Not that we were looking for a gift," but we did rejoice to see this evidence of Christian maturing.[1]

The believers in Yurimaguas decided they wanted to build a Christian camp on the outskirts of town, so they requested a SPRINT

---

1 Scripture quotation paraphrased from Philippians 4:17.

team's help. The team of nineteen helped tremendously get the project off the ground. One of them had a cross-cultural experience he wouldn't soon forget. Colleen wrote, "The SPRINT team had some fish stories, especially the one about Randy, the sixteen-year-old who was bitten on his big toe by a fish known to pack a real wallop. As he howled in pain, the rest of the Sprinters howled with delight when one of the nationals suggested that soaking it in warm urine would stop the pain! As Bert said, 'Nothing like using what's available!'" Within a month after the team left, the nationals held their inaugural session at Road to Emmaus Evangelical Camp.

The Elliots took the *Maranatha* to Iquitos and sold it for fifteen thousand dollars to a Baptist family who continued to use it for planting churches along the Amazon tributaries. One-third of the proceeds were used to support the jungle work. The remainder was set aside to invest in property for building a church in Trujillo. Colleen wrote, "I must confess some feeling of sadness as we left the boat this week. It seems like it's sort of the end of an era, and we will definitely miss the river life, even though we know well that we can't continue on with it."

Then they were faced, as Colleen put it, "with the herculean task of packing, shipping, and disposing of the things we have collected these nearly forty years in Peru. It is also the goodbyes to lifelong friends and very precious brothers and sisters with whom we have worked so long. That's the hardest part."

The next step was to find suitable living accommodations in Trujillo. After much searching, Colleen wrote,

> Bert had felt attracted to a spacious, furnished four-bedroom house we had seen in one of the better districts of Trujillo. He was especially attracted to the owners, who continued to call us. My first reaction was that it was *too* nice. "No," I said, "I really would prefer something simpler where I can put my own furniture and where we can be our ordinary selves! What would our Peruvian brothers and sisters, who have

so little, think? Or our visitors from North America, whose stereotyped image of the way missionaries supposedly live would be smashed completely if they walked into that house!" No, no, no! And besides, the rent was way too high! But eventually the rent wasn't so high, because the owners were so eager to have us as renters that they agreed to come down to half of what they were originally asking. (Likely our age and nationality were in our favor, plus the fact that the landlady thought Bert looked just like Pope John Paul II!) When we told Laura, the owner, that one of our reasons for renting a house in Trujillo was to start having Bible studies with neighbors and friends, she was delighted and told us that for four years a Catholic professor had been conducting a Bible study in their house on Tuesday evenings. She invited us to attend (which we did on three occasions). Jorge, in turn, invited her to attend the Monday night study in their house, which she did. The following week she also brought a friend. By this time I, too, had peace that it was the right house. God had led in so many of the details that it was very confirming.

The Bible studies multiplied, and people made commitments to follow Christ. They began to look for a suitable facility for Sunday services. Colleen wrote,

On October 29, 1988, we and the Osorios made a verbal arrangement to purchase the land and building that Jorge has been looking at for a long time for the multipurpose facility in Trujillo. The land measures more than a thousand square meters (all cemented) and is in a prominent location. There is a large brick-and-concrete two-story building on it that was originally a drive-in restaurant and dance hall. We envision the second-floor dance hall as a chapel auditorium and maybe one classroom, whereas the rooms downstairs would be for the office, kitchen, and dining room or whatever. The Nehemiah team that is due in February will be working on remodeling the building (which is really just a shell) and if possible construct another.

The Nehemiah team was a group of workers from their supporting churches in the Pacific Northwest. When they first saw the site, some of the more experienced construction workers thought it should be bulldozed and begun anew from the ground up. But they removed tons of debris, and with their hard labor the church building began to take shape. Centro Bíblico Trujillo (CBT) was born.

Centro Biblico Trujillo

Soon after Bert and Colleen moved to Trujillo, Pam Zarek joined their missionary team. She was from the Osorio's home church in Portland and worked primarily with women and children. The Elliots appreciated her heart for the Peruvian people and her friendship. She gave the rest of her life to ministry and died in Trujillo in 2019.

Through the years one of the ongoing frustrations for Bert and Colleen was the postal service's undependability. It was plagued by inefficiency, postal strikes, canceled flights, theft, and airports being rebuilt. In addition, because of their seminomadic lifestyle, mail went to numerous locations and was being regularly forwarded. Some letters from the US would take seven days, others four months. Sometimes both coming and going mail was "lost in transit." However, the problem finally became apparent. Colleen wrote,

> The government has discovered a real mafia (is that an English word?) among the postal employees and has discharged about 250 of them, supposedly in Lima. It was discovered that for about a year now they have been opening letters that arrive from outside the country and removed checks, money orders, and what have you. Then with the help of certain "friends" in banks or money exchange offices they cash and pocket the dollars and just destroy the letters, I guess. They are trying to get a stiffer jail sentence for them than what has been the norm in the past, but I kind of wonder if they will carry through with that. I hope they really make it stiff and also carry their investigations to some of the post offices in the provinces. I'm just sure there must be some dishonest employees in Cajamarca, because it seems strange that we generally get most of the mail that is sent to Yurimaguas. The employees there may be slow, but I think they are fairly honest.

After the Elliots moved to Trujillo, they kept abreast of pressures from communists and the drug cartel on the jungle churches. Colleen wrote,

> It is alarming to see the way coca production and drug trafficking has increased just since our last visit to the jungle in March [1987]. There is now more money in circulation and lots of new boats and outboards in evidence, but I'm afraid most of the money is being spent on liquor and

vice. It's sad to see so much drunkenness, and people are very hard. One hears the sound of the small drug-carrying planes in the predawn hours nearly every morning, and high-powered speedboats pass by on the river in the middle of the night. One night a boat tied up right next to ours at 1:30 a.m. The occupants gave a low whistle, which was answered by a similar whistle. Then, in a muted conversation but loud enough for us to hear, the transaction was made for a "couple kilos," and they took off. The believers who refuse to grow coca (and so far most of them refuse to grow it) are often threatened. I'm sure it will become increasingly hard to keep from joining the crowd. Pray that the Lord will give them courage and stamina to stand against evil in these increasingly difficult times.

In a subsequent letter Colleen noted, "One of the latest problems comes from a small village upriver from Yurimaguas, where the drug traffickers asked the town authorities to make a clandestine airport. These in turn are trying to force the believers to help them make it. Some of the brothers are considering moving elsewhere, which of course would be very costly."

Bert and Colleen were aware of the imminent danger to their lives from both the drug traffickers and communist terrorists. They prayerfully considered whether they should evacuate. As American missionaries they were attractive targets, but they became convinced they were right where God had called them to serve regardless of the inherent dangers.

Several incidents illustrate the impact of terrorist activity. The first three happened while the Elliots still lived in Yurimaguas. The others occurred after they had relocated to Trujillo. Bert recounted,

A leftist-led strike paralyzed Yurimaguas for eighteen days. They were demanding a paved road, a new hospital, and other things that the whole town wants, but it was obvious that the left was flexing its muscles and eroding the people's confidence in the government. It is scary to see how easily they have mobilized the masses and taken control of the town—communications, transport, commerce, municipal offices—everything! Even the market!

Convention in the Yurimaguas church

This month another communist group, called Tupac Amaru, attacked Juanjuy, about two hundred miles upriver from us. We understand they killed some policemen and injured others. Then they pillaged a number of stores and gave the contents to the people. They are apparently not as violent as the Shining Path group and present a sort of Robin Hood approach. Their presence in the area has brought police reinforcement to Yurimaguas as well, so we are conscious again of the clenched fist lifting itself up against the established authority. Even in the villages upriver the atheists are working hard. It is increasingly difficult to get people to listen to the good news. We are thankful that there are little groups of believers in the majority of the towns and some developing leaders, but they seem so few and so weak compared to the adverse political machine they must face. I was encouraged this morning by the words of King Asa in 2 Chronicles 14:11 [NIV], "LORD, there is no one like you to help the *powerless* against the *mighty*. Help us, O LORD our God, for we rely on *you* . . . . Do not let man prevail against you" [emphasis Bert's]. As the storm escalates around us, we ask for your earnest prayers that we may be low enough, small enough, humble enough for the Lord to show Himself strong on our behalf.

Colleen wrote, about the impact of terrorists on their friends,

Our neighbors up next to where Jorge and Donna used to live have a small print shop. At the beginning of the week they installed a new copy machine. Since the [terrorist-initiated] strike started, they have been working behind closed doors, because *nothing* is supposed to be open and no employees working. But this lady is a friend, and she agreed to copy these letters for me this morning. When I was there getting this done, a band of strikers started pounding on their door and told her, if she didn't shut down their press and close up the shop within five minutes, they would nail the door shut or damage the property in some way. They told our brother Julio the same thing. He explained he was making a coffin for someone who had died and asked them how they expected folks to bury their dead if he didn't work. But it's impossible to reason with them. They think they are fighting for a just cause, and they are trying to force everyone to join in. I keep wondering how long they will manage to stick it out, because groups take turns even at night marching through the streets and keeping watch at strategic points to make sure there is no traffic of cars, boats, or whatever. The authorities keep coming up with solutions for the things they are asking for, but we think terrorists don't really want any solutions. They just want to keep stirring up hatred in the masses for the government and ruling party.

Some two hundred believers from the assemblies upriver from Yurimaguas were enjoying a happy time together at their biannual conference in the village of Huimba, when a group of about thirty heavily armed, hooded terrorists invaded the town. The believers were able to continue their conference without interruption. There was no violence during that time. But the presence of that many armed, unscrupulous men (and women) in the village proved a very frightening experience and undoubtedly caused the prayers of the Christians to ascend with greater fervency and urgency than usual!

After moving to Trujillo, the Elliots continued to receive reports from the jungle. Colleen wrote,

A couple of policemen were killed in Yurimaguas in broad daylight, right near the main plaza, and folks are constantly being threatened. But Guillermo said the tenseness of the situation there is causing many folks to listen to the gospel who wouldn't listen before. They are seeing lots of blessing in the church. Please pray for our dear friends in Yurimaguas.

And about six months later Colleen wrote,

The communist group MRTA attacked Yurimaguas at four a.m. They blew up one whole block of buildings just off the main square, about three blocks from our old house, plus some other public buildings. They were not able to capture the navy base, but they took over the police station and emptied the jail, etc. They called the town together to the plaza for a public "judgment," with the idea apparently to

271

execute some policemen, but refrained from this when the people with one accord asked for their release. About six people died during the course of the five hour attack, but none of the believers were injured.

Colleen described the believers' response, a time of prayer and fasting:

> The main purpose of the fast was to pray for our needy country [Peru] and the people who are suffering in the red zones. Apparently more than five hundred evangelical Christians have lost their lives—in the south mostly—to say nothing of Catholic workers, etc. It is sobering to think about. The other night Gordon phoned from Lima and said that the US embassy had advised the heads of missions to tell their missionaries to sort of lay low and try to be as "inconspicuous" as possible this week especially. Today is the birthday of the president of Shining Path, and there were reports that they planned to "celebrate" with some extra violence and bloodshed. Trujillo is still quiet and peaceful, for which we are very thankful. It is just a bit difficult for people like ourselves (and Pam) to try to make ourselves inconspicuous!

Peru was experiencing incredibly difficult days. Added to communist terrorists and drug traffickers were a major cholera epidemic, hyperinflation, and economic instability. Colleen wrote, "Our local newspaper reported last week that during 1991 some six thousand Trujillanos had left Peru for other countries. We believe it, because just from our small Centro Bíblico family there has been quite an exodus—to Italy, Spain, the US, Canada, Venezuela, New Zealand, and soon even Japan."

Meanwhile life for the Elliots continued. Colleen wrote,

I knew there were days when we felt like we were one hundred years old [they were in their early sixties], but I didn't know we *looked* that old until one of our young Peruvian guests prayed one morning during devotions something like this: "Lord, You know that we are just starting our ministry, whereas the Elliots are finishing theirs and are just waiting for You to call them into Your presence any minute!" Hmm . . . ! We didn't know whether to add an amen to that prayer or not! (Decided not to!)

Last month we had to get involved in a very sad situation. A young woman from Yurimaguas [daughter of well-known believers from Papaplaya] and her eighteen-month-old son were both killed one evening when a bus struck them as they were crossing a busy street in the center of Trujillo. This girl had been baptized as a teenager and then had gotten away from the Lord when she had this affair with a schoolteacher. Shortly after that she came to Trujillo to work as a maid, and her baby was born over here. We brought a letter to her from her parents when we came from the jungle the end of November, but then we didn't see her for several months. But she had our address and telephone number. Two weeks before she was killed she came to see us, bringing her cute little boy, Erick. She came wanting counsel regarding some problems in her work, but most of all she seemed to really want to straighten out her relationship with the Lord. We were able to pray with her and listen to her as she called on the Lord for forgiveness. It was almost as if the Lord was preparing her for her sudden and unexpected death two weeks later. None of her family, of course, made it for the funeral, so we felt the responsibility to represent them at the wake and the burial, where Bert spoke lovingly and clearly of her faith and the message she had believed.

Stan Pence had led Jorge to Christ in 1975 and introduced him to Bert and Colleen. Stan then completed his training as a medical doctor and joined a medical practice in Portland. In 1991 he took his family to Trujillo to explore the possibility of becoming part of the missionary team and to work with the medical community in Trujillo. The Elliots, Osorios, and Pences had been praying about this for years. During the Penses' visit Colleen wrote,

> Stan has been kept very busy giving lectures on surgery in the different hospitals and also giving messages by interpretation at the Bible studies and chapel meetings. Stan's wife, Sharon, has the advantage of knowing Spanish. She had several craft

Bert with Jorge

classes with the women. Everyone loves them and their three lovely children. The Peruvian doctors have offered him their support when he returns in a year or so on a permanent basis. He plans to teach surgery part-time and build friendships with the doctors and their families, while helping with the spiritual aspect of the work at CBT.

Bert and Colleen were thrilled to see a strong missionary team forming in Trujillo, including Penses, Osorios, and Pam Zarek, all from Portland. The Elliots had been sent by Grace and Truth, the Penses by Cascade Community Church, and the Osorios and Pam by Spring Mountain Bible Church. The team was enhanced by key Peruvian leaders.

The Elliots embraced the Plymouth Brethren distinctives of shared, decentralized leadership by multiple leaders and the autonomy of each local church. Because CBT grew successfully around these distinctives, it was becoming the base for a church-planting movement in northern Peru.

In spring 1992, Colleen discovered a lump on her breast, which turned out to be cancerous. So the Elliots returned to Portland for her surgery and full recovery.

17

Collegio Cristiano Elliot

The Elliots' return to Trujillo in January 1993 renewed their joy in seeing God continuing to work through the ministry at Centro Bíblico Trujillo to draw people to Himself. The home Bible studies were ministering to real needs. Many accepted Jesus Christ as their Savior and were baptized. But in the midst of these spiritual victories arose the dark shadows of divisiveness. Where God is doing His greatest work, Satan loves to do his greatest damage.

While in Lima to renew his passport, Jorge was introduced to a Guatemalan who pastored a church in Callao, near Lima. He invited Jorge and Donna to visit his church for an evening service. Colleen wrote,

> Apparently Jorge was quite impressed with their joyful worship. Right then and there he decided to invite the pastor up to Trujillo to give a workshop on worship at the three-week Capacitación Bíblica course. Fortunately that didn't happen. The pastor called during our first week and

said he wanted to bring fifty people from his church with him for the workshop. Jorge told him we already had seventy people living on the premises here, and there was no way we could accommodate fifty more. So it was then that they made arrangements to come for three nights following Capacitación Bíblica. Well, Ray Benz [Colleen's brother-in-law from Seattle] and Jack Mackie [an electrician friend from Portland who made fifteen trips to Peru over the years] were here for the first meeting. Jack only lasted about five minutes before taking off for the office. I lasted about ten minutes before joining him there. It wasn't too long before Ray and Bert also followed suit and we went home. I didn't go to the other two meetings, but Bert went the next night just to hear the message so he would know what the man was teaching. He felt it was not a correct interpretation of the Scriptures at all, because he was using that verse in Hebrews 12:12 about weak knees and fallen arms to get the people to raise their hand in praise to God and dance with their feet. This is precisely what everyone was supposed to do. It not only looked a bit wild but was also very noisy. They brought huge speakers and amplifiers. I really wonder what our neighbors must have thought. The first night our people were surprised and confused. By the second night many of the young people especially were beginning to like it. By the third night they were dancing with great gusto along with the visitors. I guess that is the scary part of it all to us, along with the fact that Pam and the Osorios were very favorably impressed, as was Cecilio and a number of others.

The style of music at CBT had had a definite Latin flavor, using guitars, keyboards, drums, and contemporary choruses, some translated from English and others originally written in Spanish. So the music was already upbeat and contemporary. But this group introduced a very different style that included flamboyant dancing in front and up and down the aisles. While the form of worship was one issue, the greater concern was the division that erupted immediately, both in the church and among the missionaries. Colleen continued,

> The following Sunday (after the group had left, of course) Jorge spoke and made a plea for liberty, the liberty to worship as one feels led. Some will want to raise their hands and move their bodies and dance with their feet, others will not want to. We honestly don't know what will come of it all, but to say we are concerned is putting it mildly. It just seems like this could be a very divisive issue. Probably better not to talk about our problems with too many until we know what is going to come of it all. We honestly can't understand Jorge. This seems like such a turnaround in his strategy and workings with the middle-class people of Trujillo. We had the missionaries over for supper, and when we tried to discuss some of these issues it was pretty bad. We just desperately need your prayers if we are to work together harmoniously. Satan will do all in his power, I'm sure, to divide us.

Bert reflected on the tension in a family letter:

> The tense times have come partly because of a visit from fifty members of a church in Callao who taught and practiced dancing as part of their corporal expression of praise to the Lord. Some of our coworkers and most of the young people think it is wonderful and speak of a new joy and liberty in worship. We and some others in the congregation find it distracting and disorderly. So the Enemy has brought into our happy family fellowship an element of confusion and tension that we are trying to work through. Please pray that the Lord would give us all wisdom and humble hearts that will find the solution and restore the harmony and peace.

Colleen wrote,

> Things here have calmed down a bit in the church, though
> there is still some tension and hard feelings between the
> missionaries that we need to work on. Pray that the Lord
> will help us to be peacemakers. A couple weeks ago we had a
> session with some of the leaders at Centro Biblico, as well as
> some of the young people, in order to discuss and evaluate this
> latest trend (dancing, etc.) in the worship style. It was most
> interesting to hear the comments and evaluations of these
> folks. I think Jorge was surprised at the negative reactions
> of several of them. The session lasted until about 1:30 a.m.
> It was decided then that both sides would give a bit. The
> young people are going to respect the feelings of the older
> folks, especially with regards to the Lord's Supper. The older
> ones are to allow some freedom to the young people in their
> expressions of praise. Now at least the young people are not
> in the forefront on things, dancing and moving about with
> their hands raised, etc., as they were for a while. I think some
> of them still practice this at the back of the auditorium, but I
> don't look around to watch and therefore am not distracted
> in my own worship. It's not a perfect solution to the issue,
> but it's the one the Peruvian believers decided on, and we
> respect it. We certainly don't want to be guilty of holding
> on to our old styles and traditions just for tradition's sake.
> But we do see dangers in this more emotional trend, which
> seems to us to lead to superficiality.

While this situation was developing in Trujillo, we at Grace and
Truth became aware of the problematic attitudes and behaviors of
one of our other missionaries living in Iquitos. Fellow elder Wayne
Wiley and I traveled there to meet with him. Wayne, son of Claire
Wiley (introduced in an earlier chapter), had grown up with his
family in Mexico and spent six years in Ecuador. His fluency in

Spanish and extensive missionary experience proved invaluable in this tense situation with our errant brother. Bert flew to join and support us. The brother was unresponsive to our concerns and direction, but I was impressed to see firsthand the depth of Bert's love, patience, and grace with him.

Wayne and I then traveled to Trujillo, looking forward to relief from the previous week's tension and anticipating rich fellowship with Uncle Bert and Aunt Colleen and other missionaries there. Wayne had been in Trujillo before, an integral part of the Nehemiah team in 1989. But this was my first visit to Peru, and I was filled with anticipation. It was several days before we realized the tension among the Trujillo missionaries.

The situation exposed some fundamental questions related to ministry and missionary work. The middle-class church in Trujillo was Jorge and Donna's vision. The other missionaries joined with them as part of that vision. But did that give Jorge carte blanche authority to make unilateral decisions regarding worship practices in the church, especially in a group that values multiple leadership to discuss and evaluate anticipated changes? Should he not have worked through the proposed changes with the leadership team before presenting it to the congregation? By presenting it to the congregation first, he planted the seeds of divisiveness, and they quickly sprouted.

The Elliots found themselves in an awkward position. They deeply loved all the people involved and were by nature peacemakers. They were reluctant to interfere with Jorge's initiative. And rather than adhering to mere human tradition, they remained open to the Spirit's leading regarding appropriate expressions of worship. But from their study of Scripture, they discerned Jorge's method was neither biblical nor appropriate.

In addition, their name was quickly becoming associated with a practice of which they disapproved. "Do you know what they're doing in the church the Elliots attend?" By the time Wayne and I arrived, news of the controversy had already spread to churches and missionary colleagues elsewhere in Peru. Because of the Elliots' influence and the impact of Capacitación Bíblica, CBT had quickly become a model church. Fellow missionaries and Peruvian leaders trusted Bert and Colleen but disagreed with this new phenomenon that had been introduced at CBT. Money to build CBT had come largely through their contacts, and now it seemed Bert and Colleen's convictions about church polity were being ignored. In fact, because of the Elliots' desire not to be divisive, it looked as though they endorsed these changes.

The four primary missionary families in Trujillo were affiliated with Christian Missions in Many Lands, the Plymouth Brethren mission organization, which believes each missionary is sent by and answers to their specific sending church and its elders. As described in the preceding chapter, these four families had been sent from three different local churches in Portland, with four other Portland churches also highly invested.

Consequently, Wayne and I—from Grace and Truth—did not have the authority to speak for the elders of the other Portland churches. In fact, we realized each of the three sending churches would probably agree with the perspective of its missionary, and the controversy in Peru could easily have caused a spirit of divisiveness among our churches back in the States. So we encouraged the missionaries to continue to work toward resolution in Peru. Was that the best advice? I'm not certain. But I know the danger to our US churches was real.

Eventually the nontraditional group's influence diminished, resolving the problem, but not before some long-term friendships and ministry dreams were fractured. Was this worship experiment worth the cost? I don't think so. May the Lord forgive us for not recognizing sooner the need "to preserve the unity of the Spirit in the bond of peace" (Ephesians 4:3). Scripture doesn't prohibit change. But it calls for a loving, thoughtful, well-planned path of change, guided by the Holy Spirit.

Bert with men's Bible studies

In spite of the tension, I loved my initial visit to Peru. The people were overwhelmingly friendly. It was a thrill to watch Bert and Colleen greeting and loving people in their home, in the church, and on the streets. Their impact on these individuals was obvious.

Stan, Jorge, Bert, Wayne, Rueben, and I took a trip up one valley to hold a medical clinic, crossing a suspension footbridge over a river. As we entered the village, Stan pointed to several dead guinea pigs strung out on a clothesline and said, "That's our lunch!" He was right. Stan attended to the medical needs, Jorge cared for eyes, and Bert pulled teeth while Wayne and Rueben visited with the villagers. I held Bert's dental patients' heads still. This meaningful experience gave me a glimpse into the nature of the Elliots' earlier years.

I was privileged to preach in a couple of services with Bert interpreting. If not for Bert's humility and graciousness, that could have been intimidating!

During this visit I first met two remarkable Peruvian high schoolers. David Rengifo and Pablo Cenepo-Torres were living with Bert and Colleen as their "adopted" sons. Their families' circumstances prevented them from living at home, so they asked the Elliots to take them in. Instant parents! David was a talented musician who helped lead music at the church. Amazingly, Colleen had helped deliver baby Pablo in the jungle years before. The Elliots loved these two and poured their lives into them.

Two memorable trips highlighted this term in Peru. Bert went by himself on the first during July 1993, invited by a group of church leaders in Argentina. Here is his account of the fifteen-day trip, in which he spoke twenty times:

> I went from our rather mild Peruvian winter weather into below-zero temperatures in Argentina. I was met in Buenos Aires by one of Benito Bongara's sons and taken to the home of that happy Argentine family. They seemed to all talk at once. The different pronunciation of the "LL" kept me guessing for some time as to what was being said. Buenos Aires is about 50 percent Italian extraction, so I was fed many new-to-me kinds of Italian dishes plus strong coffee and very Argentine soda water. The next day I spoke for the first time in one of the large assemblies. The auditorium would seat over four hundred, but midweek there were only about two hundred out. Wonderful people, very warm and appreciative, and very active serving the Lord. This assembly operates a large primary and secondary school with a total student body of about 2,500. They say about 50 percent of the members of the church have been drawn in through the school. One of the elders gives full-time to the spiritual life of the school, and all the teachers have a text to meditate on

each day and include in each class session. They also operate five boarding schools in depressed areas in different parts of Argentina, each with seventy students, to whom they give board, room, and clothing through high school.

On Friday of that first week they sent me to the other side of the country to a missionary conference in a smaller assembly in a place called La Banda, Santiago del Estero. It was a busy but happy weekend with folks coming from several assemblies in the area. The assemblies there are about thirty years ahead of us in Peru. They all seem to have annexes with Sunday School classes and midweek meetings, which keep all the members busy serving the Lord. After that conference I had a free Monday before the missionary retreat started. So a lovely family drove me to the next state, Tucuman, to visit some Peruvian friends and deliver gifts from their family. It was very scenic. From Tuesday to Friday we had studies on the temple (a very beautiful model of it) and missions with about forty people. This took place in one of their out-schools that was on vacation. I met some wonderful people there, too, and was challenged as I sought to challenge them with the words of our Lord Jesus, to love Him above all else and through that love reach out to others. On Saturday I flew back to Buenos Aires for another busy weekend of meetings and making the acquaintance of more wonderful people before heading home, full of gratitude to the Lord for a marvelous trip and anxious to see my lovely wife again in Trujillo.

Colleen wrote of the trip,

I received several nice letters and small gifts from folks in Argentina who expressed their deep appreciation for Bert's ministry. One lady wrote that his messages were straight from heaven. It was really cold there (seven or eight below zero [Fahrenheit]) and only an occasional electric heater or fireplace to help the cold. Before he left, I had phoned Cajamarca and asked Andy to look for some thermal underwear. The only thing they could find was one of my thermal vests that I had purchased in England and a pair of long, black thermal bloomers (underpants) that Betty sent me once for use in high altitudes. Well, I sent these along with Bert. He said he used them nearly every day. I'm just glad he didn't have a heart attack or accident or something. It might have been a bit embarrassing, but he said they did help a lot to keep him warm. Bert was very impressed with the caliber of believers in Argentina and the progress of the work there.

The second trip could be called the Elliot Reunion Tour. It was actually a series of trips interspersed among other events of 1993. Colleen wrote,

When we returned to Peru [from the US] earlier this year, we had decided to try and visit the places we used to visit before we moved here and that we have neglected because the starting of the Bible Center in Trujillo had us pretty well committed for almost five years. We started our visits spending several weeks in May in Cajamarca and returning again in August for a large conference in the high mountains. There were about 1,500 people. The brothers provided twenty sheep and two cows as meat for the meals. The last Sunday sixty-four new believers were baptized in the cold waters of that high mountain river. The same Sunday six were baptized in Cajamarca and the next day in Trujillo (a holiday) nine more. It's encouraging to see people turning to the Lord and others growing in Him and taking greater responsibility.

In September it was exciting to return to Yurimaguas for the first time since we left five years ago. The brothers put us in our old home and kept us busy with meetings in the different churches, dinner invitations, and a constant stream of visitors at our door for counsel or medical help. It was like old times! We found that one of the newly formed churches of a different Christian tradition in town had been influencing several of the brothers from the main assembly in their particular interpretations of the Scriptures, so we dedicated many of our meetings to teaching on that subject. We also had a day at the camp with all the leaders who wanted to attend and gave ministry and answered questions about these teachings. Yesterday we had a phone call from one of the elders there, who said things have calmed down now and people seem to be more content. It was a real treat for us to be able to return to the familiar surroundings of Yurimaguas, see our old friends, and eat again some of the jungle cuisine, though I must say we did not enjoy the oppressive heat that we lived in so many years. The cool sea breeze in Trujillo has us spoiled.

Early in October we drove north to Piura and inland to the town of Morropón, where we spent a week teaching and celebrating the twenty-fifth anniversary of the assembly, which is growing and faithful to the Lord. Perhaps that was the hardest place where we started a church, and the first believers were the ones who really suffered. But they carried on amidst the persecution, the Lord added to their numbers, and now they are working together and growing. They presented us with a silver platter engraved with our names, the years 1968–1993, and the words "Because the seed sown has germinated and the fruits have increased, many thanks, beloved brother and sister." It was a very special time.

While in Argentina Bert was impressed with the impact of the Christian schools he observed there and began to share that vision. In April 1994, Colleen wrote,

The brothers in Yurimaguas have modified parts of their chapel building in order to start a Christian grade school. It is the first assembly I know of in Peru that has done this. They named it after the New Zealand missionary who is buried there, Edjar J. Burns. They have about ninety students enrolled for the school year that began this month. The school is the result of the vision of Roger Alvan [birthed before Bert's similar inspiration in Argentina]. He had a serious accident that caused him to be a paraplegic. Following the accident he finished his teacher training and bears the heavy burden of responsibility for the school. They also have an evening Bible school program.

Lord willing, we will be sending one of our Peruvian workers to Argentina for six months to study how the schools are run in the assemblies there, with the hope of starting one in Trujillo soon. The second floor of our new building would be used for this. We would appreciate your prayers that the Lord will bless and guide in this.

Stan and Sharon Pense moved back to Portland in June 1994. For several years he had been monitoring Bert's prostate specific antigen

(PSA) level. As the level increased, the Elliots decided to return to Portland in August 1994 for surgery to remove Bert's prostate. Enter Henry, a seven-year-old from Cajamarca with a badly deformed and useless arm. Stan had taken an interest in his case and lined up a hospital and doctors stateside to perform corrective surgery. It was quite a different experience for Bert and Colleen to become this young boy's "parents" while he was in the States. Both surgeries went well, and all returned to Peru after Christmas.

In preparing for another term in Peru, Colleen wrote, "We are trying to pay more attention to the two *great* commandments and are happy to be in a kingdom whose law is love."

———————◦•◦◆◦•◦———————

Among the biggest events and challenges of Bert and Colleen's thirteenth term was founding the Collegio Cristiano Elliot, using the facility at Centro Bíblico Trujillo. The Peruvians chose the name in memory of Bert's brother Jim. This grew from Bert's vision, seeded in Argentina. Bert remembered losing people from the church after they put their children in Catholic schools, because there were no evangelical schools. The church sent one of the brothers from CBT to observe the Argentine schools, and he in turn invited Argentine teachers to the Trujillo church to encourage and challenge them to start the school. They began classes in 1995 and finished the first school year with eight students. They added a grade each year until it offered all twelve grades and enrolled about 250 students. It used curriculum from A. C. E. School of Tomorrow with its God-centered program and accreditation by the Peruvian school system. Because of a steady flow of volunteers from the US who were willing to help, one of its strengths was offering English courses taught by native English speakers.

The school presented a set of opportunities and trials entirely different from those the Elliots were used to. The facility needed ongoing upgrades and expansion to keep up with the school's growth. It was an ongoing challenge to provide funds sufficient for facility maintenance, helping families who couldn't afford tuition, and keeping the school solvent. Bert wrote in the *Christian Missions in Many Lands* magazine regarding the school,

> Problems! Someone has aptly said that the only place where there aren't any is in the cemetery. We have had problems

Founding staff and some students of the Elliot Christian school

> with children, with parents and with teachers—some bad enough to make me want to close the school. But then I realized that the problem itself isn't the real issue, it's how you handle it that makes the school Christian. So we have people in the church who pray specifically for this, especially a group of sisters who meet Thursday afternoons to pray.[1]

Watching the school grow and seeing the impact on so many students' lives brought tremendous joy through the years. It was not a step the Elliots had previously envisioned. Bert wrote, "Schools

---

1 Bert Elliot, "Wildest Dreams," *Christian Missions in Many Lands*, December 1999, 9.

never were my favorite places, [but] I have seen the hand of God continually working through the school."[2]

In November 1995 the Elliots made a trip to Colombia at Jim and Sharon Fleming's invitation to speak at a missionary retreat. On the return trip they stopped in Quito, Ecuador, to visit missionaries. Of that visit Bert wrote,

> Lloyd Rodgers [missionary to Ecuador from Portland] flew me into the jungle, where we visited several Auca (Waodani) villages. At a new airstrip where Steve Saint is presently living I met three of the men who killed our men at "Palm Beach." What a joy to embrace them sincerely in the love of the Lord Jesus and tell them that Jim would do the same if he were present. All three are faithful Christians now, serving the Lord in their community. We saw Palm Beach and also Rachel Saint's home and grave [she had died just one year earlier, in November 1994]. It was an exciting day, and I shall always be thankful to Lloyd and the MAF pilot who made it possible.

Two months later, January 8, 1996 marked the fortieth anniversary of the five men's martyrdom. Lars and Elisabeth (Elliot) Gren, with her daughter, Valerie, and husband Walter Shepard, were present for the commemoration. Walt and Valerie's son Walter III, who had been living with Bert and Colleen for the past six months, traveled up by bus and joined them.

After considering all these large events, it's good to remember the continuous flow of visitors and guests through the Elliots' home. Many came for prayer and counsel. Others came for medical attention. Bert and Colleen often housed people who came from the mountains or jungle for major surgery in Trujillo. Their needs were diverse—repairing a cleft palate, removing a brain tumor, or amputating an infected leg. They not only made arrangements for

---

2   Ibid.

the procedures, but often helped with the funding as well. Stewards Ministries in the US helped with such needs on an ongoing basis. Bert wrote,

> There are many things that cool our souls as well. A couple weeks ago, while I was in the bank, thieves forced the lock on the car and stole the radio, jack, and tools. That's about the sixth time the car has been robbed in as many months. Worse than that are the many counseling sessions with different individuals that open our eyes to the suffering going on all around us. I have wept with at least three husbands this month who can't find sufficient work to support their families, with others who have marital problems, and still others with serious medical problems. And so we try to be a help, often just by listening and praying with them.

But in the midst of the heartache was always cause for rejoicing. Colleen wrote,

> Our meetings at Centro Bíblico are not terribly orthodox. We usually allow time for spontaneous prayer before breaking the bread. We use a cordless microphone for this, so folks can hear. All of a sudden in the midst of the prayer time we heard this little quivering child's voice come over the mic saying, "Thank you, Lord, because my Daddy is here with us in the Centro Bíblico." It was *so* refreshing, and I could wish some of the older ones were as spontaneous.

Bert described how the gospel continued to impact individuals' lives:

> I wish you could have heard Maggie's testimony as we stood together in the water for her baptism. For more than three years, through many stormy sessions involving a serious

Ministering with the people at Centro Biblico

Centro Biblico conference

accident in her car that killed a person and injured others, the early death of her first grandson, and many years of conflict and unhappiness in her marriage, she finally came to "simple" faith in our Lord Jesus. As I looked out over the audience, I saw many were shedding tears of joy. An ex-communist university professor was also baptized that same day, filling our hearts with gratitude to God.

293

The complexion of the missionary community changed when Jorge and Donna Osorio decided to leave Peru permanently in March 1996 to help plant Hispanic churches in the Portland area. They were certainly missed.

October 1996 found Bert and Colleen in Bolivia, invited by their nephew Steve Hawthorne and his wife, Mary. They spoke at a conference for missionaries and Bolivian workers in Cochabamba. Bert's assignment was to speak on revival. Colleen wrote, "After all his concerns about having to speak on the subject of revival at the conference, he kind of just laid aside the notes he had tried to make and spoke from his heart and from the Word. I can't remember when I have ever heard him speak more powerfully."

They toured the Hawthornes' beautiful city of Sucre, visited the clinic where Steve worked, and preached in their church. When Bert went to Potosi to preach several times, it was a good thing Steve sent along an oxygen bottle to help him cope with the fourteen-thousand-foot altitude. Bert wasn't sure how he would have endured the meetings without it.

For Peruvians, birthdays are times for celebration—to the point that Bert and Colleen almost dreaded their birthdays. Such fanfare was made, every group of friends wanting to throw a special party. Of one such gathering Colleen wrote,

A little seven-year-old boy stood on the platform clutching the microphone and said he wanted to dedicate some words and a prayer for *Don Heriberto's* seventy-second birthday (everyone howled at this point, because some of them are a bit touchy about telling their age). Then he began to pray as if he had been doing it all his life and thanked the Lord because he and his parents were now coming to Centro Biblico and that *el Hermano Heriberto* had helped his parents, and they were now together and acting better. Then he said, "Please give *Hermano Heriberto* many more years and birthdays, and keep him from the devil and from the lake of fire. . . . Amen."

It was a bit hard to keep a straight face, but at the same time it was pretty moving.

This term in Peru brought a revolution in the Elliots' method of correspondence. Long gone were the days of the manual typewriter stuffed with seven sets of thin sheets of paper and carbon to produce a family letter. They were thrilled as they graduated from the word processor to the fax machine to the computer and finally to the advent of email!

Back row: Steve (and Mary) Hawthorne, (Andrea) Hawthorne (husband Jim was absent due to ministry responsibilities), Beth (and Craig) Ewoldt, (Walt and) Valerie Shepard, (Gilbert and) Sue Gleason, Jean (and Paul) Goodrich, (Patti and) Jim Elliot. Front row: Jane and Jerry Hawthorne, Bert and Colleen Elliot, Lars and Elisabeth Elliot Gren, Ruby Elliot. Names in parentheses indicate third generation related to the Elliots by marriage.

Prompted by our invitation to a reunion of Fred and Clara Elliot's descendants, Bert and Colleen decided to come to Portland for a brief furlough for the summer of 1997. We enjoyed several days together in Manzanita on the beautiful Oregon coast. The second generation (Fred and Clara's children and their spouses) was represented by Ruby Elliot, Bert and Colleen, Lars and Elisabeth

Gren, and Jerry and Jane Hawthorne. Seven of Fred and Clara's eight grandchildren, with their spouses, were able to attend, in addition to about thirty great grandchildren. We sang praises to God, reflected on the Word, gained insight from our senior members, relished the fellowship, and appreciated the heritage God entrusted to us. Aunt Betty regaled us with her rendition of the "Wide Mouthed Frog," to the delight of all the grandchildren. We also asked her to instruct us on purity. We told stories, the children performed skits, and laughter abounded. Uncle Bert and Aunt Colleen thoroughly enjoyed every minute.

This was their first visit to Portland since Grace and Truth changed its name to Grace Bible Fellowship the previous year. They embraced the change but found themselves habitually using the old name.

While in Portland, Bert and Colleen decided to sell 7272. Although they appreciated the rental income it generated, the house was a burden. Every furlough saw them dealing with problems and regular maintenance, such as reroofing, replacing the front steps, installing electrical panels, and other projects. They also thought that, while they were in Peru, they were imposing on the Benzes and Sue and me to handle problems and finances and deal with renters.

Bert and Colleen offered the house for sale to all family members. None expressed interest except Sue and I. We had outgrown our home and decided 7272 would better meet our family's needs, so we purchased it. Whenever Bert and Colleen came home on furloughs, we always tried to make the basement apartment available. It gave them some independence and allowed us to care for them and enjoy most meals together. Colleen wrote, "We are *so* glad we made the decision to sell and they decided to buy it. It is very comforting to Bert especially to know that dear old house with all its memories is continuing on in the family."

18

Double Jubilee

To think we are called to be the fullness of God! To be in living union with Him who loves us and is filling us with His love so that all our actions are born and executed by Him and for Him. . . . My spirit longs to enter more fully into that reality with each passing day.

—Bert Elliot

Upon returning to Peru in November 1997, Colleen wrote, "After all the feelings of 'culture shock' I experienced in Lima [after returning from the US], when we got to Trujillo everything was okay, especially when we met with all those wonderful people at the Monday night Bible study. Bert said to me afterwards, 'This is where we belong.' I fully agreed."

Life soon fell into the routine of the non-routine—people coming from the mountains and jungles with severe medical problems, interpersonal struggles in the church and school, guests at most meals, constant preaching and teaching opportunities, trips to places like Chiclayo, Cajamarca, and Yurimaguas, and the challenge of housing the constant flow of people. Many of the school's English teachers from the States lived with the Elliots for extended periods. Colleen frequently wrote about her appreciation for Conchi, an indispensable Peruvian lady who helped with housekeeping and cooking. She wrote, "Bert loves company, and I think he'd have the whole world here if he possibly could. But I have to get him to stop and think about the logistics of just where he intends to put them."

Trujillo is known internationally as the "City of the Eternal Spring" due to its mild desert climate with sunny and pleasant weather year round. The average high temperature during summer months (December to March) is in the midseventies Fahrenheit, and in the winter (July to September) it is right at seventy degrees. The average annual rainfall is less than a quarter inch! Even though it is on the coast, it looks like a desert.

El Niño has a major impact on the weather in Trujillo. It is a prolonged warming of the sea surface temperatures in the Pacific Ocean and results in an abundance of rainfall. A strong *El Niño* occurred in summer 1997–1998, causing extensive flooding. Colleen wrote,

> The devastation is really impressive with big slices gouged out of the highway, and houses and chicken farms were completely swept away. There are hundreds of families in the district of Florencia de Mora who lost everything. The whole city has a muddy, dirty look. There is lots of dust around as the mud begins to dry. There was a cemetery for poor people below where the dike broke. Lots of coffins, dead bodies, bones, etc., were floating around Trujillo for a while. The city has employed soldiers to pick up and rebury the bodies! All this contributes to the contamination around the city these days.

The young people at CBT collected food and clothing to take to the flood victims. Used clothing was shipped down from the States. Christian Missions in Many Lands sent funds to help. Ministry teams made multiple trips up the valley above Trujillo to help, as Bert put it, "some of the new little villages made of mats clinging to the side of the mountains."

Around and through these occasional crises, Bert and Colleen's spiritual ministry responsibilities continued. They received frequent speaking invitations. Colleen wrote,

> On Saturday we had to make a decision about whether or not we accept the invitation to Argentina. It was a time of heart searching and crying out to the Lord. I really don't want to go and can see all kinds of reasons why we shouldn't. But Bert feels some kind of moral responsibility to the people who invited us. So we read and prayed and wrote on a paper the pros and cons. We even did what they did in Acts 1—we prayed and then drew lots!! Well, the end result of it all is that we decided to accept if the folks there still believe our presence is important to their conference.

After returning in July 1998 from the three-week trip, Colleen wrote, "We really had a wonderful time in Argentina. Everyone was so kind, and we made some wonderful friends. On our way from the airport to Benito's house, Bert asked him how many messages he would be responsible for, and he jokingly said, 'Thirty-eight!' We laughed, but he wasn't far off."

Together they did radio interviews, and Colleen spoke at several women's meetings. People were very interested in their ministry in Peru. Bert preached in several churches, at a youth conference with participants from as far away as Uruguay and Paraguay, and at a missionary conference. In the end Colleen wrote, "I'm really glad we went, but I'm also very glad to be back home."

Peruvians love to celebrate. And what occasion was more worthy of a wholehearted celebration than the fiftieth wedding anniversary of their beloved *Heriberto y Norma Elliot*! Planning began months in advance, coordinated by Pam Zarek and Norma Rengifo, a longtime

Fifty years and still in love

Peruvian coworker with her husband, Rider. Here is Bert's account of the affair:

> How can we ever describe this wonderful month of celebration, euphoria, fellowship, and joy, enveloped in the love of two families, one by blood, the other by the Spirit! It was an avalanche of love, producing gratitude and praise to the great Giver of every good and perfect gift. People came from many places to help us "exalt His Name together" for the fifty happy years of wedded love, we believe, as God intended it to be.
>
> The momentum began with our local people making plans and beginning to stockpile all the ingredients to be used on the night of Thursday, January 28, 1999. The first of

our family to arrive were Steve and Mary Hawthorne and their three children from Bolivia. Steve taught two courses in our Bible school, besides leading us to confirm our wedding vows at the anniversary. A few days before the celebration other family members arrived: Colleen's sister Joan and her husband; Ray, my sister, Jane, and later her husband, Jerry; their daughter Lynn and her husband, Drew; my sister-in-law Ruby with a very favorite cousin Pauline Parks. A dear friend Jack Mackie, who has helped us many times, came for his fifteenth visit. The total surprise was the arrival of our nephew Gilbert Gleason, bringing with him two beautifully decorated albums given by the folks in our home assembly and with at least three months of work done by Gilbert and his wife, Sue, full of pictures, cards, and letters, a fragrant potpourri of friends and lifelong memories. There were many other gifts (including a professional yo-yo, which I am enjoying), too numerous to mention.

The big night arrived, and our church building (beautifully decorated) was packed with over five hundred people. All the family marched in first to sit in the reserved seats at the front. Then came the elegantly dressed children scattering flower petals and bearing rings, who all sat on the steps of the platform in front of a beautiful cake. Then came the wedding march, and I found myself getting out of step with Colleen as all the people broke into applause. They had decorated chairs on the platform for us old folks to sit down (after we sang our song together and stole a kiss), so we could enjoy a brief message and a song written for the occasion. Steve then led us in repeating our vows, and Lynn read a brief resume of our life together. Our boy Pablo, who had flown in from DC, was the emcee for the program, which included a very humorous skit.

Colleen looked lovely in her mid-length white dress with a long gold lace jacket and a bouquet of red roses. One of the highlights for me was presenting our flesh and blood family, while they stood and faced the audience, to our spiritual family as they stood in groups—from the mountains, the jungle, and different areas along the coast—and waved their greetings, the fruit of a lifetime of abiding together in His love.

The year 1999 not only marked fifty years of marriage, but also fifty years of the Elliots' fruitful ministry together in Peru. In recognition of that, their home churches in Portland honored them with a trip to Greece, Asia Minor, and Israel in a tour group led by Dave Reid, a professor at Emmaus Bible College. Bert said it fulfilled "a dream of a lifetime."

En route to Israel, in mid-April Bert and Colleen started a four-week stop in Portland, where we celebrated their two fiftieth anniversaries in a gathering of family and friends at Grace Bible Fellowship. There an elder from each of their seven supporting Portland churches prayed for them. They visited Bert's mother's homestead in eastern Washington, guided by second cousin Ted Berney, made a quick trip to visit relatives in Vancouver, Canada, spent a couple days on the beautiful Oregon coast with Joan and Ray, enjoyed some unforgettable hours in the rain with Elisabeth and Lars Gren, and visited Jane and Jerry in Wheaton.

While the Elliots were in Portland, Focus on the Family asked permission to publish a feature article on Bert and Colleen for the inaugural edition of their magazine for seniors. Shari Strong interviewed them and wrote the article. Coincidentally, her husband Craig is a professional photographer who had visited the Elliots in Peru and taken some wonderful pictures of them and their ministry. Shari brought them the rough draft to check for accuracy. After reading the article, Colleen asked me, "What is an Energizer bunny?" Shari had described them as the "Energizer bunnies of the Peruvian mission field."[1]

---

1   Shari MacDonald Strong, "Side by Side for Jesus," Legacy, September

Bert wrote in detail about their three-week trip with Dave Reid, which began on May 22:

> For sheer pleasure, the cruise from Athens, including visits to Ephesus and Patmos and finishing in the acropolises of Corinth and Athens, takes first place. I could not stop wondering at the deep blue of the Aegean Sea and the splendor of the fourth-century Greek architecture with its labor-intensive art in both marble and granite. As we walked down the colonnaded street of Ephesus and thought of Paul coming into that cultured city with a brand new message and filling Asia with the gospel from there, I realized again that this had to be from God, and Paul had to be a chosen instrument, or it never would have impacted that imposing culture. It was exciting to set foot on Patmos as well, where John suffered banishment for his faith and received the apocalyptic vision. Corinth was another highlight, after teaching the book for some years. To actually be on the acropolis and walk through the well-preserved ruins below was both moving and instructive.
>
> What can I say about Israel! A kaleidoscope of images covering more than three thousand years of history and places I have read about since my youth, a clash of cultures, a cacophony of sounds, music, and languages, an unfinished puzzle. We climbed tels, walked through a tunnel inside the Western Wall, sang praises on the shore of Galilee as we watched the moon rising over the Golan Heights, and read the Beatitudes. (I must stop here and say that, in my view, it is precisely here in the Sermon on the Mount where the King of kings gives the Law that He writes on the hearts of all those who enter the New Covenant and whose sins He remembers no more. Here and here alone can Jew, Arab, and whoever meet together as one. To the complex problems of

1999, 11.

Israel and our world only true believers have the key. May God help us to use it boldly and wisely.)

We were loathe to leave our kibbutz right on the shore of Galilee after three days, walking where He walked. Leaving early, we passed through Tiberias, now one of Israel's diamond-polishing centers, leaving the Jordan Valley for a trip into Samaria and the tel and Roman ruins of Beth Shean, then down again to the oasis of Jericho, the world's oldest city. Next the Qumran caves, where a Bedouin shepherd found the Dead Sea Scrolls while looking for a lost goat. That find brought the world a thousand years farther back in authentic documents of the Holy Scriptures. All of Isaiah and parts of every other Old Testament book except Esther were found there. Unbelieving Israel receives them as a birthday present from God, coming as they did just as the nation was founded. That evening we floated like corks in the briny waters of the Dead Sea, so salty that it is almost impossible to maintain an upright position; your feet want to bob to the surface.

The next day we took a cable car to the top of Masada and once again were dazzled by the ruins of King Herod's Palace and the story of the 960 zealots who resisted the Roman army for three years before taking their own lives rather than being captured. We walked down the Roman ramp, Colleen doing great with the help of her cane and my arm. It was fascinating traveling up through the Judean wilderness and seeing the Bedouins with their goats and tents and now cars and tractors as well. They are now Israeli citizens. It was also strange to find a MacDonald's restaurant out there just north of Beer Sheva, but our tour group was ready for a hamburger after so many falafels, which is the Jewish and Arabic vegetarian equivalent.

Then it was *up to Jerusalem* for the last three full and fascinating days of our tour. What a thrill to meet cousin

Marilyn Bagshaw [from Vancouver, British Columbia] in Gordon's garden tomb! In that beautiful setting our group broke bread together and worshipped the One who loved us unto death and who alone can lead us through death and out again, clothed then in the power of an indestructible life.

As the tour ended, Bert and Colleen met up with Elizabeth, a neighbor from Trujillo who was now living in Israel. Bert reflected,

Our Peruvian sister gave us a view of Jerusalem that is a bit different than we saw on tour. We enjoyed meeting with a group of Latin believers, all Israeli citizens now. The next two days in Tel Aviv we were with the pastor of a Latin American church where most of the congregation were "illegal." They meet in a basement in a back alley with no signs out front. I spoke to over fifty one night, all hard-working people hoping they won't be caught and put in jail until they come up with the money for their tickets home. The pastor was trained in the Baptist seminary in Trujillo. He and his wife support themselves by working, and the Lord keeps using them to bring Latin people to Him. That is where our neighbor found the Lord a few years ago. She also took us to Joppa (Jaffa), the same port where Jonah shipped out for Tarshish and where Peter received the vision that prepared him to take the good news to the Gentiles.

Our sister Elizabeth accompanied us to the airport, where we were given the third degree by a young intelligence officer: "How long have you been in Israel? Why did you leave your tour? With whom did you stay? What were their names? The lady you are with is a Jew. Jews don't go to church, they go to synagogue!" We began to wonder if we would make our plane. We also wondered at the reason for such detail. Is this really necessary, or are they suffering from paranoia? Then we were off to Athens (two hours), New York (nine hours), Lima (seven hours), and Trujillo (fifty minutes). For once I had my fill of flying, and it was nice to be home, where we crashed and snuggled up tight to get warm in the Trujillo winter after the heat of the Tel Aviv summer.

The whirlwind trip—from departure from Peru to return in June 1999—lasted two months. The euphoria of the fiftieth anniversaries of marriage and ministry was soon replaced with the realization that it didn't imply retirement.

19

Enjoying the Fruit of Their Legacy

Life back in Trujillo for the next three years took on a routine marked by frequent and unpredictable interruptions. For example, on a typical Sunday the Elliots spent the morning at Centro Biblico Trujillo, where Bert frequently preached. For Sunday dinner they usually invited some of their guests, boarders, visiting missionaries, or national workers to a local restaurant. After a brief siesta they would provide a light supper for their house guests and then devise questions for the three home Bible studies they led each week.

Colleen was a teaching leader in the Community Bible Studies (similar to Bible Study Fellowship), which required two meetings a week—one for the leaders and the other the Bible study itself—and *Virtud* (meaning "virtue"), the biweekly women's fellowship group at Centro Biblico. She was never completely comfortable in the teaching role and found she had to spend a great deal of time studying.

In addition, Colleen managed the "Elliot Bed and Breakfast." With the help of her maid, Conchi, she provided three meals a day for an indeterminate number of people. They fed whomever was currently staying in their home, along with anyone who showed up at the last minute. The beds were in constant use. A teacher from the school might live there for a year. Medical patients from the mountains or jungle would stay for a night or a couple weeks. Family, friends from North America, or fellow missionaries on their way through town would drop in for encouragement or counsel.

Ladies with Colleen at Huanchaco

The arrival of two missionary families committed to ministering in Trujillo greatly encouraged Bert and Colleen. Steve and Lisa Twinem arrived from Canada in December 2001—with their three daughters, ages four, six, and eight—under the supervision of the faith mission Pioneers. Steve had first come with a SPRINT team that worked in Cajamarca in 1987. He caught the vision of reaching Peru and set his sights on returning. Those three cute little blond girls caused quite a stir among the Peruvians! They soon added a son to the mix. The family quickly adjusted and became a vital part of the ministry.

Ministering at the drug rehabilitation center

The second family began with Pablo Cenepo-Torres, one of the Elliots' "sons" who lived with them during his high school years. A short-term mission team from eastern Canada took an interest in him and saw great potential, so they gave him a scholarship to attend New Brunswick Bible Institute in Victoria Corner, New Brunswick, Canada. Because of Pablo's desire to serve the Lord in his home country, he continued his ministry training at Washington Bible College in Lanham, Maryland, where he earned a BA in Christian education. He returned to Trujillo to teach English at the newly founded Elliot Christian School for two years before resuming his studies at Capitol Bible Seminary in Lanham, where he completed his master of divinity degree in 2001. While counseling at a Christian camp during a summer break, he met Sarah Lemon, a recent university graduate. They fell in love and married in 2002.

Sarah's Maryland home church and ours in Portland joined in sending them to Peru as missionaries that same year. Pablo quickly jumped into ministry while Sarah worked on learning Spanish. The Elliots embraced them as valued colleagues.

Seeing an urgent need, a Peruvian brother from CBT who was a recovering addict started an inpatient drug rehabilitation center for men in nearby Huanchaco. For several years Bert spent Wednesday mornings teaching and counseling this group, and many came to know the Lord and were baptized with their families. Bert and Colleen led a Bible study specifically for members of these men's families. Some of the men experienced remarkable life changes.

But this also opened up a spiritual battlefield. One night at 11:30 a rehab center staff member called to tell Bert one of the newer men was thrashing around, saying terrible things, and acting demon possessed. It took six strong men to restrain him. They took him to the hospital, where he was given tranquilizers, to no effect. This incident caused an uproar among the other residents. Bert took another elder and went to help calm the men and reassure them of God's care.

Drug and alcohol abuse affected all strata of society, as Colleen affirmed of the small beach community of Las Delicias, twenty minutes south of Trujillo:

> It is a place where the upper crust of Trujillo have their homes. Many of them have fallen on hard times. A large percentage of the men spend their weekends with alcohol and drugs. The door opened there through a simple mountain maid working and watching the family disintegrate. She lived Christ before them and kept telling the lady of the house to go for counsel to Centro Biblico. This woman later put her trust in the Lord and immediately began telling her friends. So we have been going to her home for Bible studies once a week, and several of them come to our home for the Monday night study.

Bert tells the story of the "simple mountain maid":

> Years ago we were preaching in a mountain village where a poor little girl named Susana was converted. We almost forgot about her, but three years ago an upper-class lady came to our church and asked to speak to me. Her family was split up. Her husband was into alcohol. Her son had left home. She was a desperate woman. She came to us because Susana was her servant. It was like the story of Naaman, remember? I shared the gospel, and she received the Lord

> that night. The Lord is doing wonders in that home. The husband left the drugs, the alcohol. The family is united, and they read the Word of God every day. I believe he is not yet converted, but he does read the Word, and the children are listening. Miracles like that are very difficult to grasp—all through the testimony of a little girl from the mountains.[1]

As the Elliot school increased the number of both grades and students, it needed additional classrooms. The school purchased from friends a large house a block away on contract for $120,000. They

---

1 The biblical story of Naaman is recorded in 2 Kings 5.

were able to meet each of the payment deadlines, and within ten months they raised the money, finalized the purchase, and began to remodel the house into a school. The school now offered all thirteen grades and averaged more than two hundred students.

As the Elliots entered their seventies, they discontinued the extended ministry trips so characteristic of their younger years. They confined their travels to two- or three-day trips to places like Chiclayo, Cajamarca, Yurimaguas, Grande Porcón, and Lima to attend and sometimes speak at Bible conferences, youth retreats, church anniversaries, weddings, and wedding anniversaries and to introduce visitors to ministry opportunities in these places. Bert wrote of a remarkable August 2000 trip:

> We had ten wonderful days in Argentina to attend the first World Congress of Brethren assemblies. This all-expense-paid trip came as a surprise gift from the Lord through friends in Buenos Aires and provided us with the opportunity to meet believers from countries all over the world. The inaugural meeting was held in a civic auditorium with the presence of the president of Argentina, accompanied by several government ministers, who gave an official opening

to the congress. This was a first for an evangelical event of this kind and was very impressive. At this opening meeting and all the subsequent ones the music of a well-trained, eighty-voice choir, accompanied by an orchestra, delighted us all (including the president, who refused to leave till they had sung their last note), especially their rendition of the Lord's prayer set to Argentine music plus Handel's glorious "Hallelujah Chorus." There were inspiring messages and seminars attended by close to five thousand people. I was given the opportunity to speak following the large Breaking of Bread service on Sunday morning, as well as a couple times on a Christian radio program. We had some special invitations to several homes for those delicious barbecues for which Argentina is famous and where we enjoyed fellowship and times of singing around the piano with believers from Scotland, Australia, New Zealand, and North America, along with friends from Argentina. We thank the Lord for this, another expression of His love to us through His people.

The Mini-Amsterdam conference in Lima in fall 2001, sponsored by the Billy Graham Association, invited Bert to speak at their meetings. He initially declined, but found they had put him on the program anyway! They also scheduled Colleen to speak to the women. About 2,500 people attended. Colleen wrote, "Bert spoke from nine to ten every morning from the book of Romans. He was excellent. In fact, I don't think I have ever heard him better."

Due to the worsening condition of Colleen's knees, the Elliots traveled to Portland in summer 2002 for total replacement of her left knee. Before leaving Peru, they moved out of their rental house and put their belongings in storage, thinking they might buy a home when they returned.

During Bert and Colleen's furlough they, Sue and I, and Pablo and Sarah attended the Iron Sharpens Iron Conference at Emmaus

Bible College in Dubuque, Iowa. This provided a time for us to relax and grow together. The Elliots also attended a seniors camp at Lakeside Bible Camp on Whidbey Island, Washington.

Colleen's knee surgery was successful, and she was soon on her feet again. The Elliots returned to Trujillo in November to start a three-year term and soon found a two-story, fully finished house to purchase. On the main floor was a large combined living and dining room, a large kitchen, a half bath, and a large office that could be converted into a bedroom if needed. The half bath could also be expanded into a full bath. The second floor provided four bedrooms and two full baths. There were even finished bedroom and bathroom on what would be considered the roof. The house met all the requirements for the Elliot Bed and Breakfast and its assortment of guests.

April 2003 saw a sobering event on a school outing. The high school swimming class was finishing up at a local swimming pool. The teacher blew his whistle and told the students to take showers and get dressed. Right away they noticed a fifteen-year-old boy was missing and soon found him in the bottom of the pool. The teacher pulled him out and tried to revive him, to no avail. The boy was known to have a heart problem and had once before been evacuated from a sporting event. Students in the water would have noticed if he had struggled, so leaders assumed he went down without a struggle, having suffered a heart attack, died suddenly, and sunk to the bottom. His death devastated the teacher, students, and of course the boy's parents. Bert had to deliver the news to his mother and later said, "I will never forget her loud shriek, 'No, no! My son! My only son!'" The boy's father was a Baptist pastor who had left the ministry. He said God was now telling him to return to ministry. Students participated in the memorial service and greatly encouraged the parents.

About the same time a young woman from Las Delicias who faithfully attended CBT in her wheelchair asked to be baptized. She had been injured at birth and consequently couldn't control the

Bert and Colleen, Gilbert and Sue

movement of her head, arms, or legs. She was very intelligent and could read, but couldn't pronounce words. Her love for the Lord was obvious. To baptize her, Steve Twinem lifted her from her wheelchair, carried her in his arms down into the tank, and lowered her into the water. In her written testimony she said, "I would rather be in my wheelchair with Christ than to walk without Him."

Then came the October 2004 Luis Palau Festival in Lima, to which Palau invited Bert and Colleen as special guests. He treated them to a five-day stay on the twenty-first floor of the downtown Marriott Hotel. They felt like royalty as they enjoyed room service, buffet breakfast, and a spectacular view of the Pacific Ocean with hang gliders drifting by. They made a conscious decision to set aside any guilt feelings at the money spent on them. This was not their usual missionary accommodations! They especially appreciated the wonderful fellowship with the Palau team.

Luis Palau with Colleen and Bert

Palau publicly honored the Elliots for their sacrificial ministry by seating them on the festival platform. They marveled as they looked at the crowd of 300,000 who flooded Lima's Campo de Marta each of the two nights. Thirty-seven thousand Christians had been trained as counselors. Luis gave a simple, clear, concise explanation of the gospel. Thousands responded. Tears flowed as Bert and Colleen remembered that, when they first arrived fifty-four years earlier, Lima featured only a handful of churches, and it had been illegal to preach in public.

Now, in 2004, Lima was a city of eight million desperately in need of hope, as was all of Peru. Political unrest, periodic terrorist attacks, persistent poverty, and widespread unemployment brought discouragement and despair. In his welcoming remarks at the festival,

Peruvian Senator Walter Alejos said, "Luis Palau has arrived in Peru at a most opportune moment in time. There is a crisis of values in our country, with politicians attacking each other, daily street protests, and the people are fast losing confidence in their government."

Palau met and prayed with Peru's President Alejandro Toledo Manrique, Lima's Mayor Luis Castaneda Lossio, and members of the Peruvian Congress. Palau team member Ruben Prioetti said, "In my twenty-five years with Luis Palau, there has never been a day quite like this, where so many top leaders of a nation were eager to receive Luis and listen to his counsel on the relevance of Jesus Christ to governing a nation."

In a family letter Colleen wrote, "It was an exciting experience to observe from the inside that man of God in action."

Pablo and Gilbert

For two weeks in summer 2005, Haig and Paula Valenzuela and Sue and I led our church's mission team of twelve young people, including the Valenzuelas' son and our three children. I describe it in detail, not because it was more significant than any other team, but because it is the one I experienced firsthand.

Pablo surprised us by joining us during our layover in Houston. He had to make a quick trip to Maryland and ended up on our flight to Lima. He was especially helpful in guiding us through customs. Fifteen of our bags were lost and arrived a day late, which was a blessing in disguise. We didn't have to take them through customs or pay extra fees. The airline sent them right through.

The first morning we all enjoyed breakfast at the Elliots' home. Then we headed to Cascas, a picturesque city of five thousand in the low mountains two hours east of Trujillo. Steve and Pablo had been regularly taking turns going up there to preach on Sundays and encourage this little church.

Before leaving Portland, our team had learned three pantomimes set to music, depicting the road from a life of hopelessness to finding hope in Jesus Christ. We would perform these in a dozen different venues, and they proved effective in crossing the language barrier. Our performance would first attract a crowd, and then Pablo would give a short gospel message. Our first performance was in the plaza in the center of Cascas. The church served us dinner outside its main leader's home, surrounded by a vineyard. The church of about twenty-five met in a storefront, where we rejoiced in worship Sunday morning before returning to Trujillo.

Throughout the two weeks we performed our pantomime at the drug rehabilitation house, a women's prison where Pablo taught a weekly Bible study, and the Christian orphanage south of town. We visited the Bible study at Las Delicias, and our two married couples attended a couples study at Pablo and Sarah's home.

During the first week we spent three full days on a work project we had chosen—adding a second-story recreation room on the street side of CBT. The rest of the facility was two stories, but this section was deemed too weak to hold a brick structure. We had sent funds ahead for the church to build a flight of stairs and a light second-story structure with iron beams and a fairly light roof. Colleen described our subsequent efforts:

The team really worked hard at CBT and transformed that new room into a wonderful place for social events and recreation. That space, where the new room is, used to be a catch-all for junk. When they built the room, they transferred lots of the junk to the roof space over the bathrooms. These junk piles were always an eyesore. When Susan saw it, she said, "That has to go." I agreed 100 percent, but it looked like an enormous job to me. But Sue engineered the whole thing and began to cart things down to the street like you wouldn't believe! Bert wanted to save some of the wooden things for possible bonfires or whatever. Sue winked at me and carted most of it away. As soon as the junk reached the street, there seemed to be folks who would quickly cart it off. But what an improvement when they finished. I could hardly believe the transformation of just the roof area, to say nothing of all they did in the room itself, plus painting and building. They all worked very hard and are a great team.

Our team worked alongside the church's young people, which added to the joy. We purchased a ping pong table and foosball game. Our reward was the addition's inauguration on our last Friday night.

Bert once cautioned me about work projects: "Every team that comes down here wants a work project. It gives them a sense of accomplishment. Unless they are skilled labor, like electricians or builders, I can get most of those projects done for a fraction of the cost of bringing a team down to do them. I want the teams to see the ministry, meet the people, and get a vision for what God is doing here in Peru. Don't make the project the major focus of your time here."

On the second Saturday we traveled to Cajamarca by van. We stopped on the way at Ciudad De Dios so Bert and Pablo could speak at a young people's conference. Then we drove the nine-thousand-foot climb to Cajamarca. As we passed through each small village along the road, Bert told stories of street meetings, Bible distribution on market day, people coming to know the Lord, baptisms, and churches planted. The scenery reminded me of a description Bert once wrote of the Andes as

319

the quilt-like beauty of the farms with patches of wheat, barley, and green peas in various stages of ripening, the brilliant blue of the sky, tier after tier of mountains dropping away as we look westward toward the sea, the quaint farm houses with their quainter people dressed in wool, men riding horseback, kids herding sheep.

He pointed to a road ascending one mountain, saying, "There's a little church in the village up there. When we first went there, it was a three-hour hike over a narrow path. Now here's a road, and the church is still going."

We performed our pantomime at Centro Biblico Cajamarca and enjoyed a wonderful concert by a Christian singing group. We also performed in one of the small churches outside town. We enjoyed Cajamarca's Inca hot baths and other local sights. Of historical significance, in the Battle of Cajamarca the Spanish invaders defeated the Inca Empire, capturing and murdering the Incan emperor Atahualpa.

It was here we came to appreciate the distinctions between the coastal and mountain people and cultures.

Bert couldn't wait to take us up to the farm at Granja Porcón, eighteen miles north and at ten thousand feet elevation. Bert enthusiastically described it as

one of the only cooperatives in the area that has survived. It has become a showplace with thousands of acres of reforestation, beautiful brown Swiss cattle, alpaca, vicuna, sheep, and even a zoo with wild animals. We had the privilege for many years of sowing the Word of God in that place, and the believers there have written Scripture texts practically on every building, on the stones, and even on the chimneys. They told us that last year they had seventeen thousand visitors. The first place they take them is to the church building, where they tell them the success of the cooperative is due to the power of the Word of God that has changed lives.

The local restaurant treated us to a lunch of freshly caught, skillfully cooked trout. We walked through the zoo and "inspected" the cattle. Bert was careful to point out he and Colleen hadn't planted the church there, but their letters are peppered with accounts of their visits through the years. It was a special place to them.

We returned to Trujillo and enjoyed wonderful meals and times of fellowship at CBT and in the homes of the Elliots' Peruvian friends and Pam Zarek. We also learned about local history as we toured Chan Chan and the Moche culture's Sun and Moon Temples.

Our trip's account would not be complete without a story Colleen told:

Sue brought me ten plastic containers with freezer jam! They were piled in two large Ziploc bags. But a bunch of the containers broke, and there was raspberry jam all over everything in the suitcase. Stuart gingerly carried the two bags of jam into the kitchen. I was given the delightful job of cleaning up the mess. I scooped up as much as I could and then licked my fingers to my heart's content, because the jam was still real good. I managed to rescue about eight little containers full of jam. They are now in my new refrigerator in the freezer section. I know I will really enjoy them.

Aunt Colleen was very generous until it came to her raspberry jam. At breakfast she would very cheerfully say, "Would you like some raspberry jam?" Then she gave a look that said, "Don't you dare say yes."

20

Finishing Well

The Waodani invited Bert and Colleen to join them for a conference of thanksgiving during January 6–8, 2006, in Toñanpari, Ecuador. This marked the fiftieth anniversary of the exact dates Jim Elliot, Pete Fleming, Ed McCully, Nate Saint, and Roger Youderian camped on Palm Beach in their effort to build a friendship with the tribal group then referred to as the Auca.

The killing on Sunday, January 8, 1956, made a worldwide impact as the dedication and sacrifice of those five men motivated many to give their lives to obedient service to Jesus Christ. A generation of young men and women stepped forward to take the men's place in local church ministries and overseas missions.

The Waodani organized the conference to celebrate and give thanks for those men, who gave their lives to bring the gospel to *them*. Two years after the massacre, Rachel Saint (sister to Nate) and Elisabeth Elliot (wife of Jim), with her three-year-old daughter, Valerie, had been invited to live with them. Their intent was to learn the language, translate portions of the Bible, and introduce the Waodani to Jesus Christ.

Through the two families' love, forgiveness, and influence all the killers came to know Christ and became spiritual leaders in the Waodani church. Fear and killing had been woven into the fabric of their culture. Dyuwi, one of the killers, said they killed "because that's what the Waodani did. We lived in the ways of our grandparents." He remembered his father teaching him to kill by taking him to the Napa River and spearing someone in front of him. An unusual portion of the deaths in the community were homicides.

But the Waodani listened to these two ladies, whose loved ones they had killed, hearing the story of God, who sent His Son to be speared for their sake. It changed their lives. As Pegonca, Dyuwi's son, said in his message, "They planted a seed. They came not just to die, but to show us the way to a better life." The Waodani began to understand forgiveness and what it means to live in peace. The depth of that understanding is illustrated in the following story, told at the conference:

> What befell Omaenae, a local pastor, is . . . tragic. Among the Waodani, one group, the Tagaeidi, still lives in pagan isolation, its members holed up deep in the jungle . . . . Living in the old ways, Tagaeidi frequently kill wayward oil company employees combing the area for reserves. When Omaenae was a child, the Tagaeidi raided his village and orphaned him. By Waodani custom that act would require him to take vengeance when he came of age. He did not take it, however, converting to Christianity and preaching instead.
>
> A year and a half ago, Omaenae attended a village fiesta with traditional banana drink. In a nod to the universality of male machismo, Waodani men at parties prove themselves by chugging this thick, mashed glop in gourd-sized cups, often consuming several quarts within hours. Unknown to Omaenae, a local troublemaker named Babae added some of the outsiders' hard liquor. Innocent but copious chugging

left Omaenae, who had never tasted alcohol, very drunk. The men began to recall the terrible slayings the Tagaeidi had carried out [years previously].

Inebriated and fuming with ire, Omaenae and several men grabbed spears—precision-sharpened chonta palm measuring eight feet, notched at the tip's end. After canoeing downriver, the enraged group attacked in a drunken stupor, indiscriminately killing seventeen of the Tagaeidi, mostly women and children. Omaenae's actions were more than a horrible sin committed by the village pastor. He had put his family and friends in imminent danger. The Tagaeidi had seventeen murders to repay, and the spearing would not be selective. The villagers ostracized Omaenae.

During the conference's Saturday night session, Omaenae appeared on stage after a trilingual version [English, Spanish, and Waodani] of "I Have Decided to Follow Jesus." Village pastors and elders assembled behind him. Omaenae, formerly an admired spiritual leader, spoke somberly as he did something no Waodani had ever done: ask publicly for forgiveness and reconciliation in a culture [that once had] no word for "forgive" and no way to say "I am sorry."

As Omaenae somehow found the right words, the Waodani seemed to understand them. The others laid hands on him and prayed. They surrounded him like the arc of a curved shield. They pledged protection and promised clemency—an act the slain missionaries' families later said speaks more about the work of God in this tribe than a library's worth of books and articles has in fifty years.[1]

The conference drew an eclectic group—about ninety people from outside Ecuador, members of the local missionary community, representatives from neighboring tribal groups who were former

1   Clint Rainey, "Five-Man Legacy," *World* magazine, January 2006, accessed May 15, 2020, world.wng.org/2006/02/five_man_legacy.

Waodani enemies (Quichua, Shuar, Achuar, and Cofan), and many
Waodani. The contingent from outside Ecuador included several
relatives of the five martyrs, most notably Bert (brother of Jim, of
course) and Ken Fleming (brother of Pete).

The guests were impressed with the hospitality the Waodani
extended with assistance from longtime missionaries Lloyd and
Linda Rogers. To show off their traditional customs and folklore,
they put on a "Fiesta Tipica, Waodani style."

Sunday was the precise anniversary of the slaying. About two
hundred people met on Palm Beach. Bert observed, "The scene,
which was so violent and bloody on that Sunday fifty years ago,
was now calm, peaceful, and very beautiful." Eight young people
were baptized with two of the killers, Kimo and Dyumi, helping
with the baptism. Then everyone stood in a big circle and celebrated
communion. The table was a big plastic storage container, which
held plates of boiled platano (cooked bananas) and cups of purple
Kool-Aid. At the end of the service Bert gave a short message,
encouraging the newly baptized to keep following the Lord.

Bert noticed a theme that the various Wao wove into their
messages. It was "an appeal to the young Wao to come to Jesus.
In short this underlines that some of the tribe are sincere believers
and some are not, but are being influenced by the encroaching
civilization, where the god of this world dominates."

Ken's highlight was meeting and hugging Kimo, his brother's
killer, for the first time. Colleen said, "To see the believers, to hear
their testimonies, and to see they are following the Lord is very
thrilling to me."

Bert stood on Palm Beach and pondered the fact that this was
the very spot where his brother had been speared to death exactly
fifty years before. He reflected,

Being here brings to mind the story of John and James—
another James [that is, like Bert's brother]. When they came
to Jesus and asked Him if they could sit at His right hand

and at His left hand, He said, "It's not mine to give." But He asked them the question, "Can you drink the cup that I must drink? Can you be baptized with the baptism I am to be baptized with?" And they said, "We can." He said, "You will." Now one of those men was one of the first martyrs—James. One of them lived to be the oldest of the apostles—John. But both of them obviously drank the cup—one with a short life, the other with a long life. That is a comparison between my brother Jim and myself.[2]

I heard Uncle Bert make this comparison several times. While he highlighted the similarities regarding the lengths of both pairs of brothers' lives, I believe the similarities extend to their contrasting personalities. From day one Jesus branded them *Boanergēs*, which means "Sons of Thunder"—powerful, fervent, and aggressive. They soon proved Him correct.

Someone who was not a direct follower of Christ had the audacity to cast out demons in His name. John jumped up to stop him. The Samaritans wouldn't let Jesus and His disciples stay in their village. James and John asked if they could "command fire to come down from heaven and consume them." On both occasions, Jesus reined in their impulsive personalities. (See Luke 9:49-56.)

As Bert pointed out, James and John were also the only disciples with the arrogance to ask Jesus to make them the top officials when He formed His administration. Again Jesus reined them in and explained that they were indeed volunteering to join Him in His suffering, but not in His glory.

It should come as no surprise that James and John joined Peter as the prominent preachers in the public square following Pentecost. All three were imprisoned and forbidden from preaching. But they refused to stop. The thunder could once again be heard—this time for the sake of the gospel.

---

2   See Mark 10:35–40.

It cost James his life. His personality put him on the battle front and in harm's way. Herod discovered he could win favor with the Jewish leaders by imprisoning and killing the Christian leaders. He had James killed. Martyred as a young man, James fulfilled Christ's prediction that he would suffer for the gospel.

The trajectory of John's life contrasted sharply with his brother's. He was the last of the apostles to die and the only one to experience a nonviolent death. He pastored the church in Ephesus for years and spent time in exile on the island of Patmos. John never lost his thunder, as evidenced by his writing—he didn't hesitate to call out liars, deceivers, accusers, and the antichrist. But his gospel and three epistles are marked by the message of love. This "disciple whom Jesus loved" became known as the apostle of love. What a transformation! Tradition tells us that in John's last days his disciples carried him in their arms to church, where he would say no more than, "Little children, love one another." Eventually they grew tired of hearing the same response, so they asked, "Master, why do you always say this?" He answered, "It is the Lord's command. And if this alone be done, it is enough."

The personalities of Bert and his brother Jim parallel those of John and James. Like the apostle James, Jim Elliot was known for his thunder—powerful, fervent, and aggressive. He was handsome, athletic, scholarly, insightful, driven, and eloquent. At times he was abrasive and cocky.

In contrast, Bert's personality parallels that of the apostle John. Bert's temperament would not be described as thunderous, although if you heard him preach in the village plazas across northern Peru, you experienced thunder. But by nature he was thoughtful, sensitive, outgoing, amiable, and caring. As I traveled with Uncle Bert and Aunt Colleen in the States and in Peru, I witnessed people responding to and embraced by their love. Like John, they were God's apostles of love.

Following the Toñanpari conference the Elliots wrapped up their three-year term and flew to Portland. Missions Fest NW founder and longtime friend Bill MacLoed invited them to participate in another fiftieth-anniversary celebration. The conference (now Mission ConneXion) is an annual citywide conference encouraging churches and individuals to serve in missions. Its theme that year was "Whatever It Takes." The plenary speakers included Steve Saint (son of Nate Saint) with Mincaye, one of the Waodani killers.

The End of the Spear, the movie depicting Nate Saint's life and death, opened in theaters nationwide that weekend, adding to the excitement and anticipation at the conference. We received regular updates on the movie's success.

Bert and Colleen had two key opportunities at the conference. I interviewed them in the Friday evening plenary session, preceding bestselling author Randy Alcorn's message, and again in a Saturday workshop using a question-and-answer format.

In the Friday evening session, Bert shared that his first reaction to his brother's death was resentment:

> If we give our lives to serve God, shouldn't He protect us? But I've learned since that God takes His servants away and continues His work.
>
> Elisabeth Elliot said to me one time, "There are worse things than dying." "What could be worse than dying?" I asked. She replied, "Disobedience."
>
> The five missionary men went to the Waodani in obedience and opened the door. And then two faithful women went in, learned the language, submitted it to writing, and translated the New Testament. The power of the living Word produced real fruit. This Word is like a sword that can penetrate right through the body to the soul. A spear cannot penetrate where the Word of God penetrates. . . . We returned to Peru with a yearning to give more of ourselves to God.

Mincaye, Steve Saint, Colleen and Bert, Steve McCully

In the Saturday workshop the Elliots told their life story with vivid descriptions and anecdotes. Bert read Romans 12:1–2, then said, "I went with a passion to discover the will of God. What did He make *me* for?" He turned that around and encouraged the audience to do the same: "What did He make *you* for? And then present yourself every day as 'a living and holy sacrifice,' which means you will say, 'Not my will but Thine be done.'" When asked about retirement, Bert said, "The Lord who sent us to Peru never brought us back!"

On Sunday, Sue and I invited a group to our home for dinner. Families of three of the five men were represented—Bert and Colleen, Steve and Ginny Saint, and Steve and Ellie McCully (son of Ed McCully). They enjoyed the meal with Mincaye, one of the killers who robbed them of their fathers and brother. What a demonstration of the power of the cross and the forgiveness of God expressed to one who had hurt them so deeply.

Included at the table were some local ministry leaders, instrumental in planning the weekend—Bill and Joan MacLoed, Randy and Nanci Alcorn, and Stu and Linda Weber. It was a memorable occasion.

I couldn't help but consider the contrast between that joyful, celebratory dinner and the scene in that very room fifty years earlier. Then it had been filled with grief, agony, sorrow, and questions. At that time the Elliot family submitted their loss to the will of God and began the process of trusting Him who "causes all things to work together for good to those who love God, to those who are called according to His purpose" (Romans 8:28) Now we look back and rejoice at the hand of God in that tragedy.

Women's leadership training in Trujillo

That five-month furlough saw delightful visits to 7272 from Colleen's sister Joan and her husband, Ray; Bert's sister Jane and her husband, Jerry; their sister-in-law Ruby; and their sister-in-law Elisabeth with her husband, Lars.

Upon the Elliots' June 2006 return home to Trujillo their next three years assumed a routine that Bert described:

What a high privilege it is to be in His service! I don't do as much of the preaching as I used to, but we have a number of younger men who do a great job, and I enjoy listening. My present activities mainly consist of (1) bringing a message every Wednesday morning to some thirty men who are trying to break drug addiction, (2) helping lead a home Bible study on Thursday mornings in a small beach town a short drive south of Trujillo, (3) a Bible study in our home Friday evenings, and (4) meeting several hours every two weeks with five or six men who care for the needs of the assembly. Last but not least are the many visits and calls from folks here and also phone calls from our brothers and sisters in other parts of Peru seeking solutions to their questions or just wanting fellowship. So we are trusting in the promise of Psalm 92:14–15 [NIV]: "They will still bear fruit in old age, they will stay fresh and green, proclaiming, 'The LORD is upright; He is my Rock, and there is no wickedness in Him.'"

Colleen keeps really busy, not only managing the house, but meeting with the leadership in a group like Bible Study Fellowship and meeting with the women's meeting of the church. She also is my chief secretary, keeping up with all the correspondence. She is a wonderful woman, a true companion in every sense of the word, and my love and respect for her continues to grow.

At one point their routine was interrupted by thieves who broke into their house through an office window. They stole Colleen's computer, Bert's laptop, and a money belt with their passports, bank cards, and some money. The Elliots were home at the time but were distracted by a long-distance phone call and unaware the robbery was happening. That probably protected them from being hurt in a confrontation, but this disconcerted them, and they went to great trouble replacing the stolen items and safeguarding their accounts.

For a few years, Bert and Colleen enjoyed annual three-week visits each February from Lars and Elisabeth (Elliot) Gren. Lars brought books for them to read aloud together and DVDs to watch each evening. Elisabeth was suffering from advanced dementia and had difficulty carrying on a conversation, but she and the cook, Conchi, got along famously. Elisabeth especially enjoyed when Colleen played the piano and they could sing old hymns together, which Elisabeth recalled flawlessly. These visits provided vacations for Bert and Colleen, giving them an excuse to take breaks from many of their ongoing responsibilities.

Back row: Jerry, Lars, Bert.
Front row: Ruby, Jane, Elisabeth, Colleen.

In 2009, anticipating the sixty-year mark of the Elliots' ministry in Peru, I approached Dr. Randall Roberts, the president of Portland's Western Seminary, and asked if Western would consider awarding Bert an honorary doctorate in recognition of his faithful and exemplary service. The board of directors approved unanimously.

Bert's initial reaction was to decline graciously, as he didn't think their accomplishments were unusual. They had simply done what they determined God asked of them. Once he and Colleen decided to accept the honor, he received a fair amount of teasing even from Colleen. It was ironic that one who struggled with academics and never finished college should now become Dr. Herbert I. Elliot. Colleen wrote:

> We have been quite surprised by all the fuss being made about our many years in Peru. Our first reaction was to decline the honorary doctorate. But the family persuaded us otherwise and provided free airline tickets, using frequent flier miles.
>
> So on April 21 we left Peru for a memorable three weeks in the US, which included receiving the degree just mentioned in a very beautiful and Christ-honoring graduation service, as well as many other wonderful events.

Colleen and Bert, Joan and Ray

At the graduation ceremony Scott Reavely, president of Western's board, said to me, "Gilbert, I've been to a lot of graduations, and we've conferred many honorary degrees, but this one was special. To honor Bert, who so faithfully served in simple obedience without any fanfare, truly touched my heart." Bert and Colleen served as the right kind of examples for "average" followers of Jesus, proving that for most of us substantial, supernatural impact is achieved through simple daily faithfulness, listening to Jesus and loving people in His name.

Colleen continued describing their Portland trip and what followed:

> We especially enjoyed the big family breakfast for relatives from far and near on the morning of May 2 and an open house that afternoon for over two hundred family and friends, organized by our niece and nephew, Sue and Gilbert Gleason.
>
> In addition there were many invitations to different homes for wonderful meals and delightful fellowship, and also a very special trip by train to Seattle to visit my sister Joan, where we were again celebrated by friends and relatives. The three week in the Northwest afforded us many wonderful memories to bring back to Peru.
>
> On May 14 we started our long journey back to Trujillo, hoping to arrive in time to take in part of an important conference for national elders and workers from the Brethren assemblies around the country. Because of flight delays we were only able to be here for the last day of the conference, but there, too, another surprise awaited us. One of our colleagues had written a small book in Spanish about our lives here, and this was presented to us that morning in another celebration of our sixty years.
>
> What can we say to all the attention?? In our daily reading we recently read the words of David in the last chapter of 1 Chronicles when he presented to the Lord all his treasures for the building of the temple. He blessed the Lord, to whom belong all the glory and dominion and power, and

ended his ode of praise with words something like, "Who am I and who are my people that we could give You all this? In reality, everything comes from You, and we only give You what we have received from Your hand." That's the way we feel. The long years we have enjoyed together here in Peru are definitely a gift from the Lord's good hand, and to Him alone belongs all the praise.[3]

Through the years, Bert and Colleen were frequently asked to sing together for special occasions. Usually they sang hymns, but one folk song was often requested and became their signature song. I heard them sing it for more than thirty years, and each time it seemed to fit them even more appropriately—especially their rendition at their sixty-year anniversary celebration—"Side by Side," originally written by Harry M. Woods.

You can find the song lyrics online. Bert and Colleen could identify with the singer's experience of material poverty, uncertainty, and grief, but their delight was that they traveled life's road together, "singin' our song . . . side by side."

---

3   Scripture quotation paraphrased from 1 Chronicles 29:14.

21

Side by Side

The diagnosis was serious. The prognosis grim. In fall 2011 Bert developed a bladder infection that did not respond to oral antibiotics. After initial testing, Bert immediately and confidently declined treatment. He wanted to stay home in Trujillo for treatment by Dr. Willy, a member of their church. There he would wait on the Lord for healing, if that is what He desired.

On November 3, with Colleen and friends, Bert celebrated a special eighty-seventh birthday at his favorite restaurant in Huanchaco.

To avoid stairs, Bert and Colleen soon moved their bedroom to the first floor, and it quickly became apparent Bert required full-time care. An eager helper was designated full-time to attend to Bert during the day. Pablo lined up a team of a dozen or so men to take turns looking after him at night. Isabelle, a longtime coworker from Iquitos, gave daily massages and attentive care to both Bert and Colleen while Conchi efficiently ran the kitchen, as she had for years.

Christmas Day brought a beautiful turkey dinner. Bert joined the table for a few bites, but his energy was quickly fading.

In early January 2012 I received a call from Jack Dryden, a medical doctor and Bert and Colleen's close friend. He was arranging to take his son John to make a "house call" to Trujillo. He asked if I would like to go with them. Yes, I would. We wanted to encourage Bert and Colleen and provide respite for those providing round-the-clock care. Jack also planned to look at Bert's medical treatment and see if a second set of eyes might help. His specialty was not geriatrics, but he could consult resources in the States.

When we arrived, Uncle Bert sat in his reclining chair in the living room. His greeting was warm but omitted the robust bear hug to which I had become so accustomed. The Elliots' support team was impressive. The love in the room was tangible. We were convinced Bert wouldn't have received better hospice care anyplace else in the world.

Jack talked with Bert's doctor and consulted with his colleagues in the States. I was impressed with Jack's humbleness as he interacted with the Peruvian doctor, affirming and encouraging him. He expressed confidence that Bert was receiving the best treatment possible.

Jack, John, and I joined the care rotation, hoping to give others a break. One time Isabelle and I both heard Bert, in his weakness, mutter a barely distinguishable request. She looked at me. "¿En inglés?" To which I responded, "¿En español?" We shared a good laugh.

Bert repeatedly, anxiously asked for help to stand up and then sit down, to take his sweater and shirt off and then put them back on again, to have his legs moved or his back rubbed. He would murmur, "It hurts . . . but God is so good."

I told Aunt Colleen we planned to have a memorial service in Portland and would love for her to come if she was up for it. We talked through the service details; she chose the hymns and asked that I give the message. She didn't promise she would attend.

"I will make you fishers of men if you follow Me."

Colleen sorrowed as she watched Bert's steady decline, but the continuous flow of visitors brought strength to their souls. Those from the church sang favorite hymns, prayed, and took communion with the Elliots. Delegations of believers from various regions of Peru came to pray for and honor them.

In the midst of all this activity, they celebrated their sixty-third wedding anniversary. That "love so amazing" that drove them to commit to each other for life on that bitter-cold stormy night in 1949 Portland had reached full maturity as they reveled in God's love while they enjoyed their final days together on earth.

Bert's sister, Jane, came from Wheaton for Bert's final days. At 1:45 p.m. on February 17, Bert went home to be with his Lord, where he experienced firsthand the full reality of gaining what he could not lose.

Bert's first memorial service was that evening. Friends and family reviewed his life, especially his years in Peru. The next day, a Saturday, the church played his recorded messages as people came to pay respects. In another service that evening Pablo reminded attendants of Bert's love for the Lord: "Someone once introduced him by saying, 'I present to you a great servant of the Lord, Heriberto Elliot.' To which Bert responded, 'I am a servant who has a great Lord.'"

The next morning, after the church service at Centro Biblico, everyone walked in a colorful procession, accompanying Bert's casket to the cemetery where he was laid to rest.

The Portland memorial service was set for March 31 to give Colleen time to recover and make plans. She and Jane flew to Wheaton mid-March, where they had scheduled cataract surgery for Colleen. However, on the day of surgery doctors discovered her heart rate was dangerously high. They took her to the emergency room, where they found she had two blood clots in her lungs. They canceled the surgery and prescribed a blood thinner.

The sisters-in-law arrived in Portland on the Wednesday evening preceding the scheduled Saturday memorial service. They were delighted to once again enjoy the hospitality of 7272 (our home) with its many memories. Thursday they laughed and cried their way through a plethora of photos for the memorial service.

That evening they had dinner in Jack and Marilyn Dryden's Vancouver home with the Dryden family. They had a wonderful time, although Colleen commented to Marilyn, "I don't want to go to that memorial. They will say good things about us, and it will make me feel uncomfortable."

The Dryden's son Andy brought the ladies home. He walked Colleen and Jane to the bottom of the steps and then, at Colleen's request, went back to the car to retrieve the memorial bulletins.

Jane stepped aside to admire our yard's flowers. Sue opened the front to welcome them home. When she looked down, Colleen had both feet on the bottom step and was holding the rail with both hands. She suddenly closed her eyes, sat down hard on the cement, fell back, hit her head, and passed out. Sue and Andy both called 911. That brought the fire department from a station only three blocks away. Colleen revived a bit, and Jane talked with her. I received word at the church office, where I was working late, and arrived even before the ambulance. Colleen was conscious and responding. The ambulance transported her to Oregon Health and Science University, the state-of-the-art Portland hospital for brain trauma. I accompanied Colleen in the ambulance and could hear her responding to the EMT's questions. But by the time we arrived, Colleen was unconscious.

Jack and Marilyn met Sue, Jane, and me at the hospital as we awaited news. Colleen sustained a fractured skull with extensive bleeding and was in a coma. Because she was on a blood thinner, doctors were unable to stop the bleeding. Early in the morning they reported that she had experienced severe brain damage. If she survived, she would not have any brain activity. After consulting Colleen's sister Joan, the family decided to take her off life support. She passed away early Friday afternoon, exactly six weeks after Bert.

Former missionary colleague Sharon Fleming said, "When I heard Bert passed away, I couldn't imagine Colleen without Bert. Then when I learned Colleen passed away as well, I thought, 'God must not have been able to imagine it either.'"

I was prepared emotionally for Uncle Bert's death. But Aunt Colleen's caught me off guard. I had been relying on her presence on the front row to give me strength to make it through the service. Through the years I knew I could always count on her to be in my corner. Now, when I needed her most, she was gone.

As tragic and unexpected as Colleen's death was, a joint memorial service for Bert and Colleen seemed so natural. Her sister Joan put together an insert about Colleen to add to the bulletin. I began the service by informing the audience of Colleen's passing, as many had not yet heard. We accepted God's sovereign act as a divine expression of His love for this couple.

Side by side

The first hymn we sang, chosen by Colleen, was "May the Mind of Christ My Savior." Just as Bert and Colleen had sung this song at their union, gathered family and friends also changed the first-person singular "I/me" to first-person plural "we/us." What Bert and Colleen sang as their life's desire at their wedding, we sang as their life's triumph at their memorial service. The song's message is so important and meaningful that I encourage you, before continuing, to return to chapter 3 and ponder its words.

Their niece Kathleen (Benz) Miller reflected that same sentiment when she gave testimony in the service that they were the "truest examples of Jesus" she knew. She made several statements about their acts of service for the Peruvians and ended each sentence with "just as Jesus did." That was their heartbeat.

The Elliots' friend Luis Palau spoke, noting how their life demonstrated Paul's message in 2 Corinthians 4:18: "We look not at the things which are seen, but at the things which are not seen; for the things which are seen are temporal, but the things which are not seen are eternal." Luis said, "They lived that way, and they left us a great example that—the rest of our lives—we should live that way."

I centered my comments around Romans 12:1–2 (NASB): "Therefore I urge you, brethren, by the mercies of God, to present your bodies a living and holy sacrifice, acceptable to God, which is your spiritual service of worship. And do not be conformed to this world, but be transformed by the renewing of your mind, so that you may prove what the will of God is, that which is good and acceptable and perfect." Bert often referred to this passage as his life's guiding principle. Indeed, daily presenting themselves as instruments for God's service culminated in a life that proved that the will of God is good and acceptable and perfect. Their entire life was an act of divine worship. The service was a wonderful tribute to their life well lived.

The next issue we faced was the disposition of Colleen's body. It was inconceivable not to return it to Peru to be buried next to her beloved Bert. The funeral home began the complicated process of gaining permission to transport, which required authorization from the Peruvian embassy in San Francisco.

Before Colleen's death, she had planned to return to Peru accompanied by Pat Guttman, whose sister Pam Zarek was the Elliots' close missionary colleague in Trujillo. They had already purchased tickets for the end of April. Sue decided to use Colleen's ticket, and our son Jim joined them. Coincidentally, Colleen's body arrived in Lima at the same time.

At her service in Trujillo, Steve Twinem highlighted Mark 10:45 (NIV): "For even the Son of Man did not come to be served, but to serve, and to give his life as a ransom for many." Serving others was a major focus of Colleen's life. Steve said, "Greatness is best defined and displayed in service."

It was a privilege for Jim and Sue to attend, along with Bert and Colleen's nephew Eric Benz, who had come down from Florida. After the service was a another procession to the cemetery, where Colleen was laid to rest next to Bert—side by side once again.

"He is no fool who gives what he cannot keep to gain what he cannot lose."[1]

Let's consider the question: Is Jim's statement as true for the life long-lived as it was for the young martyr?

———————————

". . . and they shall become one flesh" (Genesis 2:24). As I was preparing my message for Uncle Bert's memorial service before Aunt Colleen died, I rehearsed the phrases in my head. I found myself automatically referring, not to Bert, but to the two of them together. They were inseparable in my thought processes. My notes said, "Bert had an incredible love for the Peruvians." As I rehearsed it in my mind, it spontaneously became, "Bert and Colleen had . . ."

My editor, Brian Smith, and I were just completing the first major edit of the manuscript when he made this observation in an email:

> I don't know if you thought about this, but dozens of times you chose singular over plural when describing something that belonged to both Bert and Colleen—for example, "Bert and Colleen's life," "Bert and Colleen's heart." As an editor I noticed these and considered changing to plural, but many times I left these singular. This points to the unity they became and brought to their life assignments. They were powerful as one, while still recognizing, respecting, and celebrating their separate individuality. You already highlight

---

1   Jim Elliot, as quoted in Elisabeth Elliot, ed., *The Journals of Jim Elliot* (Old Tappan, New Jersey: Revell, 1978), 174.

this, but I'll say it again in this context: It is fitting—and maybe an expression of their oneness—that they died so close together.

Their love for each other is what God had in mind when He created man and woman and introduced marriage. They knew their love for each other was a gift from God and was an expression of His love for them. In return they had an intimate and overwhelming love for Him.

It was that love that motivated the simple obedience and submission demonstrated in their life. It motivated them to strive to discover "what God made them for"—to watch God use ordinary people like them (and us) to do the extraordinary when we are in His hands. It motivated them to fight for unity and harmony within the Christian community. It motivated them to discover His purpose in the deep valley of loss. It motivated them to walk faithfully for sixty-two years of marriage and ministry together. That love filled them so abundantly that it spilled over onto the Peruvians and to friends and family. Indeed this

> Love so amazing, so divine,
> demands my life, my soul, my all.
>
> —Isaac Watts

Acknowledgements

No book reflects the solitary efforts of one individual. *Love So Amazing* represents the contribution of many. I have heard stories and insights—from too many to mention—that have added to my understanding of Bert and Colleen's life.

My readers gave invaluable input: Dr. Mary Wilder, Marshall Christensen, John Banner, Lynn and Marcia Ruark, Mike and Barbara Goertz, Dr. Steve Hawthorne, Ruth Nelson, and Korrie Hooper. I appreciated having access to the Elliot, Collison, and Benz family letters—more than one thousand in all. I also valued having the Benz emails (another thousand, I'm sure) and Joan's booklet on the Collison family history. Phyllis Sahlin loaned me her hardcopy correspondence from Bert and Colleen after the advent of email—those handwritten notes added by Colleen were always insightful. Elisabeth Elliot's writings about the Elliot family proved valuable as well.

I am thankful for the Grace and Truth / Grace Bible Fellowship church family, who prayed for, supported, and loved Bert and Colleen for their sixty-two years in Peru and shaped their lives even before that. The couple always considered Grace their home church. I also appreciate Grace Bible Fellowship's serving alongside Sue and me in ministry for the past forty years.

On behalf of Bert and Colleen, I want to thank their family, friends, partnering churches, and missionary colleagues who stood beside them. The Elliots knew they enjoyed the privilege serving in Peru because a great army of people linked with them, prayed for them, and sacrificially supported them.

On their behalf, I also want to thank the people of Peru who loved Bert and Colleen and were loved by them. These people brought life and fulfillment to the Elliots' ministry as they came to know Jesus and ministered alongside them.

Tom Syfrett graciously used his cartography skills to produce the two maps of Peru, which feature the important towns and rivers in Bert and Colleen's unending travels.

My editor, Brian Smith, remembers Bert and Colleen visiting his church when he was a teenager, although his vivid memory is, not of Bert's preaching, but of Bert and Colleen singing together! His editing skills transformed the book. Thank you, Brian, for all your perceptive insights and encouragement, and for embracing Bert and Colleen's story. Your fingerprints are on every page. I sensed a kindred spirit that kept me going.

To my longsuffering children, Stuart and Marissa, Clara and Leon, and Jim and Victoria, thank you for your encouragement and patience as you had to listen to unending stories about Uncle Bert and Aunt Colleen and deliberations regarding the book. You were privileged to spend special time with them when they stayed with us during furloughs. And a special thank you to Stuart and Marissa for all their work on the photos and cover design.

A special note of love and appreciation goes to Aunt Jane Hawthorne and Aunt Joan Benz, sisters to Bert and Colleen, respectively. Your faithful love toward Sue and me through the years and your encouragement throughout this project have been deeply felt.

And lastly to Sue, who encouraged me to write this book. Thank you for standing beside me all these years and for your help with *Love So Amazing*. Your input at the beginning shaped the book. Your love for your Uncle Bert and Aunt Colleen gave me inspiration to undertake the task and motivated me along the way.

Soli Deo gloria.

About the Author

Gilbert A. Gleason grew up on the Navajo Reservation in northern Arizona, where his parents were missionaries. That experience enriched his understanding of the opportunities and challenges of missionary life. Because there wasn't a high school nearby, he attended Yucaipa High School in southern California.

He graduated from Biola University and then moved to Portland, Oregon, where he graduated from Western Seminary. He married Sue Elliot in 1979 and has pastored Grace Bible Fellowship since 1981. They have three married children and four wonderful grandchildren. Gilbert enjoys bike riding and hiking.

Gilbert teaches mission classes for Perspectives on the World Christian Movement, which has included being adjunct faculty at Western Seminary and Trinity University. For many years he served on the board of Eagle Fern Camp and is currently on the board of the Elisabeth Elliot Foundation.

Gilbert now focuses on teaching the Bible and telling the story of Bert and Colleen Elliot.

For update information visit gilbertgleason.com.